# Bloom's Modern Critical Views

*Bloom's Modern Critical Views*

# ISABEL ALLENDE

*Edited and with an introduction by*
## Harold Bloom
Sterling Professor of the Humanities
Yale University

**CHELSEA HOUSE**
P U B L I S H E R S
A Haights Cross Communications Company
Philadelphia

Printed and bound in the United States of America
10  9  8  7  6  5  4  3  2  1


Library of Congress Cataloging-in-Publication Data

Isabel Allende / editor, Harold Bloom, contributing editor, Robertson
Erskine.
    p. cm. -- (Bloom's Modern Critical Views)
    ISBN 0-7910-7039-5
    1. Allende, Isabel--Criticism and interpretation. 2. Allende,
Isabel.
Casa de los espairitus. I. Erskine, Robertson. II. Series.
    PQ8098.1.L54 Z695 2002
    863'.64--dc21

                                    2002009105


Chelsea House Publishers
1974 Sproul Road, Suite 400
Broomall, PA 19008-0914


http://www.chelseahouse.com

Contributing Editor: Robertson Erskine

Cover: Associated Press, AP

Cover design by Terry Mallon

Layout by EJB Publishing Services

# Contents

# *Editor's Note*

My Introduction allows itself to question the generally prevalent judgment that Isabel Allende is a major novelist.

Patricia Hart assures us that, for Allende, storytelling is an act of love, while E. Thomson Shields Jr. endorses the novelist's vaunt that her work, and her precursors', is written with "ink, blood, and kisses."

"Female creativity" in Allende is exalted by Doris Meyer, after which Catherine R. Perricone considers signifiers other than the verbal in *Of Love and Shadows*. *Eva Luna* is credited by Edna Aguirre Rehbein as an instance of total narrative-control, while Norma Helsper sees the union of family and the Chilean nation in *The House of the Spirits*.

Susan de Carvalho commends Allende as artist-protagonist, praise exceeded by Roni-Richelle Garciacutea-Johnson who discovers in Allende the authentic freedom of feminism. In turn, Claudia Marie Kovach credits Allende with ultimate justice, and Philip Swanson defends her from those who do not find her feminist enough!

To Lynne Diamond-Nigh, *Eva Luna* fuses writing and true listening, after which Catherine F. Perricone returns to praise *Paula*.

Carolyn Pinet commends the dog Barrabas in *The House of the Spirits*, while Caroline Bennett finds nothing but magic splendor in Allende's resort to magic.

# Introduction

What will happen with this great empty space that I am today? What will fill me now that not a whiff of ambition remains, no project, nothing of myself? The force of the suction will reduce me to a black hole, and I will disappear. To die.... The idea of leaving the body is fascinating. I do not want to go on living and die inside; if I am to continue in this world I must plan the years I have left. Perhaps old age is a new beginning, maybe we can return to the magic time of infancy, to that time before linear thought and prejudices when we perceived the universe with the exalted senses of the mad and were free to believe the unbelievable and to explore worlds that later, in the age of reason, vanished. I have very little to lose now, nothing to defend; could this be freedom at last? I have the idea that we grandmothers are meant to play the part of protective witches; we must watch over younger women, children, community, and also, why not?, this mistreated planet, the victim of such unrelenting desecration. I would like to fly on a broomstick and dance in the moonlight with other pagan witches in the forest, invoking earth forces and howling demons; I want to become a wise old crone, to learn ancient spells and healers'secrets. It is no small thing, this design of mine. Witches, like saints, are solitary stars that shine with a light of their own; they depend on nothing and no one, which is why they have no fear and can plunge blindly into the abyss with the assurance that instead of crashing to earth, they will fly back out. They can change into birds and see the world from above, or worms to see it from within, they can inhabit other dimensions and travel to other galaxies, they are navigators on an infinite ocean of consciousness and cognition.

This passage from Isabel Allende's *Paula*, a memoir that is also an elegy for the tragic loss of her young daughter, is a kind of touchstone for the placement of this novelist. It has many of the qualities that move nearly all of the essayists in this collection to ecstatic celebrations of the exemplary (for them) achievements of Isabel Allende. She is their Latin American feminist novelist and spiritual guide. Benignly respectful of Allende and her work as I am, I nevertheless will indicate a few sober doubts and reservations in this brief introduction. I can locate no aesthetic achievement in the immensely popular *The House of the Spirits*, or in *Paula*, or in the recent *Daughter of Fortune* (Oprah's Book Club).

There are several diverse perplexities that beset me when I read Isabel Allende (rereading her is simply not possible). One is that her literary precursors, Gabriel García Márquez and William Faulkner (to a lesser degree), haunt her pages. To speak of "feminist realism" or "magical feminism," as her admirers do, is an evasion.

Perhaps this might matter less if any of her fictive characters were more than a name on a page. Again, I go against not only the enthusiasts reprinted in this book but an immense chorus of worldwide journalistic reviewers. Try the test of distinguishing between the personalities of Nivea, Clara, Blanca, and Alba: four generations of women whose strength, endurance, and mystical powers are fiercely asserted throughout *The House of the Spirits*. I challenge anyone to contrast the four: are all these women one woman?

I think it scarcely possible to disagree with the humane political and social stances of Isabel Allende. The passion and sincerity of these stances are palpable, admirable, and totally irrelevant to any responsible judgment as to aesthetic and cognitive achievement. The issue between the essayists collected here and this volume's editor is quite simple, and has no relation I can see to my lamentable status as an agèd white male, ludicrously labeled as a "patriarchal critic" by bevies of *feministas*. Are novels like *The House of the Spirits* and *Daughter of Fortune* permanent works of literary art, or, alas, are they Period Pieces, popular romances for our age of Ideology and Information?

In fairness, I quote from a crucial passage in *The House of Spirits* at its most harrowing:

> Ana Díaz helped her to resist while they were together. She was an indomitable woman. She had withstood every form of cruelty. They had raped her in the presence of her lover and tortured them together, but she had not lost her capacity to smile or her hope. She did not give in even when they transferred her

to a secret clinic of the political police because one of the beatings had caused her to lose the child she was carrying and she had begun to hemorrhage.

"It doesn't matter," she told Alba when she returned to her cell. "Someday I'll have another one."

Is this imaginative literature, or is it something else? Journalistically and historically, it has the accents of truth, and morally it is heroic, but is it persuasive as novelistic art? Is Isabel Allende truly comparable to Gabriel García Márquez, or are we to seek her peers at a very different level, in the cosmos of supermarket fiction? I cannot pretend to outvote the essayists brought together here, but I raise these questions because I must observe that few others will do so.

PATRICIA HART

# "Magic Books" and the Magic of Books

Quede claro, pues, que a mí me gustan estos narradores
[Tolkien, Verne, H.G. Wells, Kipling, Stevenson, Salgari, Poe,
Zane Grey, Conan Doyle, etc.] por las mismas razones que a
los niños, es decir: porque cuentan bien hermosas historias, que
no conozco razón más alta que ésta para leer un libro. ...
—Fernando Savater, *La infancia
recuperada*

Soy un lector simple que busca entretenerse con lo que lee. Me
parece una falta de respeto aburrir al lector. ...
—Isabel Allende, in *Informaciones*

No discussion of *La casa de los espíritus* would be complete without
mention of the so-called "libros mágicos" from the "baúles encantados" of
Uncle Marcos. Allende's capacity for forging phrases with the sonorous
memorability of epic epithets "la bella Rosa," "la gran casa de la esquina," "el
túnel de libros," etc.), which in their simple straightforwardness suggest all
sorts of impossible enchantments, is evident. In the early life of Clara del
Valle (described in that portion of the book in which magic is presented most
literally), the "libros mágicos" are presented as if they were quite literally

From *Narrative Magic in the Fiction of Isabel Allende*. © 1989 by Fairleigh Dickinson University
Press. Reprinted by permission.

magic, capable of transporting a young reader to a distant place or time, or of preserving him from other worldly evils. But as the story progresses, the "magical" title acquires a more metaphorical acceptance, related to the power these tales hold over the childish imagination of their readers. By Blanca's generation some of the specific books are actually identified, and it turns out that they are not unpronounceable incantations in forgotten mystical tongues, but rather universal classics that have delighted children and adults for generations:

> ... Sandokán, Robin Hood ... el Pirata Negro, las historias verídicas y edificantes del Tesoro de la Juventud ... el diccionario de la Real Academia de la Lengua Española ... historias imposibles, los duen-des, las hadas, los náufragos que se comen unos a otros después de echarlo a la suerte, los tigres que se dejan amaestrar por amor, los inventos fascinantes, las curiosidades geográficas y zoológicas, los países orientales donde hay genios en las botellas, dragones en las cuevas y princesas prisioneras en las torres. (126–27)

In fact, the wide variety of this reading matter testifies to the astonishing capacity of children who read almost anything. There is magic in the reader, but the most literally magic aspect of the books is their capacity to "poblar los sueños" of those who open them (23).

The transmission of these "magic books" is depicted as an act of love in the novel, either from mother to daughter (as in the cases of Clara to Blanca, and Blanca to Alba), or from one lover to another, as when Blanca commemorates her first stirrings of adolescent love for Pedro Tercero, offering the books to him as proof of affection (126).

Later, the retelling of these very tales is also an act of love. Blanca and Pedro Tercero, for example, shout them good-naturedly into the age-deafened ears of old Pedro García, something that he, we are told, "agradecía mucho" (127). In exchange, he responds lovingly with some of his own oral folklore. Blanca also expresses her love for her daughter Alba by trying to reconstruct remembered tales from the trunk. Although her poor memory magically transforms them and they miraculously metamorphose into something completely different, the act of love is still the same, and the final effect is much appreciated by Alba:

> [Blanca] le contaba [a Alba] los cuentos de los libros mágicos de los baúles encantados del bisabuelo Marcos, pero que su mala

memoria transformaba en cuentos nuevos. Así se enteró Alba de un príncipe que durmió cien años, de doncellas que peleaban cuerpo a cuerpo con los dragones, de un lobo perdido en el bosque a quien una niña destripó sin razón alguna. (269)

Moreover, reading these "libros mágicos" has another magic effect: it stimulates the young reader to write or create on his or her own, and a mention of reading the books is frequently linked to an urge to write, within the text. For example, in one paragraph we are told of young Clara's voracious reading habits:

... Leía mucho ... y le daban lo mismo los libros mágicos de los baúles encantados de su tío Marcos, que los documentos del Partido Liberal. (73)

In the very next sentence the author calls attention to Clara's nascent practice of writing things down in journals:

Llenaba incontables cuadernos con sus anotaciones privadas, donde fueron quedando registrados los acontecimientos de ese tiempo que gracias a eso no se perdieron borrados por la neblina del olvido. (73)

Already, some of the deeper magic of these "libros mágicos" begins to emerge. They stimulate the readers in their turn to learn how to tell a good story, and the telling of tales results in two effects of paramount importance within the cosmos of *La casa de los espíritus*. First of all, tale-telling entertains honestly, and such entertainment brings teller and listener closer together. Second, it can preserve history, whether that of a family, country, or continent.

The magically stimulating effect of the "libros mágicos" can be seen again when the reading of them, along with syndicalist literature, helps Pedro Tercero García to develop spiritually and intellectually and to pass from childhood to adolescence. In this period, the boy "leyó y releyó mil veces los libros mágicos de los baúles encantados del tío Marcos" (139). At the same time, this period of intense reading is the birth of Pedro Tercero's creative productivity, and prompted by the magic of the books and the magic of his love for Blanca, the youth begins composing his first songs.

The "libros mágicos" also have an important catalytic function in Alba's beginnings as a writer. Blanca attempts to recount the tales from memory to

her young daughter, with the confusing results that have already been
mentioned. In spite of the oddity of these tales, they enchant the tiny Alba,
who wants to hear them repeated:

> Cuando Alba quería volver a oír esas truculencias, Blanca no
> podía repetirlas, porque las había olvidado, en vista de lo cual, la
> pequeña tomó el hábito de escribirlas. Después anotaba también
> las cosas que le parecían importantes, tal como lo hacía su abuela
> Clara. (269)

Again we see the magic function of books, how they stimulate the
imagination toward artistic creation—a phenomenon quite literally
inexplicable according to natural law and therefore eminently magic. In this
sense, the books from the "baúles encantados" come to stand for all
childhood reading in general. The very looseness of the designation, "baúles
encantados" in the plural lets the imagination fill in exactly how many trunks
it takes to hold the treasures of childhood reading, and exactly how many and
what are the books contained. Some of the books are identified, but no index
of them is ever given, and in this way Allende contrives to make these magic
trunks miraculously expand or contract to hold the childhood favorites of
each individual reader.

The connection between the "libros mágicos" and the stimulation of
artistic creation can now be seen more clearly on page 73, where the magic
books, Clara's notebooks, and the rarely intrusive "yo" (belonging to the
older, retrospective Alba) all join together. After mentioning the "libros
mágicos" and the notebooks of Clara, the narrator adds, "y ahora yo puedo
usarlos para rescatar su memoria" (73). It is as if these two sources, beloved
childhood readings and family oral history, are presented here as the raw
ingredients of the novel we hold in our hands. These two sources do not
contain the actual motivation for Alba's "writing" this book, but they
certainly do contain her raw materials.

Reading the "libros mágicos" stimulates the imagination of a child;
moreover, within the world of this novel it is a fairly significant factor in
determining who will later turn out well and who will not. For example,
Jaime and Nicolás are saved in part from the unimaginative rigors of their
strict "colegio inglés" by such stimulating reading. By contrast, Esteban
Trueba's bastard grandson, Esteban García, in being excluded from his
physical birthright within the family is also excluded from the spiritual
birthright represented by the magic tales. His frustrations cannot find the
creative, constructive outlets that Pedro Tercero forges through song and

political activism; rather, his distorted soul resorts to torture and force. The seeds of the adult Esteban García will become are already present in the child, and at our first view of him we can already perceive a dangerous inability to imagine the suffering of others. He is described as "ocupado en ensartar los ojos a un pollo con un clavo" (170). The child, unsupervised and uninstructed by maternal tales lovingly told, so completely lacks the imagination to suppose the pain of the creature he tortures that when he discovers his grandfather dead, he tries to do the same to the old man until Blanca stops him.

Rather than finding compassion, morality, and idealistic adventure in the stories told to him as a child, Esteban García finds embitterment. Instead of the loving accounts of the del Valle history that Nívea tells Clara during the latter's period of muteness, instead of the fascinating adventures that Uncle Marcos relates, instead of the confused but well-intentioned stories that Blanca tells Alba, by contrast, Esteban García's childhood has been poisoned by the bitter tales that his grandmother, Pancha García (the first woman raped by Estaban Trueba) whispered into his ear from the time he was old enough to understand:

> Su abuela, Pancha García, antes de morir alcanzó a envenenarle la infancia con el cuento de que si su padre hubiera nacido en el lugar de Blanca, Jaime o Nicolás, habría heredado Las Tres Marías y podría haber llegado a Presidente de la República, de haberlo querido. (170)

A childhood imagination is such a delicate thing, according to this novel, that malicious stories, told in a susceptible period of childhood, can serve to permanently deform a young character.

Such serious consequences are seen in the "pious" lie Blanca tells Alba about her "father," Jean de Satigny. Because Blanca invents a very believable tale in which the count dies of a fever in the northern desert, Alba actually has nightmares:

> Soñaba con un hombre joven ... caminando por el desierto a pleno sol. En su sueño el caminante acortaba el paso, vacilaba, iba más ymás lento, tropezaba y caía, se arrastraba de rodillas un trecho sobre las ardientes arenas, pero finalmente quedaba tendido en la inmen-sidad de aquellas dunas lívidas, con las aves de rapiña revoloteando en círculos sobre su cuerpo inerte. (236)

This is clearly a frightening, even damaging effect from adult abuse of the power of storytelling, and Alba reproaches her mother for this when she discovers at last that her father was really Pedro Tercero García:

> Alba … sacó un hilo de voz temblorosa para preguntar por qué no le habían dicho antes que Pedro Tercero era su padre, así se habría ahorrado tantas pesadillas de un conde vestido de blanco muerto de fiebre en el desierto. (317)

But fortunately, this abuse of storytelling is counterbalanced by a loving and careful use of the power of books and tales for the most part in the rest of Alba's childhood:

> [La historia del conde] fue uno de los pocos infundios que tuvo que soportar en su infancia, porque … su tío Jaime se encargó de de-struir el mito de los niños que surgen de los repollos o son transportados desde París por las cigüeñas y su tío Nicolás el de los Reyes Magos, las hadas y los cocos. (318)

By truthfully answering Alba's serious questions about sex, Christmas, and what is under the bed at night, her uncles have not spoiled a childish fantasy world for her, but rather they have permitted her to enjoy the books of enchanted stories, while at the same time knowing that not everything in them is literally true. Thus Alba, the most modern and moderate of the Trueba/del Valle women, enjoys a synthesis between the fantastic and spiritual ways of her grandmother and the practical intelligence of her grandfather. In a way, a wise use of storytelling has been an important factor in seeing to it that Alba falls heir to much of the best of each grandparent.

Other characters are not always so fortunate in the effects that reading and hearing tales have on them. For example, Blanca is determined to convert her passion for her childhood love, Pedro Tercero García, into "un amor de novela" (276). This romanticism causes her to fear the prosaic realities of daily life with someone and ultimately nearly costs her that great love forever.

La Nana as well is adversely affected by a series of "folletos terroríficos" that she cannot even read but whose pictures nevertheless serve as the inspiration for the horrifying costumes with which the good woman does herself up in an attempt to frighten the child Clara out of her muteness. Even pictures can tell a story, and in this case they have a disastrous effect (76).

The "libros mágicos" themselves can have a negative effect if taken too seriously. It has already been mentioned that Alba's reading of the magic books was tempered by her uncles, who always kept her "en un estrecho contacto con las prosaicas verdades de la existencia" (236). Young Clara, by contrast, did not have such a balancing force against the extravagances of her Uncle Marcos, and thus her reading actually leads her to interpret the worst from the most traumatic incident in her childhood—the moment when she accidentally witnesses kindly old Dr. Cuevas performing an autopsy on her sister Rosa.

> El doctor Cuevas, ese hombronazo bonachón y dulce, de amplia barba y vientre opulento, que la ayudó a nacer y que la atendió en todas sus pequeñas enfermedades de la niñez y sus ataques de asma se había transformado en un vampiro gordo y oscuro como los de las ilustraciones de los libros de su tío Marcos. (40)

Once again, pictures have inflamed a suggestible imagination, just as they did in the case of La Nana, and without the counter-balancing effect of an adult to carefully help separate some of the fantasy from reality (without crushing the enjoyment of the fantasy), the imagination is overstimulated to unhealthy ends.

But the telling of tales is not only an important part of childhood in *La casa de los espíritus*. It is also a privileged part of the adult world. Those adults who can tell a good story are given a special position in the narrative, whereas those who use storytelling for malicious ends are veritable personifications of archetypal evil.

Nívea, Clara, and Blanca all tell the best stories they know to their children, stories handed down both from family history and from the magic books of Uncle Marcos. But some other mothers in the book, though often well-intentioned, simply have no good stories to tell. The illiterate Pancha García, for example, can only recount her own poisonous family history over and over. Thus she becomes, as has already been mentioned, one of the first sources for Esteban García's monumental resentment and hatred. On a lesser scale, Ester Trueba tries to be a good mother to Esteban, and on her death, the young man's fondest memory is of her reading with him, "se había inclinado con él sobre las páginas de un libro" (81). But unfortunately, Ester lacks imagination in her choice of reading matter, and as she gets older and more ill, she sits day after day, "sin más compañía que las lecturas piadosas de sus libritos píos de vidas y milagros de los santos" (43). Although her intentions are very good and although the "milagros" alluded to seem to promise magic sparks, the dismal reality of these books is a sadistic distortion of morality that is at least one factor in pushing daughter Férula toward her masochistic relish of self-humiliation.

In fact, books are so important in *La casa de los espíritus* that figures are frequently characterized by what they read. The mention of Ester's bedside reading matter helps to flesh her out immediately in our imagination as someone of limited and somewhat morbid intellectual horizons. By contrast, Alba's beloved Uncle Jaime lives in a "túnel de libros," a monument to a love of reading. What is more, the ultimate statement of intimacy between uncle and niece is seen in the phrase, "compartían los mismos libros" (295). It does not matter that they totally disagree about all they read; this mutual passion for books so unites them that it transcends differences of opinion:

> ... Ambos se perdían en una oratoria confusa que los dejaba agotados, acusándose mutuamente de ser más testarudos que una mula, pero al final se daban las buenas noches con un beso y quedaban ambos con la sensación de que el otro era un ser maravilloso. (296)

Jaime's veneration for books has been apparent since his childhood days in English schools, where one of the "extrañas manías" that sometimes separated him from other boys was that, "no le gustaba que ... le pidieran libros prestados ..." (167). In a novelistic universe where books play such an important role, it is no wonder that a reluctance to part with valued books foreshadows a great man to be.

By contrast, the unlikable Jean de Satigny is a determined dilettante when he reads, and is damned with the physical description of his hands, "manos ... de un hombre que no tiene nada interesante que contar" (236).

As the book comes closer to contemporary times, another important function of storytelling begins to emerge: tale-telling as a motivation for action, specifically as a force for political and social change. Through his political awakening, Pedro Tercero becomes convinced of the need for social change among the residents of Las Tres Marías. Initially he passes out syndicalist pamphlets that leave the workers confused and indifferent. But then a "magic" story intervenes, recounted by old Pedro García from the stories of his oral tradition:

> Un día el viejo ... les contó ... el cuento de las gallinas que se pusieron de acuerdo para enfrentar a un zorro que se metía todas las noches en el gallinero para robar los huevos y devorarse los

pollitos. ... Pedro Tercero ... se quedó toda la tarde pensativo,
rumiando el cuento del zorro y las gallinas, y tal vez ese fue el
instante en que el niño comenzó a hacerse hombre. (128)

Eventually, Pedro Tercero writes a song that recounts the story, and from
that point on, the tale comes to represent his songwriting as a whole. By
taking an oral tradition, transforming it to the best of his abilities, and
adapting it to his own special talent—song—Pedro Tercero has begun to
grow into a man. And within the world of this novel, developing artistically
is clearly seen as one of the highest goods. Besides, Pedro Tercero discovers
to his surprise that by telling his parable in song, he achieves much more
than through the prosaic distribution of pamphlets. His father notes this
development proudly:

Cuando escuchaba canturrear algunas de las canciones de gallinas
y zorros, sonreía pensando que su hijo había conseguido más
adeptos con sus baladas subversivas que con los panfletos del
Partido Socialista que repartía incansablemente. (157)

In fact, teaching through storytelling is an ancient, time-honored custom in
Christianity, and was a favorite pedagogical method of Christ himself
according to the Bible. *La casa de los espíritus* takes the ratio of good parables
to Christ-like behavior very literally, and the use of parables becomes for
example, a good test to determine the virtue or hypocrisy of a priest within
the book. The most favorably presented priest in the story is, of course,
Padre José Dulce María, the renegade Jesuit whose specialty is transforming
biblical parables into calls to socialism. Even after he is banished by the
Compañía de Jesús to a forgotten corner of the world, his conviction remains
strong and his methods unwavering: "ni por eso renunció a transformase las
parábolas bíblicas en panfletos socialistas" (125).

Later, these parables and other books join with the "libros mágicos" to
aid in Pedro Tercero's spiritual formation and in the development of his
imagination and character. The priest also fulfills the important function of
guiding Pedro Tercero into an outlet for his creativity: "también le enseñó a
cultivar su habilidad natural para versificar y a traducir en canciones sus
ideas" (139). Later, it is once more Padre José Dulce María who convinces
Pedro Tercero that he can overcome the loss of three fingers from his right
hand and continue making music.

By contrast, the most dislikable priest in the book, Padre Restrepo, is
condemned by his distance from simple Christian parables and virtues.

Instead of telling straightforward tales to inspire his parishoners to do good, Padre Restrepo uses the power of the pulpit to abuse the patience of his hearers with stories that reflect a diseased imagination and a total lack of reality contact:

> —¡Tú, desvergonzada que te prostituyes en los muelles!—y acusaba a doña Ester Trueba, inválida debido a la artritis y beata de la Virgen del Carmen, que abría los ojos sorprendida, sin saber el significado de aquella palabra ni adónde quedaban los muelles. (10)

Instead of using his eloquence to uplift his hearers, inspire them, or even at least to entertain them, Padre Restrepo chooses to describe such delicacies as the suffering of Hell in such vivid detail that it inflames Ester and Férula Trueba to unhealthy fantasies, while the more sensible Nívea del Valle simply feels sick and worries about fainting.

Another character who uses storytelling to provoke action is Nicolás Trueba. For the imaginative Nicolás, storytelling is first and foremost an art of seduction. After practicing it with success on the country lasses at Las Tres Marías, Nicolás plies his storytelling to great advantage back in the capital. There he woos urban damsels with a fabrication about having learned to dance flamenco in the caves of Sacramonte. As the following passage shows, he was a very convincing teller of tales:

> Nicolás andaba esos días con la novedad del baile flamenco, que decía haberlo aprendido de los gitanos en las cuevas de Granada, aunque en realidad nunca había salido del país, pero era tal su poder de convicción, que hasta en el seno de su propia familia comenzaron a dudar. (195)

Such powers of deception are hardly surprising in a fellow who spent his adolescence arguing both sides of every issue with his brother Jaime (168). Still, Nicolás's powers of storytelling are limited to the same degree that his own spirit is limited, deformed by his later life, and lacking in the ability to imagine the sufferings of others, especially Amanda. This is so much the case that when he eventually sits down to write a book, it sounds without a doubt to be one of the most boring ever printed:

> Después de corregidas e impresas, las mil y tantas cuartillas manuscritas se redujeron a seiscientas páginas de un voluminoso

> tratado sobre los noventa y nueve nombres de Dios y la forma de
> llegar al Nirvana mediante ejercicios respiratorios. (242)

Here is an example of a book that is quite literally about a magical subject but that nevertheless could certainly never qualify as a "libro mágico." Nicolás writes, but he does not *tell*; by not availing himself of the storytelling arts, he creates a book that exists literally only as a physical object, not as a transcendental means of arriving at a different reality that is to be found, for example, in an adventure tale, it is no wonder that this highly unimaginative tome soon ceases to be considered as a book at all, and is reduced to its purely physical dimensions:

> Los cajones de la edición terminaron sus días en el sótano donde
> [la pequeña] Alba los usaba como ladrillos para construir
> trincheras. (242)

The "libros mágicos" of Uncle Marcos miraculously capable of holding an entire world within themselves, but by contrast, Nicolás's book is nothing more than the pages and binding, a physical mass. It is not enough that a book be about magic for it to be a magic book. Part of what constitutes a "libro mágico" is that it must stimulate the imagination.

But according to the morality of this novel, even works that stimulate the imagination must do so wisely in order to be considered "magic." When the stimulation is random, manipulative, or malicious, then the books in question are not magic at all. Consider with what scorn the text speaks of the books that Jean de Satigny brings to Las Tres Marías. Every piece of literature that this man introduces produces a negative effect, from the "revistas de moda," which promote styles totally impractical for the active country man or woman; to the "folletines de guerra que se habían popularizado para crear el mito del soldado heroico"; and the "novelas románticas para Blanca" (236), which as was discussed earlier, are a factor in her nearly losing the love of her life, Pedro Tercero. All of these types of reading matter are abuses of storytelling, distortions of reality and emotional manipulation. Within this novel, storytelling is viewed almost as a sacred responsibility, associated with acts of love and the very perpetuation of life itself. Therefore it is no surprise that corrupt stories and books should emanate from a character who is presented as morally degenerate.

If the characters within *La casa de los espíritus* can be judged by the stories they tell and the books they read, then Esteban Trueba poses a special problem. The narrator and *lazarillo* throughout much of this novel, he tells a tale of his own life that is first and foremost compelling reading. His, we are certain, are the hands of a man who *does* have something interesting to relate, and his story proves it. Does this mean that the association of good storytelling with a strong moral base falls down in the character of Esteban Trueba? This question can be answered by remembering *when* it is that Trueba begins to tell his story. Although his tale begins chronologically when he was a young man, this is not the point in time from which he is "writing." Rather, as the novel explicitly states, Trueba begins writing all of these remembrances only *after* Alba has returned home, mutilated by her captors, and therefore after Trueba has been forced to change some very deeply held prejudices and beliefs. His written narration, then, is part of his spiritual regeneration, and he can be allowed within the morality of the book to tell a good tale because that is literally part of his expiation for past sins.

Even before his spiritual epiphany, the brusque Trueba associated the telling of personal tales with intimacy. He defines his friends thus:

> Con ellos discutía mis negocios, hablaba de política y a veces de la familia. (278)

But before his spiritual regeneration, brought about through recognition of his errors, Trueba is guilty of some gross abuses of storytelling. Probably the most glaring of these are his terrifying stories of what would happen if the socialists were to win the election. Fittingly, it is his bookish son Jaime, who lives in a "túnel de libros," who is most offended by his father's tactics:

> La única vez que Jaime perdió la paciencia fue cuando una mañana encontró la ciudad tapizada de afiches truculentos donde aparecía una madre barrigona y desolada, que intentaba inútilmente arrebatar a su hijo a un soldado comunista que se lo llevaba a Moscú. Era la campaña de terror organizado por el Senador Trueba y sus correligionarios. ... Aquello fue demasiado para Jaime. ... Cerró su túnel ... y se fue a dormir al hospital. (297)

This distortion of storytelling into which Trueba falls is nothing new in terms of his political methods. Earlier in the novel, he kept his workers in line at election time with a mixture of alcohol, rare friendliness, and lies. But this distortion of truth and the abuse of the power of a story cleverly told to move the masses is especially condemned within this book as it pertains to the Right in general and the leaders of the coup in specific.

As the Junta takes power after the coup, a successive degeneration of storytelling occurs until even words, the most basic unit of storytelling, fall into degeneration.

The first action of the military leaders after the coup is to attempt to find "witnesses" to swear to a story that is completely false within the novel, i.e., that el Presidente has committed suicide in a drunken stupor. It is fitting that it should be Jaime, with his love for books and veneration for tales that convey beautiful truths, whose last act of courage is to refuse to appear on nationwide television and propagate the story:

> —Haga esa declaración usted mismo, conmigo no cuenten, cabrones—respondió Jaime. Le sujetaron de los brazos. El primer golpe le cayó en el estómago. (327)

Through fear of retribution, moreover, Alba's first act when the military seizes control is to begin destroying Jaime's "túnel," along with all of the other written records that she foresees may be dangerous. Alba, with her grandmother's clairvoyance, senses that the military will launch an attack on these very documents and will destroy directly and indirectly much personal and national history, in the process of contraverting one of the sacred duties of storytelling. As the Junta continues in power, censorship begins to attack the language itself:

> La censura que al principio sólo abarcó los medios de comunicación, pronto se extendió a los textos escolares, las letras de las canciones, los argumentos de las películas y las conversaciones privadas. Había palabras prohibidas por bando militar, como la palabra compañero, y otras que no se decían por precaución, a pesar de que ningún bando las había eliminado del diccionario, como libertad, justicia y sindicato. (337)

The destruction of the language is symbolized by the death of el Poeta. The cause and effect, according to the novel, is clear: "Estaba enfermo y los acontecimientos de los últimos tiempos agotaron su deseo de seguir viviendo" (341). In addition to their crimes against humanity, the leaders of the coup are guilty of literal "lèse culture," and the body of world literature was truncated as a result.

Eventually, the destruction of truth becomes so great that all important events begin to be told by means of a blackly magical conundrum:

> [La] casa azul [del Poeta] estaba medio en ruinas. ... No se sabía
> si era obra de los militares, como decían los vecinos, o de los
> vecinos, como decían los militares. (341)

After so many lies, the truth of any important historical event becomes all but impossible for an outsider to determine. Did Allende kill himself, as the army claims, or did the army kill him, as the Allendes claim? Did the economy of Chile fail because the wealthy withdrew their money, or did the wealthy withdraw their money because the economy was failing? Did the upper-class women march in the streets because no food was being delivered, or were both a ploy to harass the Allende government? Again, it is not the role of this study to answer such historical questions. But what is appropriate is to point out how neatly the conundrums Isabel Allende comes up with in her book match the frustrating situation she depicts in her novel. In *La casa de los espíritus* the situation is at last reduced to the ultimate conundrum, which Esteban Trueba himself articulates:

> El país está en guerra, guerra contra el comunismo internacional,
> o contra el pueblo, ya no se sabe. (366).

As the moral pretext for the coup and the resultant Junta disintegrates, the storytelling becomes more and more distorted, and less convincing, until finally it deteriorates into obvious lies that can only be believed by those making a conscious effort to avoid the unpleasant truths:

> Los periódicos dijeron que los mendigos en las calles, que no se
> veían desde hacía tantos años, eran enviados por el comunismo
> internacional para desprestigiar a la Junta Militar. (336)

With answers like this one, the Junta begins to feel free to say anything with impunity, even to change world history and national boundaries in the schoolbooks the children study.

No moral storytelling can come from this entity so opposed to clear speech and the direct transmission of a tale. The closest thing to literature that the Junta is capable of producing is a document of terror, "una lista negra que manejaba la policía política" (338)

Eventually, the Junta steals from the people their most precious words and stories. For Isabel Allende, this is the ultimate crime. This is seen most clearly after Alba has been tortured. The final effect of such destruction of the truth is the loss of words themselves, and the loss of words, for Alba, is the spiritual equivalent of death:

> Nadie resistía mucho tiempo [en la perrera] ... antes de perder ...
> el significado de las palabras ... o, simplemente, empezar a morir.
> (362)

But it is at precisely this point in the narration that the real importance of storytelling become most clear. On the surface, destruction has proved stronger than creation, and the agents of evil have burned in a demonic pyre all the "libros mágicos" that filled so many of the del Valle and Trueba children with dreams. Without their stories, their language, their words, the moral storytellers of *La casa de los espíritus* must surely die, mustn't they? But no, such a grim outcome is far from being Isabel Allende's message. Pedro Tercero García, that teller of parables through song, escapes into exile. Of course this escape requires a degree of moral compromise, but nevertheless, he lives. The Junta may declare him a nonperson, smash his records the way soldiers deliberately smashed Esteban Trueba's record collection for sheer pleasure, and even prevent his name from being mentioned, but they cannot prevent his songs from living on in the hearts of his listeners. The same is true of the words of el Poeta, and for those of el Presidente. Alba, who survives solitary confinement and torture by "writing" in her head the history of her country along with that of her family, proves stronger than the forces that seek to blot out her tale.

The "libros mágicos" that began this chapter can be physically destroyed by the "pira infame" that burns "por error," along with the supposedly politically damaging works when Alba is arrested (23, 353). But the imaginative, creative forces that the books have inspired are not so easily blotted out. The triumph of Alba's survival is at least in part her continued ability to tell her own story and that of the women and men who shared her fate in prison. It is by preserving memory and continuing to tell this tale that the hopeful predictions found in el Presidente's last words can be fulfilled.

By writing, Alba manages to overcome her strict desire for vengeance and to forgive, just as Esteban Trueba manages through his writing to arrive at a much-needed absolution that enables him to die in peace. Thus, writing according to *La casa de los espíritus*, can be a spiritual experience.

The stimulations for a writer can be many, but the foundations for writing, as seen in this novel, come from two basic sources, both rooted in childhood. The first source is based on the stories of family history, which in this book the mothers are especially responsible for transmitting. The second one is drawn from the "libros mágicos," the childhood books that filled the childish imagination the way no other books read later are ever quite able to do. In order to transform these basic sources (the first of which influences content, and the second, style), something magic is needed. Perhaps the influence of the "libros mágicos" is one of the most literally magic in all of the so-called "magical realism" of this book, because it may be from their stimulus that the desire to write arises. Most people who read voraciously as children experience at one time or another the desire to write something as good as their childhood favorites. In the case of Alba, this stimulus combines with a good education (something her mother and grandmother lacked), a rich family history, and living through a historical moment whose telling is important to many people. This mystical configuration, according to the fiction of the book produces Alba's narrative, and it is a magic one indeed, somehow much greater than the sum of the parts that make it up.

I have shown the "libros mágicos" in *La casa de los espíritus* have a number of important implications: they stand for the magical adventure of childhood reading, for the well-told, compelling tale, and even as models for the writing of fiction. Moreover, I have shown how the "magic" aspects of these books—their ability to inspire the readers and even to stimulate them to write—is constant from the beginning to the end, with even more importance at the end. Once again, this goes to disprove the idea that a bit of magic is dropped into the book to get things going at the beginning, but that it is abandoned later on for a more realistic mode of narration. If anything, the "libros mágicos," though physically destroyed by the end, have a more literally magic power at the end of the book than they did at the beginning.

What are the "magic" books in Isabel Allende's personal "baúles encantados"? Surely they are some of the same ones that Alba read. Yet as the "baúles" magically expanded with her later reading, one can guess at others they stretched to encompass—Gabriel García Márquez, William Faulkner, Henri Troyat.... But in the end, part of the magic of this secret store is that it is hers alone, and of dimensions that only she really knows. "Alba no soy yo," she has said on various occasions (*Der Spiegel*, Vera Jarach, Michael Moody, for example). Therefore, we cannot ascribe to her all of the literary make-up of her character, Alba. What is more, an important part of Allende's writing background—her experience in journalism—is not shared by Alba, but rather is more similar to the background of the protagonist of *De amor y de sombra*, Irene Beltrán. But in spite of this, one assumption seems very safe to make in conclusion to this look at books, storytelling, and writing within

*La casa de los espíritus.* That is that for Allende, telling a good story is an act of love, and that in addition to all of the other things that this book is, it is also Isabel Allende's gift of love to us.

E. THOMSON SHIELDS, JR.

# *Ink, Blood, and Kisses:* La casa de los espíritus and the Myth of Disunity

In an April 1985 address at Montclair State College, "A Few Words About Latin America," Isabel Allende gave her own perspective on Latin American literature: "In these books, written with ink, blood and kisses, reality and fantasy go hand in hand, as they do in real life in Latin America." It would be hard to imagine a better metaphor for Allende's first novel, *La casa de los espíritus,* than "written with ink, blood and kisses." Ink—words, narratives, myths—do not come easily, especially in Latin America, a land of both blood and kisses, of violence, coups, rapes, murder and of love, love-making, family, and ritual. Myth creation, if it aspires to tell as much truth as possible, does not happen with simple strokes on typewriter keys, particularly if the myth must bring together violence and love without glossing over one to emphasize the other. The new myth created cannot conform to old ways, old prejudices—it cannot present a false sense of unity if it wishes to tell more truth than the myths that came before. Therefore, in order to write a new myth for *La casa de los espíritus,* Allende must write a myth based on ink, blood, and kisses. The new myth must find some way to bring together what we usually consider to be irreconcilable elements, violence and love. In other words, the new myth must be a myth of disunity.[1]

Allende portrays the myth of disunity nowhere better than in the scene where *el viejo* Pedro García tells the story of the fox and the hens:

From *Hispanófila: Literatura-Ensayos* (May 1990): 79-86. © 1990 by University of North Carolina. Reprinted by permission.

23

> Un día el viejo Pedro García les contó a Blanca y a Pedro
> Tercero el cuento de las gallinas que se pusieron de acuerdo para
> enfrentar a un zorro que se metía todas las noches en el gallinero
> para robar los huevos y devorarse los pollitos. Las gallinas deci-
> dieron que ya estaban hartas de aguantar la prepotencia del zorro,
> lo esperaron organizadas y cuando entró al gallinero, le cerraron
> el paso, lo rodearon y se le fueron encima a picotazos hasta que
> lo dejaron más muerto que vivo.
>     —Y entonces se vio que el zorro escapaba con la cola entre las
> piernas, perseguido por las gallinas—terminó el viejo. (128)

But the scene does not end with the old man's folktale of strength through
unity. Each of the two listeners—Blanca, the landowner's daughter, and
Pedro Tercero, the old man's grandson—reacts to the story in his or her own
way:

> Blanca se rió con la historia y dijo que eso era imposible, porque
> las gallinas nacen estúpidas y débiles y los zorros nacen astutos y
> fuertes, pero Pedro Tercero no se rió. Se quedó toda la tarde
> pensativo, rumiando el cuento del zorro y las gallinas, y tal vez
> ese fue el instante en que el niño comenzó a hacerse hombre.
> (128)

Normally, in a world which emphasizes unity, we would force ourselves to
choose one reaction over the other. But Allende does not give us a signal as
to how we should react to Pedro García's story. Blanca's laugh is as valid a
response to the story as Pedro Tercero's meditations. Instead of
editorializing, making one of the two reactions the "accepted" reading,
Allende presents both ideas as equal. What Allende gives is a new myth, the
myth of disunity. Through ink—through her juxtaposition of the two
reactions on equal terms—Allende brings together blood and kisses. For
what is more violent than laughing at someone's beliefs, as Blanca does? And
what is more loving, as Pedro Tercero eventually does, than to turn someone
else's beliefs into the theme song of one's life?

   This one scene encapsulates, in good mythic form, the entire argument
of *La casa de los espíritus*. The full plot of the novel is too complex to
summarize here, but what can be done is to show how this same scene—the
uneditorialized juxtaposition of two perspectives on the same action—occurs
throughout the work. For example, when Estaban Trueba, the landowner,
first goes to his plantation, *Las Tres Marías*, he works hard in an attempt to

forget the memory of his dead fiancée, Rosa. However, the memory rests too strongly in Esteban's mind, and he decides—consciously or unconsciously—that only sex will help ease his pain. In order to find the sexual outlet he feels he needs, Esteban rapes a young *campesina*, Pancha García, the sister of his overseer. In this moment, we feel for Pancha as a victim of the master's brutal violations, like her mother before her and her gandmother before that (57-58).

Allende could very easily leave the story here, a vulgar Marxist myth of the proletariat victimized by the bourgeoisie and its capitalist values. But nothing happens this simply in Allende's world. Esteban not only victimizes, but he becomes victimized himself through the very same act. Years later, the illegitimate grandson of Pancha's rape returns to cause havoc in Esteban's life. Esteban says:

> Un día estaba en el corredor, fumando un cigarro antes de la siesta, cuando se acercó un niño moreno y se me plantó al frente en silencio. Se llamaba Esteban García. Era mi nieto, pero yo no lo sabía y sólo ahora, debido a las terribles cosas que han ocurrido por obra suya, me he enterado del parentesco que nos une. Era también nieto de Pancha García, una hermana de Pedro Segundo, a quien en realidad no recuerdo. (182)

Esteban García, the child (or, rather, grandchild) of rape, leads Esteban Trueba into a fight with Pedro Tercero—the same Pedro Tercero who appropriates the story of the fox and the hens—a fight from which Trueba never completely recovers. Trueba fights Pedro Tercero, Blanca's lover, in order to defend Blanca's honor. However, both men end up being brutally beaten by one another. Instead of being the traditional forceful Latin American male, the *macho*, Trueba, from this point on, begins to reform, accepting more and more of his family's liberal ideals even though he himself remains a political conservative to death.

Once again, it would be easy to posit a myth of unity—victimizer becomes victim, and both the individual and the world become better for the lesson learned through the experience. But again, no single unifying myth acts as a static measure for *La casa de los espíritus*. Esteban García returns once more, this time to rape Esteban Trueba's granddaughter, Alba, while she is in prison for political crimes. Ironically, Trueba has sponsored Esteban García's entrance into the police force, where García gains the opportunity to have charge of Alba while she is incarcerated. After the rape scene, the novel ends with the revelation that Alba is pregnant, but because she has also slept with her lover, Miguel, she cannot be sure whose child she carries. "[Estoy] gestando a la criatura que tengo en el vientre," says Alba, "hija de tantas violaciones, o tal vez hija de Miguel, pero sobre todo hija mía" (379-80). The final result arrived at through this storyline of violence (the rape of Pancha), love (Trueba fights Pedro Tercero over the honor of his daughter), and again violence (Alba's rape) is the "blood and kisses" myth. The child Alba carries is the daughter of either, neither, and/or both Esteban García and Miguel. The child embodies the myth of disunity.

We need to remember, though, how Allende creates her myth. Blood and kisses do not stand alone, but become unified by ink. Ink—words, narrative—serves as the unifying agent by which such disparate elements can be brought together in the same story. For Allende, words have the mystical power to create such transformations. "De manera muy primitiva," writes Allende in her essay "La magia de las palabras," "le atribuí a la palabra el poder de resucitar a los muertos, reunir a los desaparecidos, reconstruir el mundo perdido" (448).[2] With this in mind, we can look at the novel's overall narrative structure—not the plot, but the manner in which the story is told— and can see how ink transforms blood and kisses into more than just literal acts of violence and love; blood and kisses also become metaphors for the more abstract ideas of the real world and the fantastic.

Allende writes *La casa de los espíritus*, not in her own voice, but through the persona of Alba. Still, as with everything in the novel, the narrative structure cannot be described as simple first-person narrative. In fact, not until the last pages of the book does Alba break into an open presentation of her own voice. Most of the novel, though written by Alba, consists of material she gleans from the notebooks of her grandmother, Clara, interspersed with the memoirs of her grandfather, Esteban Trueba. The difficulty of such a structure occurs in the fact that a variety of voices come together in one history—Clara's notes retold through Alba's "objective" third-person narrative, Esteban's first-person memoirs, and Alba's first person epilogue. Each voice points the reader in a different direction. Clara's notes concerning her spiritualist friends and their séances point the reader to a world of souls, what Allende (in the opening quotation to this essay) has termed the fantastic element. Esteban's memoirs, on the other hand, concentrate on the political/economic realities of the physical world. Even when he talks about love, Esteban talks about work in the same breath—such as when he works in order to forget the memory of his dead fiancée, Rosa. Finally, when Alba turns to personal narrative in her epilogue, we might expect that the words of a woman who loves both her grandmother and grandfather equally could create some sense of unity. However, no unity appears, at least in the traditional sense. Alba writes:

> Quiero pensar que mi oficio es la vida y que mi misión no es prolongar el odio, sino sólo llenar estas páginas mientras espero el regreso de Miguel, mientras entierro a mi abuelo que ahora descansa a mi lado en este cuarto, mientras aguardo que lleguen tiempos mejores.… (379)

Alba can only fill pages with the stories given to her by her grandparents, an activity which fills the days until a better time comes. A traditional myth would tell us who is right and who is wrong, but this new myth does not tell us what to think. Nor does it create a picture of Hegel's thesis, antithesis, and ultimate synthesis. Both Clara's and Esteban's versions of the events have validity, but they are neither combined into some new "correct" point of view nor is either given predominance. Despite the lack of traditional unity in *La casa de los espíritus*, Allende has not simply recorded stories without giving them some purpose. Her purpose, though, is not the traditional one of judging actions, giving them values, for such a purpose would be exclusive, not inclusive. Exclusionary acts matter to Allende because exclusion occurs first on the fringe. Exclusion disenfranchises those who are not part of a central tradition, and Allende fills *La casa de los espíritus* with people who live on the extreme borders of society—women, *campesinos*, Marxists, spiritualists, and so on. Allende's structure, instead of excluding the fringe element, brings it into focus. With her ink, Allende brings together the extremes—blood and kisses.

To understand how *La casa de los espíritus* brings the fringe into the narrative tradition, a short overview of Roland Barthes' theory of language can be used. In *Writing Degree Zero*, Barthes states:

> We know that language is a corpus of prescriptions and habits common to all the writers of a period. Which means that a language is a kind of natural ambience wholly pervading the writer's expression, yet without endowing it with form or content: it is, as it were, an abstract circle of truths, outside of which alone the solid residue of an individual *logos* begins to settle. It enfolds the whole of literary creation much as the earth, the sky, and the line where they meet outline a familiar habitat for mankind. It is not so much a stock of materials as a horizon, which implies both a boundary and a perspective; in short, it is the comforting area

> of an ordered space. The writer literally takes nothing from it; a language is for him rather a frontier, to overstep which alone might lead to the linguistically supernatural; it is a field of action, the definition of, and hope for, a possibility. (9)

Language, then, is a horizon beyond which people generally do not go. Allende's project, however, steps into the area Barthes calls "the linguistically supernatural." To step into this area can be discomforting, and such a step has the feeling of being a supernatural act; but exploring the linguistically supernatural expands the horizons of language by making what was once considered incomprehensible a part of everyday life. Allende, in "A Few Words About Latin America," says, "In America we are still inventing our own language...." To invent language, Allende must go beyond the accepted limits, the traditional limits, and explore new linguistic areas usually thought to be beyond comprehension. Allende, by positing a world where two linguistic extremes can coexist—violence and love—expands the linguistic playing field, and in the same act, enfranchises what was once only the fringe element.

This expansion of language's playing field I have called the myth of disunity. I do not call *La casa de los espíritus* a pluralistic myth because, again in the traditional sense, it is not. Traditionally, pluralism means that by positing a variety of ideas, by looking at an issue from a number of different perspectives, we will achieve a complete picture of "the truth." But no such truth, no *logos* appears in Allende's novel. Just at the moment we would expect a conclusion, during the last sentences of Alba's epilogue, Allende deprives us of just such an easy satisfaction:

> Clara los escribió para que me sirvieran ahora para rescatar las cosas del pasado y sobrevivir a mi propio espanto. El primero es un cuaderno escolar de veinte hojas, escrito con una delicada caligrafía infantil. Comienza así, «Barrabás llegó a la familia por vía marítima …». (380)

Just when we would expect some form of resolution, Allende takes us back to the beginning of the novel, ending by repeating the book's very first sentence. Instead of closure, which would imply some form of *logos*, the process of ink, blood, and kisses starts again. It may appear that closure comes through the use of a circular process, but not here. When Allende goes back to the beginning of her novel, she gives us a sign that we must rewrite the same story again—a story already lived by the history's characters; a story written by Clara, Esteban, and Alba; and a story rewritten by Alba. The writing of this book never stops, never finds a point of completion because in each return to rewrite the story, readers approach the work with new knowledge—for example, knowing that Alba creates/edits the story. The unity of *La casa de los espíritus* becomes its disunity, its ability and need to contain within its narrative structure those things which cannot be reconciled to one another—violence and love, the fantastic and the real, the various rewritings (rereadings) of its own history.

Finally, the idea of unity in disunity, alongside the idea of the linguistically supernatural, helps to explain Clara's last words to Alba. As she lies dying, Clara is reported as saying, "Cuando ese momento llegara, quería que estuviera tranquila, porque en su caso la muerte no sería una separación, sino una forma de estar más unidas. Alba lo comprendió perfectamente" (257). Through these words, we more completely understand the novel's title—*La casa de los espíritus*. For Clara, death does not mean becoming a ghost—*un espectro, un fantasma*. Ghosts are limited creatures, stuck haunting one place. They are separated from the world, for whatever reason, and are condemned to be seen or felt, but never heard. On the other hand, spirits, *espíritus*, inhabit everything, appropriate everything. Clara, when she dies, will become a spirit. She will live within and beyond the limits of language. As a spirit, she will be everywhere, will become part of the linguistically supernatural. In effect, by leaving her physical body, Clara will embody the myth of disunity in its most complete, its most unified, form. As a spirit, she will be more unified because she will hold more of the universe's irreconcilable elements. And Alba "lo comprendió perfectamente."

Myth, violence, and love. Ink, blood, and kisses. Reality and fantasy hand-in-hand. Latin America. For Allende, taking in the fringes of society— accepting Clara, Esteban Trueba, Esteban García, Rosa, Alba, and all the other characters in *La casa de los espíritus*—means accepting words such as these, even if we do not understand them. "El único material que uso son palabras," writes Allende in "La magia de las palabras" (447). All we have to help us understand the world are words. And words control us, not so much by what they say, but by what they do not say. For Allende, only by expanding the horizon of language will we be able to say all that needs to be said. Only by accepting the myth of disunity can language open itself enough to include all those as equals who now live on or beyond language's borders. Irreconcilable plurality, this is the message, the unity, of *La casa de los espíritus*.

## NOTES

1. By myth, I mean a closed construct proposed through a text for widespread social acceptance. Myth is that aspect of a work which gives the writer's vision of a universal, as opposed to private, perspective of "truth."

2. The term *desaparecidos*, disappeared ones, has political connotations, particularly for Allende, who is the niece of the former president of Chile, Salvador Allende. The word is used to name those who have disappeared without a trace, usually assumed to have been abducted by the government for political reasons. It is interesting to note that Allende's second novel, *De amor y de sombra* (Barcelona: Plaza y Janes, 1984), uses as its central theme the idea that government abductees are just one among many types of *desaparecidos* a repressive social system can create. In *De amor y de sombra*, *desaparecidos* are usually those who either place themselves or are placed by others on the fringes of society.

## WORKS CITED

Allende, Isabel, *La casa de los espíritus*. Barcelona: Plaza & Janes, 1982.

———. "A Few Words About Latin America." Trans. Jo Ann Englebert. Montclair State College, April 1985.

———. "La magia de las palabras." *Revista Iberoamericana*. 51 (1985): 447-52.

Barthes, Roland. *Writing Degree Zero*. Trans. Annette Lavers and Colin Smith. New York: Hill and Wang, 1977.

DORIS MEYER

# "Parenting the Text": Female Creativity and Dialogic Relationships in Isabel Allende's La casa de los espíritus

In *The Newly Born Woman* [*La Jeune Née*, 1975], the French feminist critic Hélène Cixous speaks of a woman's symbolic bisexuality, "that is to say the location within oneself of the presence of both sexes, evident and insistent in different ways according to the individual..." (85). For Cixous, this "gift of changeability" (88), this "capacity to depropriate herself without self-interest" (87), is potentially liberating and radically different from the traditional man's need to prove himself, to "gain more masculinity: plus-value of virility, authority, power, money, or pleasure, all of which reenforce his phallocentric narcissism at the same time" (87). As portrayed by Cixous, hierarchical Western society has trapped and, ironically, victimized man on a psychic level, ensnaring him in his own "rigid law of individuation" (96). Woman, on the other hand has managed to stay in touch with her bisexual unconscious by "liv[ing] in dreams, embodied but still deadly silent, in silences, in voiceless rebellions" (95). Breaking this silence by the act of writing, woman can "displace this 'within,' explode it, overturn it" (95), externalize the private world of the feminine Imaginary and "spread values over the world, un-quoted values that will change the rules of the game" (97). Cixous's "sorties" into the terrain of feminist theory are not an exercise in utopianism; *The Newly Born Woman* is a political text with an autobiographical impulse. "I come," writes Cixous, "biographically, from a

From *Hispania* 73 (no. 2) (May 1990): 360-365. © 1990 by University of Southern California. Reprinted by permission.

rebellion, from a violent and anguished direct refusal to accept what is happening on the stage of whose edge I find I am placed, as a result of the combined accidents of History" (70). As a Jewish Algerian French woman, Cixous is committed to bringing about a non-hierarchical, non-repressive future, "defeating [masculine domination], yes, but in order to espouse ... a union that is the opposite of rape and masculine abduction" (116).

A similar vision of a "newly born woman" engendered by personal experience emerges from Isabel Allende's first novel, *La casa de los espíritus* [1982]. Like Cixous, Allende believes literature can help transform society: "We are a new people. Out of so much accumulated, shared suffering, out of so many forms of violence and oppression, a tremendous force is arising which, as it gathers momentum, will change our relations of dependence. We have the audacity and candor of the young. Imagination and a sense of the magical will not only serve to seduce the readers of the ill-named *literature of the Boom*; we will also be able to use these qualities in building an original society, one that is happier and more just" ("A Few Words" 10). In the early 1970s, Allende witnessed the beginning of a democratic movement for socioeconomic change in Chile, only to see it crushed by an alliance of conservative forces. Her response in this novel is a direct refusal to accept the patriarchal oppression historically practiced by the upper classes and the military in Latin America.

In addition, and of central interest to this paper, Allende creates a feminocentric novel that—in the tradition of the self-conscious text—represents through discourse two empowering and transforming female experiences associated with renewal: giving birth and being reborn. In other words, *La casa de los espíritus* focuses both on the physical experience of creating a text (within the text) and the psychological experience of creating a new self. Central to this female-centered approach to the novel is a narrative strategy that symbolizes a dual psychosexual inheritance at the most profound creative levels, as suggested by Cixous.

*La casa de los espíritus* is the story of four generations of a Latin American (implicitly Chilean) family told by two narrators. The primary voice, representing 90% of the narration, is that of Alba, the youngest member of the Trueba family. Despite occasional subjective references, her voice is essentially objective assuming the tone of an omniscient narrator who recounts the history of her family. Only when she reaches the present [ca. 1974] in the epilogue of the novel does she reveal how and why she is writing. The secondary voice is that of her grandfather, Esteban Trueba, who interrupts Alba's narrative from time to time with his own testimony. In the epilogue we learn that the elderly Esteban has, in fact, just died, and that it was he who urged Alba to write the family story: "Empecé a escribir con la ayuda de mi abuelo," she says, "cuya memoria permaneció intacta hasta el último instante de sus noventa años. De su puño y letra escribió varias páginas y cuando consideró que lo había dicho todo, se acostó en la cama de Clara" (378).

In addition to her grandfather's memory, Alba has her grandmother Clara's notebooks, her mother Blanca's letters, and assorted records and family documents to help her piece together her narrative. Like Isabel Allende, Alba identifies with her foremothers and finds in their writing a timeless mirror of female experience:

> En algunos momentos tengo la sensación de que esto ya lo he vivido y que he escrito estas mismas palabras, pero comprendo que no soy yo, sino otra mujer, que anotó en sus cuadernos para que yo me sirviera de ellos. Escribo, ella escribió, que la memoria es frágil y el transcurso de una vida es muy breve y sucede todo tan de prisa, que no alcanzamos a ver la relación entre los acontecimientos, no podemos medir la consecuencia de los actos, creemos en la ficción del tiempo, en el presente, el pasado y el futuro, pero puede ser también que todo ocurre simultá-neamente, como decían las tres hermanas Mora, que eran capaces de ver en el espacio los espíritus de todas las épocas. Por eso mi abuela Clara escribía en sus cua-dernos, para ver las cosas en su dimensión real y para burlar a la mala memoria" (379).

This sense of the community of female experience across the boundaries of time and space conveys a message of female empowerment that subverts historical stereotypes of submissive women and mocks androcentric individualism. Alba—who perceives this strength and survives because of it—is a symbol of female self-awareness and potentiality on the eve of a new era. Unlike most contemporary feminist authors who reject or exclude the hegemonic patriarchal voice as *non grata* other, Allende is, on the whole, conciliatory; indeed Esteban Trueba's testimony is essential to the novel's theme of self-renewal and rebirth. Nearing death, Esteban writes, with Alba, in order to explain the past, but he also writes out of his own need to exorcise the sins of selfishness and pride that drove him to violence and cost him the love of his adored Clara. His testimony, like his refurbishing of the eccentric house built for Clara and neglected since her death, is an effort to renounce authoritarianism and seek communion with the spirit of his indomitable wife. In Allende's metatext, Esteban represents the androcentric vision of history, the perspective within Latin American (and Judeo-Christian) culture that has traditionally imposed its discourse of power and law of privilege. The intersection of Esteban's aging, disillusioned voice—no longer dominant— with that of his young, vibrant granddaughter—no longer muted—points toward a transformation in "the rules of the game." Indeed, Allende's ingenious blending of the two narrative voices not only clearly situates the female voice within the context of a *machista* culture but it also displaces and subverts the power of that culture.

One might interpret this narrative strategy as a novelistic rendering of the "double-voiced discourse" described in socio-ideological terms by the Russian critic M. M. Bakhtin as "social heteroglossia" or "another's speech in another's language serving to express authorial intentions but in a refracted way" (324-26). Elaine Showalter has adapted Bakhtin's concept of the "double-voiced discourse" to her theory of gynocritics in order to illustrate the internalized duality of female literary expression, generated in the language and culture of a "dominant" order but from the perspective of a "muted" group within that order (204). Applied to the discursive relationships of *La casa de los espíritus*, this dialogic approach to the novel reveals an ironic twist: the muted voice (Alba) has become the dominant one in the novel, and vice-versa.

Allende explicitly traces the emergence of this confident female voice through Alba's coming-to-awareness of the silent but unrelenting rebellion of her grandmother Clara. Other female ancestors were non-conformist in various ways, but only Clara managed to create her own magical space in which she opted to remain silent, commune with the spirits, practice clairvoyance and write a detailed diary that ignored historical chronology. As Marjorie Agosín has accurately observed, Clara's "estética de silencio" was not a capitulation to society's efforts to muzzle women but rather a positive act implying a rejection of hypocrisy and violence and a commitment to non-traditional forms of communication (450). Her bizarre habits of dress, her refusal to let her headstrong husband control her life, and her unswerving devotion to her children, her friends and her work with the disadvantaged were Clara's ways of affirming her own values and autonomy. Clara's rebellion, however, was a private one, and the space she created for herself was a world apart.[1] Discourse, for her, was metaphysical and ahistorical, "[un] delicado equilibrio que ella mantenía entre los espíritus del Más Allá y las almas necesitadas del Más Acá" (148), and social reform was a personal not a political crusade. She neglected her own household in order to bring food and clothing to the needy, but she knew that her good will was not enough. As she explained to Blanca, "Esto sirve para tranquilizarnos la conciencia, hija … Pero no ayuda a los pobres. No necesitan caridad, sino justicia" (124).

Alba adored her grandmother as "el alma de la gran casa de la esquina" (250, and when Clara died, the child understood that they would be separated in flesh but not in spirit. Years later, when Alba was raped and tortured and left to die in a military prison isolation cell, Clara's spirit appeared to her urging her to fool death and write herself into life again. She must testify, Clara told her, to the events she had witnessed and write her way out of the "cramped confines of patriarchal space"[2] into the liberating space of female truth. Alba's text, inscribed only in her imagination, would be her private refuge in a world of madness, just as Clara's diaries had liberated her from Esteban's uncontrolled violence. Silently and alone, Alba began to create her secret text of life and hope.

After being transferred to a woman's concentration camp, she found unexpected support among her co-prisoners who cared for her and encouraged her to write, giving her a precious notebook and pencil. In writing her own story, they said, she would write for them all. This protective female community, united in mutual concern and support, reinforced Alba's will to survive. As Nina Auerbach has noted, communities of women bound by hospitality and sympathy "possess a power of quasi-magical self-sustainment that blooms of apparent death" (11). By writing, Alba transcended her own personal tragedy, achieving a new level of collective historical awareness that was far stronger than her grandmother's evasive rebellion.

Alba's act of communal affirmation fulfills the generative, transformational relationship, of reader/text/author, central to Allende's novel. Alba "reads" the "texts" of female experience (such as Clara's, Blanca's, Ana Díaz's) and, inspired by this polyvocal female testimony, she "authors" her own text and consequently "en-genders" her own selfhood. Her awareness of the social context of gender is highlighted by her identification with Clara, as cited earlier and as represented by the circular structure of the narrative, which begins and ends with words from her grandmother's notebooks. By taking Clara's words and making them her own, Alba both accepts and adapts them to suit her own intentions, which respond to a different historical context. Her language is thus a result of dialogic interaction, an experiencing of self vs. other which is, according to Bakhtin in "Discourse in the Novel," the natural orientation of all human discourse:

> As a living, socio-ideological concrete thing, as heteroglot opinion, language, for the individual consciousness, lies on the

borderline between oneself and the other. The word in language
is half someone else's. It becomes "one's own" only when the
speaker populates it with his own intention, his own accent, when
he appropriates the word, adapting it to his own semantic and
expressive intention. Prior to this moment of appropriation, the
word does not exist in any neutral and impersonal language ...
but rather it exists in other people's mouths, in other people's
contexts, serving other people's intentions: it is from there that
one must take the word, and make it one's own (293-94).

The expropriation of language, and thus the act of becoming, necessarily
involves "reading" the various heteroglossia, or different languages, of the
world around one. This is illustrated by Alba who feels compelled to write
out of understanding that "cada pieza [del rompecabezas] tiene una razón de
ser tal como es" (379) and that she has to break the relentless chain of hatred
that links different generations and social classes in unending violence.
Esteban Trueba, the secondary narrator, also comes to understand the
destructive nature of his rage and is able to die happily with Clara's forgiving
spirit by his side. Essential to both characters' transformed vision is the
dialogic interaction between themselves and among others: Alba must
understand the "language" of Colonel García just as Esteban must prostrate
himself before Tránsito Soto.

The blending of two narrative voices, representing two opposing
"languages" is also an example of what Bakhtin refers to as "hybridization":
"one of the most important modes in the historical life and evolution of all
languages. we may even say that language and languages change historically
primarily by means of hybridization, by means of a mixing of various
'languages' co-existing within the boundaries of a single dialect, a single
national language ..." (358-59). Such intentional novelistic hybridization,
according to Bakhtin, "is *an artistically organized system for bringing different
languages in contact with one another*, a system having as its goal the
illumination of one language by means of another, the carving-out of a living
image of another language" (361).[3] A classic example of this would be
Cervantes's *Don Quijote* in which the dialogue between Don Quijote and
Sancho has a transformational effect on both protagonists and the
concomitant effect of making the reader question the monologic, univocal
world-view of the protagonist or others like him. Allende's narrative
juxtaposition achieves a similar effect: not only are the fundamental tenets of
androcentrism (the primacy of the male over the female, logos over eros,
vertical hierarchy over lateral relationships) repudiated, but the traditional

family/State structural reinforcement of the nationalistic romance, so popular in Latin America in the early and mid 20th century, is called into question.[4]

In a recent essay on feminist literary criticism and the discourse of power in Latin American women's literature, Jean Franco points out that critics should focus less on defining a female voice or style in writing and more on women's relationship with the institutions of power, be they literary or otherwise. To quote Franco:

> No se trata de averiguar si las escritoras tienen temas específicos o un estilo diferente a los hombres, sino de explorar las relaciones del poder. Todo escritor, tanto hombre como mujer, enfrenta el problema de la autoridad textual o de la voz poética ya que, desde el momento en que empieza a escribir, establece relaciones de afiliación o de diferencia para con los 'maestros' del pasado. Esta confrontación tiene un interés especial cuando se trata de una mujer escribiendo 'contra' el poder asfixiante de una voz patriarcal (41).

Franco places the word "contra" in quotes to indicate the internalized nature of the patriarchal voice and the paradox of the female writer's struggle against its persuasive authority in an effort to give birth to the sense of "otherness" within. In an article written in response to Franco's, Francine Masiello points out that Bakhtin's double-voiced discourse is particularly suited to Latin American reality and feminist concerns:

> En el caso de América Latina esta clase de discurso doble emerge por dos razones: en primer lugar, a las mujeres aisladas de los centros del poder (y se enfatiza, de manera radical, la distancia entre la mujer y el discurso hegemónico), les toca inventar un lenguaje híbrido que reconozca las estructuras del poder a la vez que ofrezca una alternativa a las mismas; *la voz de la mujer, por consiguiente, siempre se desdobla para hacerse sentir.* En segundo lugar, esta pluralidad recuerda la violencia trazada en la sociedad civil, de manera que la identidad femenina no se limita a una espacio privilegiado único; más bien, se utilizan la pluralidad de los márgenes y las zonas periféricas para redefinir a la mujer como actante político y social (56-57; emphasis added).

By structuring *La casa de los espíritus* as a double-voiced discourse in which the grandfather represents the internalized patriarchal culture and the granddaughter the newly born feminist, Allende embodies this emergence of a polyvocal feminist text which expresses the hope of a ethically transformed community. By giving voice to the oppressor in addition to the dominant voice of the oppressed, Allende symbolically portrays the "parented" female text as defined by Elaine Showalter:

> *If a man's text, as [Harold] Bloom and Edward Said have maintained, is fathered, then a woman's text is not only mothered but parented; it confronts both paternal and maternal precursors and must deal with the problems and advantages of both lines of inheritance.* Woolf says in *A Room of One's Own* that 'a woman writing thinks back through her mothers.' But a woman writing unavoidably thinks back through her fathers as well; only male writers can forget or mute half their parentage (203; emphasis added).

Alba effectively comes to grips with both her paternal and her maternal precursors by making peace with her grandfather and collaborating with him in writing the family history.[5] She is the child of the independent Blanca and revolutionary Pedro Tercero García, but she is also profoundly affected by the vivid memories of her grandmother Clara and grandfather Esteban. Their memories make up the majority of the text as "ventriloquated" (in Bakhtin's terminology) by Alba and ultimately by Allende, whose identification with Alba is patent.

Although Alba is the dominant narrative voice, she interprets the experiences of many women divided by class, race and economic situation, who, like herself, have been oppressed by patriarchal culture in Latin America. If they have something in common, it is not an ideology but a spirit or moral affiliation that values nurturing relationships over the exercise of power.[6] Without rejecting the paternal inheritance, Allende's novel calls for a revaluation of the maternal generosity epitomized by the anonymous woman of the slums who comforted Alba on the night of her release from prison: "Le dije que había corrido mucho riesgo al ayudarme y ella sonrió. Entonces supe que el colonel García y otros como él tienen sus días contados, porque no han podido destruir el espíritu de esas mujeres" (377).

NOTES

1. In an article entitled "Texto, ley, transgresión: especulación sobre la novela (feminista) de vanguardia," Francine Masiello offers a reading of early feminist novels by María Luisa Bombal, Norah Lange and Teresa de la Parra in which she discusses the subversive, anti-patriarchal nature of their female protagonists: "... en lugar de reducirse a un objeto dentro del discurso del otro (del marido, del hijo o del padre), las protagonistas de Bombal, Lange y Parra eluden el compromiso erótico para proteger su libertad. Dicha libertad les permite a las mujeres redefinirse no en términos de la herencia o el acto procreador, sino en términos del cuerpo propio y la identidad que éste produce. Son modos de producir una nueva identidad, de reclamar el cuerpo de la mujer como territorio independiente" (814). Her description evokes the character of Clara and suggests that she is the soul-sister of the protagonists of these earlier novels. Like them, the product of an earlier generation of women not accustomed to activism, Clara expresses her defiance by retreating into her own imaginary world and by building relationships with other women.

2. Elaine Showalter, in her article "Feminist Criticism in the Wilderness," discusses the concept of "female space" which has recently received much attention by feminist critics, including Cixous for whom this signifies the "wild zone" or repressed female consciousness. According to Showalter, "through voluntary entry into the wild zone, other feminist critics tell us, a woman can write her way out of the 'cramped confines of patriarchal space.'" [Here, Showalter cites Mari McCarthy.] The images of this journey are now familiar in feminist quest fictions and in essays about them. The writer/heroine, often guided by another woman, travels to the "mother country" of liberated desire and female authenticity ..." (201). Allende's novel is not a classic linguistic example of entering the "wild zone," yet it has much in common with the theoretical grounding of this concept and its liberating psychological effect on women.

3. Bakhtin acknowledged that the decentralizing concept of "heteroglossia and multi-languagedness" fundamental to his theory of the dialogic novel could not be espoused by a "sealed-off interest group, caste or class, existing within an internally unitary and unchanging core of its own" (368). Such groups—like the Latin American oligarchy that produced its own mythology of power—cannot tolerate threats to their hegemony. Bakhtin did not, however, see the application of his theories

to the issue of gender. This has been successfully accomplished in a recent book by Dale M. Bauer entitled *Feminist Dialogics: A Theory of Failed Community*, although, as her subtitle suggests, she concentrates on novels in which the feminist interpretive process ends in failure because "they [the resisting female characters] do not come fully to self-awareness of their differences with dominant ideology, and this failure of engagement dooms them to silence, a failure in tandem with the failure of community" (167).

Bauer points out the crucial nature of the triangular relationship between reader, text and author in Bakhtin's approach to discourse analysis and relates it to the internal dialogics of feminism: "The feminist struggle is not one between a conscious 'awakened' or natural voice *and* the voice of patriarchy 'out there.' Rather, precisely because we all internalize the authoritative voice of patriarchy, we must struggle to refashion inherited social discourse into words which rearticulate intentions (here feminist ones) other than normative or disciplinary ones" (2).

4. Again, I am indebted here to Francine Masiello's article, cited in note 1, in which she draws a contrast between the discourse of feminist novels of the vanguard period and that of the traditional nationalist romance. In her words, "... las novelas femeninas nos obligan a reconsiderar la creatividad del individuo relacionada con la dinámica familia-Estado ... [Estas novelas] cuestionan los principios que organizan la familia dentro de la obra literaria. Echan una mirada al malestar de la hija de familia y cuestionan tanto la lógica de la familia como la obligación de la mujer de asegurar la reproducción de la especie dentro del sistema estatal establecido" (812-13). Undoubtedly, the novels of Bombal, Lange and Parra are important precursors to the re-vision of culture and history portrayed by later feminist authors such as Allende. A notable difference in these two generations of female novels is the increased emphasis in the 1980s on the socio-historical context of the female experience as well as the tendency of today's protagonist to turn her defiance outward and participate in a restructuring of society.

5. Allende's text is "parented" in the literary as well as the cultural sense. She was evidently influenced by the feminist tradition of novels of a generation before her and also by the patriarchal tradition of family sagas in the traditional nationalist romance style. The hybridization or dialogic relationship between the two literary traditions has resulted in "the carving out of a living image of another language" (as Bakhtin put it) in the literary context.

6.  This psychosocial dichotomy of moral values has been analyzed by Carol
    Gilligan in her groundbreaking study *In a Different Voice*, published the
    same year as Allende's novel.

## Works Cited

Agosín, Marjorie. "Isabel Allende: *La casa de los espíritus*." *Revista
    Interamericana de Bibliografía* 35 (1985): 448-58.

Allende, Isabel. "A Few Words about Latin America." An address to
    Hispanic students at Montclair State College, April 1985. Trans. Jo
    Anne Engelbert. Typescript courtesy of translator.

——. *La casa de los espíritus*. Barcelona: Plaza & Janes, 1982.

Auerbach, Nina. *Communities of Women: An Idea in Fiction*. Cambridge, MA:
    Harvard University, Press. 1978.

Bakhtin, M. M. "Discourse in the Novel." *The Dialogic Imagination: Four
    Essays*. Ed. Michael Holquist. Trans. Caryl Emerson and Michael
    Holquist. Austin: University of Texas Press, 1981. 259-422.

Bauer, Dale M. *Feminist Dialogics: A Theory of Failed Community*. Albany:
    State University of New York Press, 1988.

Cixous, Hélène and Catherine Clément. *The Newly Born Woman*. Trans.
    Betsy Wing. Minneapolis: University of Minnesota Press, 1986.

Franco, Jean. "Apuntes sobre la crítica feminista y la literatura
    hispanoamericana." *Hispamérica* 45 (1986): 31-43.

Gilligan, Carol. *In a Different Voice: Psychological Theory and Women's
    Development*. Cambridge, MA: Harvard University Press, 1982.

Masiello, Francine. "Discurso de mujeres, lenguaje del poder: Reflexiones
    sobre la crítica feminista a mediados de la década del 80." *Hispamérica*
    45 (1986): 53–60.

——. "Texto, ley, transgresión: Especulación sobre la novela (feminista)
    de vanguardia." *Revista Iberoamericana* 132-33 (julio-dic. 1985): 807-
    22.

McCarthy, Mari. "Possessing Female Space: "The Tender Shoot."" *Women's
    Studies* 8 (1981): 368.

Showalter, Elaine. "Feminist Criticism in the Wilderness." *Critical Inquiry (Special Issue: Writing and Sexual Difference)* 8 [Winter 1981]: 179-205.

CATHERINE R. PERRICONE

# Iconic/Metaphoric Dress and Other Nonverbal Signifiers in De amor y de sombra

The applications of concepts and terms associated with psycholinguistics provides a useful way to evaluate the human discourse[1] which characterizes Isabel Allende's *De amor y de sombra* and its impact upon readers. Immediately drawn into the narrative, the reader questions how this interest is so rapidly aroused and successfully sustained until the novel's conclusion. A partial answer lies in Allende's use of iconic and metaphoric signifiers so much a part of the daily human experience; namely, dress and nonverbal signs.

In this study it will be shown that Allende's use of dress and other nonverbal signifiers functions in her narration in much the same fashion as gestures do in speech. Since nonverbal signs form an integral part of daily life, their meaning is readily accessible to readers, providing them with a more immediate grasp of the novelist's plot, characterization and theme.

What psycholinguists have written about gestures, one of the most frequently used nonverbal signifiers, is particularly germane to this study. As described by Mc Neill in *Psycholinguistics: A New Approach*, gestures enact or depict ideas through patterns of movement. Although usually concurrent with the spoken word, they may somewhat precede verbal expression[2] (211-12) and whether iconic or metaphoric, they exhibit a meaning "relevant to the concurrent sentence meaning" (ibid). Iconic gestures are linked to

From *Critical Approaches to Isabel Allende's Novels.* © 1991 by Peter Lang Publishers. Reprinted by permission.

material actions, and metaphoric gesticulations exhibit images of abstract concepts (16; 230-31). While these iconic and metaphoric gestures provide experts with a means "to see in comparatively pure undistored form, the mental operations of speakers as they utilize the linguistic code" (210), in practical terms they are means to enhance and complement the spoken word; at times they even surpass or supplant the verbal mode in their ability to convey a message. The following examples illustrate how Allende's analogous use of dress and other nonverbal signifiers immediately attracts and sustains reader response throughout *De amor y de sombra*.

The first of these nonverbal signifiers is dress. While "el hábito no hace el monje," it is what draws one's attention to the individual. This is its iconic value, symbolizing as it does an individual's profession. As an iconic signifier it is a nonarbitrary sign; that is, the outward sign perforce of a certain type of profession. Allende uses this kind of nonverbal signifier on numerous occasions to convey a particular image of a character, among them: 1) the long silk dress of half a century ago to introduce the old actress, Josefina Bianchi (11); 2) the fashionable clothing of Beatiz Alcántara, vain mother of Irene, the central figure of the novel (13); 3) Irene's brightly colored skirts and gaudy jewelry and youthful attitude (71); 4) Professor Leal's sockless feet exhibiting eccentricity (29-30); 5) the workman's clothes of Professor Leal's priest-son to indicate his worker role (27); 6) the impeccable white attire of Mario, the homosexual (86); and 7) the uniforms of various military men as symbols of their profession as suggested by their titles of sergeant, lieutenant, and captain.

The nonverbal signifier of iconic dress immediately engages the reader. She makes a first judgement about the person and later expands upon it or changes it because of subsequent information. The reader decides early, whether the character is eccentric (Josefina, Professor Leal), a part of the military establishment (Sgt. Rivera, Lt. Ramírez, Capt. Morante), vain (Beatriz), or a young and stylish person (Irene). Allende subsequently takes the reader from this iconic stage, in which only the external is viewed, to a metaphoric level, where dress embodies an idea, a philosophical or political stance or a particular attitude. For example, when Irene Beltrán, the fashion and news editor for a woman's magazine,[3] learns of the death of some "desaparecidos" and of Evangelina Ranquileo, the adolescent who had been the subject of one of her interviews, Irene's fashionable clothing changes to a simple cotton dress (136) and later to nondescript slacks. Sgt. Rivera saw little resemblance between the woman he remembered and the one who stood before him (230). The fashionable clothes of the "liberated woman"[4] no longer hold any importance for her. Her attire reflects her transformation into a more mature and caring individual. As gestures synchronize with speech to convey meaning, attire analogously indicates this change in Irene. In Professor Leal's case, his apparently eccentric refusal to wear socks is actually a sign of his rejection of the Franco regime. Having vowed to never wear socks while Franco lived, he is unable to accustom himself to wearing them after the caudillo's death. On a deeper metaphoric level, one could conclude that the trauma he experienced in the ranks opposing Franco was still with him: there is no way to undo the psychological effects of the tragic past (28-33).

The homosexual Mario's white and impeccable clothing contrasts dramatically with the soiled clothes he would have worn as a miner. His clothing symbolizes his complete rejection of that sordid existence, a graphic metaphor for his new life as a hairstylist and owner of the beauty salons. Beatriz's clothing assumes a metaphoric value as more is revealed of this woman's excessive concern for clothes and physical appearance. In fact, her life goal, as exemplified by her attire, is to be beautiful and desirable. In contrast with Beatriz is the worker-priest, who eschewing religious garb and donning the shabby clothes of a laborer, attempts to become like one of the poor whom he serves.[5] At the same time, his actions demostrate a Christianity reminiscent of the simplicity of apostolic times.

A final example of the metamorphosis of the iconic into a metaphoric signifier is found in the military uniform, which is undoubtably one of the most visible indicators of a person's profession. In the metaphoric stage, the uniform becomes a sign of the military mentality and its penchant for order and disciplines as well as pride and ostentation, as exemplified by its sharply pressed creases, the medals which adorn the jacket, the epaulets and military chevrons indicating rank, and the shining shoes. Lt. Ramírez is the example par excellence of the career officer whose perfect uniform is a metaphor for his extreme interpretation of the military way of life. On the other hand, a crumpled and torn uniform, muddy shoes, a tie askew or missing can be a visible metaphor for a lack of order and pride in what one does, and ultimately a rejection of the military norm, as is the case with Pradelio, Evangelina's foster brother's disheveled appearance when he is found in a cave by Francisco and Irene.[6] The uniform has now become for him a degrading symbol of the military life in which he had once taken so much pride.

Each of these examples of dress as iconic and metaphoric signs complement Allende's narration and draw the reader more deeply into the story, but one of the most significant cases is that suggested by military attire. In an interview with Levine and Engelbert, Allende herself recognized "[m]achismo … [as] a global attitude that has political consequences" and commented: "Of course. Have you ever seen anything more **machista** than the military mentality? It is the synthesis, the exaltation, the ultimate exaggeration of **machismo**. There is a direct line from **machismo** to militarism." (20)

The concept of militarism leads to another type of nonverbal signifier: action. The act precipitating the largest portion of *De amor y de sombra* is one which deals with the military and consists of Evangelina's physical attack on Lt. Ramírez. Evangelina Ranquileo, subject to strange epileptic-like seizures ever since her "brother's" enlistment into the army, knocks Lt. Ramírez to the floor during one of her trances (77). Humiliated by this act which occurs in front of his subordinates, the lieutenant later has her arrested. On one level, this unintentional act (there is nothing to indicate that Evangelina knew what she was doing) was an iconic act, a nonarbitrary sign of violence— a punch to the lieutenant's nose, an act which knocked him onto the floor. It, however, also has a metaphoric sense. It is the complete annihilation of Ramírez's military **machismo**. As he sees it, he is irrevocably humiliated by the personal attack and he must respond with a violent act that will restore his **machismo**. Hence he performs the brutal rape of Evangelina just before she dies. Only by a perverse sexual act can this affront to his **machismo** be undone.

Another act frequently used by Allende is that of flight, and is evinced in a number of examples such as the following:

1. the homosexual, Mario, who flees the life of a coal miner;
2. Francisco's parents, the Leals, who had to flee Franco's Spain;
3. Eusebio Beltrán, who flees from his wife Beatriz;
4. Beatriz, who flees into the arms of various men;
5. Javier Leal, who takes flight in suicide;
6. Pradelio, who escapes from prison and flees to the mountains; and finally
7. Irene and Francisco who must flee their country and seek refuge in Spain.

On the iconic level all of these represent an escape to another existence. The metaphoric value of each type of flight becomes apparent upon closer examination. Again gestures synchronize with the linguistic mode or anticipate what will be said. The act of flight precedes a change. Mario's flight[7] anticipates and effects a completely new existence in the city, where he can follow what Nature seems to have preordained.[8]

The departure of the Leal couple, is a metaphor for all those individuals who have had to flee an intolerable political situation. The fact that Francisco, one of Leal's sons, and Irene must flee the land that had brought them safety, in order to return to their parent's country, emphasizes the vicious circle of tyranny that has characterized so much of twentieth century Hispanic political life.

Eusebio Beltrán's flight becomes a metaphor for those individuals who because of their personality, character or lack thereof, are not satisfied with ordinary daily existence. Their lives must be filled with new places and things at all costs. Beatriz, his wife, represents the middle class values and lifestyles that Eusebio rejects, hence his flight from his wife. Beatriz, on the other hand, metaphorically flees her status as an abandoned woman by fleeing into the arms of other men. From these actions, it may be inferred that she attempts to convince herself of her sex appeal and selfworth.

Pradelio's flight to the mountains is a natural response to being incarcerated.[9] On the iconic level, it is a nonarbitrary sign of flight to gain freedom. When he learns that his "sister" Evangelina, with whom he had been involved in an incestual relationship, has disappeared, he flees his mountain refuge to roam the countryside in search of her. With the second flight, he jeopardizes his own life for a more important objective, the life of another.

Javier's act of flight through suicide symbolizes all those who cannot cope with failure even when it is blameless. It is noteworthy that, like gestures which may anticipate speech, his silent and morose preoccupation with tying knots in a cord prefigure the desperate act of a man unable to carry out the traditional male role of caring for the financial needs of his family.

Another nonverbal signifier under the general heading of act is the mix-up of the two Evangelinas at birth in the hospital. Indeed, it was this incident which initiated the majority of the narrative's action and highlighted an intrinsic part of Latin American life. It is important to note that this was the first time either of the two mothers had gone to the hospital to have a baby. At the same time Mamá Encarnación (certainly a symbolic name), the midwife, was incarcerated for practicing medicine. That this mix-up occurred can be viewed as a metaphor for the superiority of the old, traditional way of doing things over the new. The subsequent refusal of the hospital officials to admit what was an obvious mistake shows the entrenchment of bureaucracy in Latin American life.[10] The fact that the two mothers would not simply exchange their children when they returned home, as was suggested by their husbands, demonstrates a blind adherence to the bureaucratic rules and regulations.

By the time Irene and Francisco go to investigate the story of Evangelina Ranquileo's strange attacks, fifteen years have passed since the birth of the two Evangelinas. There is no one answer for the noonday seizures: the townspeople think she is a saint with miraculous powers; a Salvation Army follower attributes them to divine punishment for her stepfather's alcoholism; the Catholic priest believes she is simply crazy; and Mamá Encarnación observes that she is beginning puberty and needs a man (62-65). Whatever the reason may be, the fact that the attacks occur at noon offers further conjecture over their significance. The number twelve symbolizes cosmic order and salvation. Corresponding to the number of signs of the Zodiac, it is also linked to the notions of space, time, and the wheel or circle (234). These seizures, in contrast, present the opposite states: chaos, ruin, and a suspension of time and space during their trance-like moments. Taken as a whole, these attacks disrupt natural order. Nevertheless, just as when the sun is overhead, the earth's revolutions cause the day inexorably to move towards sunset, twilight and night, these attacks provide the symbolic apogee after which events also move inexorably toward Evangelina's rape and death, the discovery of other "desaparecidos" while searching for her, and Francisco's and Irene's exile.

There are other several nonverbal signifiers which complement Allende's narrative style and engage the reader more effectively in this Latin American saga.[11] Gustavo Morante had been Irene's sweetheart since childhood. While at an isolated military outpost, he had written her letters everyday even though he could not mail them. The act of writing the letters serves as an iconic signifier of his physical affection. The letters take on metaphoric value when presented to her upon his return. Dramatically indicative of his undying affection, they become nothing but a bundle of mute linguistic signs, a metaphor for her rejection of Gustavo when she refuses to read them, and conversely a sign of her love for Francisco.

Throughout the novel Allende permits readers to draw their own conclusions about the characters from the actions and activities in which these individuals partake, rather than by their conversations or interior monologues. Serving to exemplify this technique are several of the female characters. Evangelina Ranquileo's mother, symbolically named Digna, is indeed characterized by her activities. As the first to rise and the last to retire, busy throughout the day, she is immediately recognizable as a self-sacrificing individual. When Allende writes: "Digna Ranquileo **sintió compasión por su marido**" (25; emphasis added), she reinforces this impression for the reader. Later she writes: "Para él reservaba la mejor porción de cazuela, los huevos más grandes, la lana más suave para tejer sus chalecos y calcetas" (25). Taken as an iconic image these activities symbolize any busy person; metaphorically, they symbolize the loving concern of a wife and mother for her husband and children.

The second female character whose activities symbolize her is Evangelina Flores, who is actually Digna Ranquileo's daughter. A carbon copy of her real mother, from the time she was twelve years old and began puberty she fought political repression through a dramatic series of events:[12]

> Se presentó en la asamblea de las Naciones Unidas, en ruedas de prensa, en foros de televisión, en congresos, en universidades, en todas partes, para hablar de los desaparecidos y para impedir que el olvido borrara a esos hom-bres, mujeres y niños tragados por la violencia. (264)

Franciscos's mother, Hilda Leal, is also characterized by certain activities. She, for example, was always at her husband's side at union meetings "**con sus palillos incansables en las manos**" (emphasis added) y la lana dentro de una bolsa sobre sus rodillas" (31). Once again the image of a woman constantly busy and thinking of others is evinced by nonverbal signifiers.

Silence itself is a dramatic nonverbal signifier that conveys as much or more than words. Noteworthy here is Hilda Leal's silence after the explosion that could have killed her and her newborn child; she was, in fact, seriously injured, having saved her son's life by protecting him with her body. When she recovered, she refused to speak of the Civil War (31), her silence standing as a sign of the horror of war, her own rejection of those cataclysmic events, and offering a means of healing the wounds they had caused. Her husband immerses himself in a similiar silence after his son Javier's suicide (124). In both instances external silence stands as a metaphoric signifier of the thoughtful processes happening within which bring healing and acceptance of what cannot be changed.

The revealing silence of another couple juxtaposed with their equally silent actions experienced by the reader at the time of Evangelina's attacks show once again that Allende finds certain nonverbal acts more effective than lengthy narration or dialogue. She wrote:

> El padre (Hipólito Ranquileo), oscuro, desdentado con su patética expresión de payaso triste, observaba abatido desde el umbral, sin acercarse. La Madre (Digna) permanecía al lado de la

cama con los ojos entornados, intentando tal vez escuchar el silencio de Dios (74).

One final act deserves special mention. When Francisco and Irene are preparing to leave the country, Rosa, Irene's faithful "nana", gives her a small package containing soil from the family garden. The iconic value of this act lies in the fact that one enjoys the physical presence of a part of one's country no matter where one goes; the metaphoric value symbolizes a love and longing undiminished by time or space. This gathering of garden soil replicates Isabel Allende's action upon leaving Chile.[13]

In conclusion, Isabel Allende in *De amor y de sombra* has used dress and other nonverbal signifiers to complement her narrative in the same way that gestures are either mimetic or anticipatory of the meaning of speech. The use of these iconic and metaphoric signs, so much a part of everyday experience, immediately arouses and sustains the reader's interest throughout the novel, and the humane discourse that results from this technique leaves an unforgettable image of Latin American life in the reader's mind.

## NOTES

1.  Humane discourse refers to narration without any complex word games or temporal or spatial displacement. Allende's humane and accessible discourse coincides with the social focus of her novels. In a speech at George Mason University, she stated:

    "A los escritores de Latinoamérica se les reprocha a veces que su literatura sea de denuncia, ¿por qué no se limitan al arte y dejan de pre-ocuparse de problemas irremediables? ...Creo que mi respuesta está en que conocemos el poder de la palabra y estamos obligados a emplearlas para contribuir a un mejor destino de nuestra tierra." Quoted by Mario Rojas, "La casa de los espíritus de Isabel Allende: una aproximación sociolingüística." *Revista de Crítica Literaria Latinoamericana*. 11. 21-22 (1985): 205-213.

    See also Marta Traba's "Hipótesis sobre una escritura diferente", fem 6.21: 9-12, in which she discusses the feminine writer's deep concern for establishing contact with her readers.

2.  McNeill gives various examples of iconic and metaphoric gestures. Emphasizing the co-presence and shared meaning of gesture and speech, he demonstrates an iconic gesture accordingly:

a) and he bends it way back (hand appears to pull object back [19]),

b) description of a cartoon event: he goes up through the pipe this time (hand rises quickly and fingers open [ibid]).

The simultaneous statements and gestures refer to a physical activity connected with the material, visible world, hence their classification as iconic gestures. After referring to I.A. Richard's classic definition of a metaphor as described in his *Philosophy of Rhetoric* (quoted in McNeill, 164) and later defining a metaphoric gesture as "the entification of abstract ideas" (232), McNeill provides the following examples of this type of gesture:

a) I want to ask a question (hand forms a question [231]),

b) That book is packed with meaning (one hand pushes against the palm of the other [ibid]),

c) various pictorial illustrations of mathematicians describing concepts of direct limit, inverse limit, etc., (233-35).

3. This is an autobiographical note. Allende worked for *Paula*, a Chilean women's magazine, until she was dismissed; however, she continued her journalistic work, doing interviews and recording as does the protagonist of her novel. See Michael Moody's "Isabel Allende and the Testimonial Novel" (39).

4. Irene is "liberated" in her sexual freedom—she tells Francisco that she is not a virgin and also has sexual relations with him. She is an independent woman making her own living as a journalist, and it was her decision to use one floor of her mother's home as a residence for the elderly.

5. Of course, his dress reduces his visibility in his efforts to assist the victims of political repression.

6. Pradelio was so respectful of his commanding officer Lt. Ramírez, that Pradelio informed him about Evangelina. He obviously had not anticipated that Ramírez would order an investigation of the events. This is a classic example of military meddling into civilians' lives.

7. There is a great deal of irony to be found in the fact that it was the prostitute chosen to teach Mario about sex, who urged him to leave home in order to escape the fate of his father and brothers (87-88).

8. Allende portrays Mario very sympathetically. In a society which denigrates the homosexual as a coward and a misfit, the novelist makes him a brave man who assists in the escape of political personae non gratae. In particular, he helps Irene and Francisco leave the country after they have become enemies of the state.

9.  Lt. Ramírez holds Pradelio partially responsible for what Evangelina did to him and puts him in prison. A fellow soldier, Sgt. Rivera, helps him escape. Rivera is subsequently murdered because he had been seen speaking with Irene. A notebook he had kept of events relating to Evangelina and other "desaparecidos" disappears with him. Irene, however, had taped the conversations and given them into the safekeeping of Josefina Bianchi. Ultimately the content of the tape is published in the newspaper and the tragedy of the "desaparecidos" is revealed. Allende based the whole episode of the finding of the "desaparecidos" on an actual event occurring in Lonquén, a village not far from Santiago, in 1978. (See Moody, 40.)

10. History bears testimony to this. Since the days of the conquistadores and the establishment of the Casa de Contratación and the Consejo de las Indias, the government has endeavored to monitor every facet of Latin American life from religion to commerce.

11. Although not precisely like the baroque saga of *La casa de los espíritus*, as described by Tatiana Tolstoi in her review of the novel, *De amor y de sombra* does offer a dramatic account of the political reality that has characterized Latin America since the age of the Caudillos.

12. It may only be coincidental, but the number 12 seems to have its intended symbolic value of order and salvation as previously described in conjunction with Evangelina Ranquileo's noonday seizures.

13. In a prefatory biographical note to *La casa de los espíritus* the following quotation from Allende appears:

    "... Cuando hice la maleta para irme de Chile eché unos puñados de tierra del jardín en una bolsa (emphasis added). En Caracas la puse en un macetero y planté en la tierra chilena un nomeolvides. Durante estos años no ha hecho más que crecer y crecer. Como mi nostalgia."


WORKS CITED

Allende, Isabel. *De amor y de sombra*. Barcelona: Plaza y Janés, 1984.

————. *La casa de los espíritus*. Barcelona: Plaza y Janés, 1982.

————. "El valor de la palabra." Speech given at George Mason University, 19 March 1984.

Cirlot, J. E. *A Dictionary of Symbols*. Jack Sage, tr. New York: Philosophical Library, 1962.

Kendon, A. "Gesticulation and Speech: Two Aspects of the Process of Utterance." In *The Relation Between Verbal and Nonverbal Communication*, M.R. Key, ed. The Hague: Mouton, 1980, 207-227.

Levine, Linda and JoAnne Englebert. "The World is Full of Stories." *Latin American Literature and Arts Review* 34 (1985): 18-20.

McNeill, David. *Psycholinguistics: A New Approach*. New York: Harper & Row, 1987.

Moody, Michael. "Isabel Allende and the Testimonial Novel." *Confluencia: Revista Hispánica de Cultura y Literatura* 2.1 (1986): 39-43.

Richards, I. A. *The Philosophy of Rhetoric*. New York: Oxford University P, 1936.

Rojas, Mario. "*La casa de los espíritus* de Isabel Allende: Una aproximación sociolingüística." *Revista de crítica literaria latinoamericana* 11.21-22 (1985): 205-213.

Tolstoi, Tatiana. "Une Saga Baroque." *Quinzaine Litterarie* 417 (1984): 7.

Traba, Marta. "Hipótesis sobre una escritura diferente." *fem* 6.21: 9-12.

EDNA AGUIRRE REHBEIN

# Isabel Allende's Eva Luna and the Act/Art of Narrating

Cuando escribí *Eva Luna*, por primera vez me senté a escribir una novela y quise escribir una novela en varios niveles. Una novela que fuera como contar un cuento y que fuera la protagonista contándoles a otros el cuento de su propia vida. En *Eva Luna* puse muchas cosas: quería decir, por ejemplo, lo que significa poder contar, cómo a través del contar se van ganando espacios, se va ganando gente, se seduce a un lector.... el poder contar cuentos es como un tesoro inagotable...[1]

In *Eva Luna*, Isabel Allende's third novel, the author focuses on two closely linked aspects of story-telling and/or of narrating. On the one hand, she experiments with the **act** of narrating by creating a story in which the roles of Eva Luna, the protagonist, Eva Luna, the narrator, and the role of the character in the soap opera *Bolero* (written by the protagonist) are at first separate, but then seem to converge into **one**. The resulting intertextuality and self-reflexivity create various levels of fictionalization leading the reader to question "reality" within this fictional setting. The other aspect which Allende examines is the **art** of narrating, as she experiments with the text and demonstrates that the slightest manipulation of language can create or transform reality. An individual's adeptness in utilizing language, thus constructs a particular reality. These two aspects of narration, so skillfully

From *Critical Approaches to Isabel Allende's Novels*. © 1991 by Peter Lang Publishers. Reprinted by permission.

crafted by Isabel Allende, are inseparable as they work together to create or change textual "reality" to meet the narrator's liking.

Though at first this work appears to be like many other narratives, it is clear that Allende intends the novel to be more than merely another autobiographical first person account told by the narrator. Allende's intentions for the novel are clearly stated by her protagonist at the end of the novel when Eva states that perhaps all of what has taken place in the story has occurred "de acuerdo al principio de que **es posible construir la realidad** a la medida de las propias apetencias."[2] In the same way that Eva Luna can mold "la Materia Universal" (250) into anything she wishes, Allende and Eva also mold reality according to their liking.[3] In this text, the very act of narrating becomes integrated with the plot of the novel, as the protagonist first learns to tell stories orally, then blossoms from a state of illiteracy, learning to read and then to write, and finally, writes her own story. For Eva, the narrator, and for Eva, the protagonist, the text becomes one long process of learning about the power of expression, be it in written or spoken form.

The importance of revealing or telling about events is seen throughout the novel as other characters also occupy themselves with this activity. Rolf Carlé, the Austrian immigrant who becomes a photo journalist in South America, finds it extremely important to reveal the true story when he reports on political activities. His desire to tell the "official truth" is often frustrated either because the government will not allow it, or because to do so would compromise and endanger the guerrillas' lives.[4] Huberto Naranjo, the guerrilla leader, occupies himself with obscuring the true story, molding it to conform to his needs and even changing his name when necessary (216). Eva acquires this **gift** of story-telling from her mother, Consuelo, who often engaged in this activity (25).

Eva's skill is very powerful as it not only serves as entertainment for herself and others, but becomes crucial to her survival. She at times uses it in exchange for food and shelter. Allende explains, "Eva Luna, la protagonista de mi novela cambia sus cuentos por comida, por techo, después por amistad, por amor ..."[5] Toward the end, this skill becomes her profession when she begins working as a writer. More significant, however, is the fact that throughout her life Eva, the protagonist, relies on her stories to remove her from difficult situations. As she struggles to survive, she relies on their magical power to transport her from the harsh reality by which she is surrounded, to a prettier, more acceptable world which exists only in her dreams or memory. It is through this process, for instance, that as an adult she is able to continue experiencing the "existence" of her mother who died when she was only a small child (123). Isabel Allende's complex story is a reflection of her own belief in the magical power of the word and the narrative[6] as Eva, the narrator, becomes the active agent involved in molding reality and consequently the outcome of the novel.[7]

At first glance, the novel appears to be merely another first person account of someone's life: Eva narrates her life story. The first chapter provides background information on Eva's mother, Consuelo, who was orphaned and raised by monks and then went to work for various people; it also tells of Eva's birth. Already in this first chapter Allende introduces the key role played by story-telling and the concept of a reality made pliable and changeable through the use of language. Eva's mother, Consuelo, is clearly gifted with the magical powers of story-telling.

> Mi madre era una persona silenciosa, capaz de disimularse entre los muebles, de perderse en el dibujo de la alfombra, de no hacer el menor alboroto, como si no existiera; sin embargo, en la intimidad de la habitación que com-partíamos **se transformaba**. Comenzaba a hablar del pasado o a narrar sus cuentos y el cuarto se llenaba de luz, desaparecían los muros para dar paso a increíbles paisajes, palacios abarrotados de objetos nunca vistos, países lejanos inventados por ella o sacados de la biblioteca del patrón; colocaba a mis pies todos los tesoros de Oriente, la luna y más allá, me reducía al tamaño de una hormiga para sentir el universo desde la pequeñez, me ponía alas para verlo desde el firmamento, me daba una cola de pez para conocer el fondo del mar. Cuando ella contaba, el mundo se poblaba de personajes, algunos de los cuales llegaron a ser tan familiares, que todavía hoy, tantos años después, puedo describir sus ropas y el tono de sus voces. (25; emphasis added)

Eva continues,

> Ella (la mamá) sembró en mi cabeza la idea de que la realidad no es sólo como se percibe en la superficie, también tiene una dimensión mágica y, si auno se le antoja, es legítimo exagerarla y ponerle color para que el tránsito por esta vida no resulte tan aburrido. (26)

At the end of this first chapter, it is also apparent that Eva, like her mother, believes in her own ability to transform reality. She explains, "Una palabra mía y, ¡chas!, se transformaba la realidad" (28).

The second chapter begins with the life story of Rolf Carlé, a young Austrian boy whose life develops parallel to Eva's. The narrator alternates between a chapter about herself and one about Rolf throughout the remainder of the novel until the last three chapters when their lives intersect and they fall in love. In subsequent chapters, the reader learns about Rolf's own involvement in story-telling through his use of film.

By the third chapter, Eva has actively begun using her story-telling to achieve a number of goals. Eva describes how she told stories to Elvira, her **madrina**: "Me enrollaba junto a Elvira y le ofrecía un cuento a cambio de que me permitiera quedarme con ella" (58). To Huberto Naranjo, the street-wise young boy who helps her survive, who later gets involved in guerrilla warfare, and then becomes Eva's lover, she offers some of her stories as entertainment and compensation for taking care of her: "Me acurruqué entre los papeles y le ofrecí un cuento en pago de tantas y tan finas atenciones" (63). It is through Huberto's insistence that she begins to learn to read (110). Eva's ability to create or invent continues to become stronger and more evident. Later, when she finds herself alone again and feeling totally abandoned, Eva resorts to using her imagination to "magically" retrieve her mother who died when she was young.

> Escondí la cara entre las rodillas, llamé a mi madre y muy pronto percibí su aroma ligero de tela limpia y almidón. Surgió ante mí intacta, con su trenza enrollada en la nuca y los ojos de humo brillando en su rostro pecoso, para decirme que esa trifulca no era nada de mi incumbencia y no había razón para tener miedo, que me sacudiera el susto y echáramos a andar juntas. Me puse de pié y le tomé la mano. (123)

And "… la presencia visible de [su] madre …" (126) continues to accompany her through her troubled days in the streets while she looks for a home.

It is not until she goes to live with Riad Halabí, however, that she actually learns to read and the next phase of her creativity is initiated. Halabí, who finds her on the streets, takes her to work with him in his home in Agua Santa. He becomes like a father to her and takes a special interest in educating her, finding her a tutor, buying her many books, and teaching her to read (140-141). Halabí not only teaches her to read and write, rather more notably, he is the one who makes her an "official" person by acquiring a birth certificate for her. Later Eva reflected on his generosity,

Riad Halabí me dio varias cosas fundamentales para tramitar por mi destino y entre ellas, dos muy importantes: la escritura y un certificado de existencia. No había papeles que probaran mi presencia en este mundo, nadie me inscribió al nacer, nunca había estado en una escuela, era como si no hubiera nacido, pero él habló con un amigo de la ciudad, pagó el soborno correspondiente y consiguió un documento de identidad, en el cual, por un error del funcionario, figuro con tres años menos de los que en realidad tengo. (145-146)

Her interest in reading becomes a passion and consequently, she begins to write her own stories. She states,

Yo devoraba los libros que caían en mis manos, … mis historias aparecían anhelos e inquietudes que no sabía que estaban en mi corazón. La maestra Inés me sugirió anotarlos en un cuaderno. Pasaba parte de la noche escribi-endo y me gustaba tanto hacerlo, que se me iban las horas sin darme cuenta y a menudo me levantaba por la mañana con los ojos enrojecidos. Pero ésas eran mis mejores horas. Sospechaba que nada existía verdaderamente, la **realidad era una materia imprecisa y gelatinosa que mis sentidos captaban a medias** … Me consolaba la idea de que **yo podía tomar esa gelatina y moldearla para crear lo que deseara,** no una parodia de la realidad, como los mosqueteros y las esfinges de mi antigua patrona yugoslava, sino un mundo propio, poblado de personajes vivos, donde **yo imponía las normas y las cambiaba a mi antojo. De mí dependía la existencia** de todo lo que nacía, moría o acontecía en las arenas inmóviles donde germinaban mis cuentos. Podía colocar en ellas lo que quisiera, bastaba pronunciar la palabra justa para darle vida. A veces sentía que ese universo fabricado con el poder de la imaginación era de contornos más firmes y durables que la región confusa donde deambulaban los seres de carne y hueso que me rodeaban. (173-174, emphasis added)[8]

Eva becomes conscious of her own power as the reader of these stories and of the fact that she alone has the power to *create* everything that occurs in her narrative. At times, her imagined environment becomes preferable to the harshness of life itself.

Eva's ability to change her perception of "reality" to her liking continues to become further developed as she gains confidence through reading. Upon moving into an apartment with Mimí, Eva invents an entire family tree for herself by acquiring old photographs of "toda una familia" and placing them on her wall, thereby creating for herself a valid past as well (206). The hardest photograph to find, however, is that of Consuelo, her mother. She decides on a portrait of a beautiful woman and feels that one is appropriate because the woman in it "era lo bastante hermosa como para encarnar a mi madre." (207) She goes on to state, "así *deseo* preservarla en mi recuerdo" (207; emphasis added).

Aside from the obvious fact that the previous citation reinforces how Eva is again engaging in molding reality to her liking, this quote represents a pivotal point in the novel because it is one of the first times that the narrator uses the present tense as she relates her life story. Previously, she has been looking back in time at events in her life, in her mother's, and in Rolf's, so she has used the past tenses. It is at this point in the narrative that the lives of Eva, the narrator and Eva, the protagonist begin to converge, and Allende begins to communicate this merging of narrative time and of the protagonist/narrator through her meticulous use of the language. Gradually, in this chapter, and then more suddenly in the next two, there is a shift from the re-telling of events from the past to the recounting of events in the present, as they occur at that moment. This evolution from past to present is seen again just a few pages later as Eva tells of her responsibility for her **madrina**. She explains that upon coming to the capital city, she finds her **madrina**, who has been living in terrible conditions in a public nursing home. With Mimí's help, they move her to a privately run attractive care unit. "Mimí pagó la primera mensualidad," states Eva, adding, "pero ese deber *es mío*" (209; emphasis added).

Shortly thereafter Eva begins to work as a secretary in the military uniform factory and at night, encouraged by Mimí, she writes stories in her **cuaderno de cuentos** (207). She begins to see Huberto more, but only when he decides he can come out of hiding. After one of their passionate encounters, Eva reflects on their relationship, once again using the present tense.

> Para Naranjo y otros como él, el pueblo parecía compuesto sólo de hombres; nosotras debíamos contribuir a la lucha, pero estábamos exluidas de las decisiones y del poder. Su revolución no cambiaría en escencia mi suerte, en cualquier circunstancia yo tendría que seguir abriéndome paso por mí misma hasta el último de mis días. Tal vez en ese momento me di cuenta de que la mía es una guerra cuyo final no se vislumbra, así es que más vale darla con alegría, para que no se me vaya la vida esperando una posible

victoria para empezar a sentirme bien. Concluí que Elvira tenía
razón, hay que ser bien brava, hay que pelear siempre. (214;
emphasis added)

Whereas previously the narrative has described Eva's life in retrospect, this
passage clearly creates the impression that Eva, the narrator is now
recounting Eva, the protagonist's life as it is unfolding and developing before
her. By merging narrative time in this way, the author dissolves the gap
between Eva, the protagonist and Eva, the narrator. At this point in the
novel, the **two** become **one**.

This evolution of narrative time is intensified in the subsequent
sections as Eva quits her work at the uniform factory and dedicates herself to
writing on a regular basis. Mimí, who believes in fortune telling, reads Eva's
future and affirms that her "destino era contar" (229). Mimí encourages Eva
to begin writing screenplays for the soap opera in which she appears and
purchases a typewriter for her. The next morning, as Eva anxiously sits down
to write, she is filled with a flurry of emotion and inspiration.

> Desde que la maestra Inés me enseñó el alfabeto, escribía casi
> todas las noches, pero sentí que ésta era una ocasión diferente,
> algo que podría cambiar mi rumbo. Preparé un café negro y me
> instalé ante la máquina, tomé una hoja de papel limpia y blanca,
> como una sábana recién planchada para hacer el amor y la
> introduje en el rodillo. Entonces sentí algo extraño, como
> una brisa alegre por los huesos, por los caminos de las venas bajo
> la piel. Creí que esa página me esperaba desde hacía veinti-tantos
> años, que yo había vivido sólo para ese instante, y quise que a
> partir de ese momento mi único oficio fuera atrapar las historias
> suspendidas en el aire más delgado, para hacerlas mías. (230)[9]

She explains:

> Se ordenaron los relatos guardados en la memoria genética desde
> antes de mi nacimiento y muchos otros que había registrado por
> años en mis cuadernos. Comencé a recordar hechos muy lejanos,
> recuperé las anécdotas de mi madre cuando vivíamos entre los
> idiotas, los cancerosos y los embalsamados del Profesor Jones;
> aparecieron un indio mordido de víbora y un tirano con las
> manos devoradas por la lepra; rescaté a una solterona que perdió
> el cuero cabelludo como si se lo hubiera arrancado una máquina

bobinadora, un dignatario en su sillón de felpa obispal, un árabe de corazón generoso y tantos otros hombres y mujeres cuyas vidas **estaban a mi alcance para disponer de ellas según mi propia y soberana voluntad.** (230-231; emphasis added)

Allende adds to the text's complexity by allowing Eva to detail the recording of these events which have already been written by the narrator and have been read previously by the reader in this same novel, thereby leading the reader to question the reliability and chronology of the narrative. Eva explains that

Poco a poco **el pasado se transformaba en presente y me adueñaba también del futuro,** los muertos cobraban vida con ilusión de eternidad, se reunían los dispersos y todo aquello esfumado por el olvido adquiría contornos precisos. (231; emphasis added)

As she continues to write she begins to speculate about her own future: "Sospechaba que el final llegaría sólo con mi propia muerte y me atrajo la idea de ser yo también uno más de la historia y tener el poder de determinar mi fin o inventarme una vida" (231). It is as if narrative time, the action being retold, has now caught up with the present events and Eva Luna has begun to recount **her** life as it takes place. The implication, therefore, is that she is now beginning to tell her life story as it will transpire in the future, though it has not yet occurred. Eva Luna is now in total control of her destiny: all she needs to do is to write it in order for it to occur in her narrative "reality."

When Eva Luna and Rolf Carlé finally meet at a dinner party, she is asked to supply more of her **cuentos.** Eva's creative powers and the author's utilization of the present tense amidst passages narrated in the past tense are further evidenced. The following passage illustrates Allende's techniques:

Mimí **dice** que **tengo** una voz especial para los cuentos, una voz que, siendo mía **parece** también ajena, como si brotara desde la tierra y me subiera por el cuerpo. **Sentí** que la habitación **perdía** sus contornos, esfumada en los nuevos horizontes que yo convocaba. (234; emphasis added)

Whereas the early segments of the novel conveyed the idea of a narrator who was telling about her life as it had happened many years back, the interjection of these comments in the present tense make the text seem like a conversation in the present with some momentary descriptions of past events.

In Chapter Eleven, Eva, who has become involved in helping the guerrillas with their greatest effort against the government, finds that Rolf, who had previously merely been documenting the events, is also now involved in the struggle. While out in the countryside, waiting for the attack to occur, Rolf asks her to tell a story she has never told before. She willingly begins to tell about "una mujer cuyo oficio era contar cuentos" (258). This unmistakably is a reference to herself, Eva the story-teller. The story she continues to tell, however, is even more engaging and insightful as it seems to correspond very closely to the narrator's/protagonist's life story. She states that the young woman met a man who was very sad and was burdened by his past, so he asks her to create a new history for him. She consents, but after she has told the new story of Rolf's life, Eva comments:

> Por fin amaneció y en la primera luz del día ella comprobó que el olor de la tristeza se había esfumado. Suspiró, cerró los ojos y al sentir su espíritu vacío como el de un recién nacido, comprendió que en el afán de complacerlo le había entregado su propia memoria, ya no sabía qué era suyo y cuánto ahora pertenecía a él, sus pasados habían quedado anudados en una sola trenza. Había entrado hasta el fondo en su propio cuento y ya no podía recoger sus palabras, pero tampoco quiso hacerlo y se abandonó al placer de fundirse con él en la misma historia... (258)

The story that Eva tells Rolf is indicative of what has happened in the novel with respect to her own life and Rolf's, for earlier, Eva too had helped Rolf accept his painful past by changing it for him through her **cuentos** (238-239). Eva and Rolf have become intertwined just as have the two characters in her **cuento**.

After the guerrillas' successful maneuvers against the government, Eva and Rolf become concerned over how the government will present the news about the occurrence, so they decide to tell the story in the next episode of her soap opera. Eva and Rolf explain that they can avoid any problems with the government censorship because, "siempre se puede alegar que es sólo ficción y como la telenovela es mucho más popular que el noticiario, todo el mundo sabrá lo que pasó en Santa María" (272). Thereby, Eva uses her fictional media to depict a true incident. Eva's soap opera, **Bolero**, becomes very popular and receives enormous attention. Mimí plays herself in the television story, while Eva,

> ... escribía cada día un nuevo episodio, inmersa por completo en
> el mundo que creaba con el poder omnímodo de las palabras,
> transformada en un ser disperso, reproducida hasta el infinito,
> viendo mi propio reflejo en múltiples espejos, viviendo
> innumberables vidas, hablando con muchas voces. (273)

At the end of the novel, Eva and Rolf leave the city for a while because they
are concerned about possible repercussions from the telecasting of their
episode depicting the guerrilla actions. While in Colonia, the couple fall
passionately in love. Eva describes their kiss, saying;

> Se acercó a grandes pasos y procedió a besarme tal como ocurre
> en las novelas románticas, tal como yo esperaba que lo hiciera
> desde hacía un siglo y tal como estaba describiendo momentos
> antes el encuentro de mis protagonistas en *Bolero*. Aproveché la
> cercanía para husmearlo con disimulo y así identifiqué el olor de
> mi pareja. (280)

The narrator ends the story by stating that they loved one another for a while
until their love faded. But then she interjects,

> O tal vez las cosas no ocurrieron así. Tal vez tuvimos la suerte de
> tropezar con un amor excepcional y yo no tuve necesidad de
> inventarlo, sino sólo vestirlo de gala para que perdurara en la
> memoria, de acuerdo al principio de que es posible construir la
> realidad a la medida de las propias apetencias. ... Escribí que
> durante esas semanas benditas, el tiempo se estiró, se enroscó en
> sí mismo, se dio vuelta como un pañuelo de mago y alcanzó para
> que Rolf Carlé—con la solemnidad hecha polvo y la vanidad por
> las nubes—conjurara sus pesadillas y volviera a cantar las
> canciones de su adolescencia y para que yo ... narrara ... muchos
> cuentos, incluyendo algunos con final feliz. (281-282)

The novel is a prime example of Isabel Allende's belief in the magical
power of words and in the concept that books have their own spirit to exist
as they wish. Eva, the narrator, is completely in control of the narrative and
capable of molding and defining time and reality as she wishes. Allende
demonstrates that the act and the art of narrating consist of the skill and
talent to change language in order to achieve the desired textual "reality."

## NOTES

1. Isabel Allende, personal interview, 5 January 1989.

2. Isabel Allende, *Eva Luna* (Barcelona: Plaza y Janés, 1987); 281. Emphasis added. Other references to the novel will be from this edition and will appear within the text.

3. Already in Allende's first novel, *La casa de los espíritus* (1982), the author's emphasis on the process of narration is evident. This first novel, is in fact the product of the author's continous narration in the form of a letter to her grandfather. The second novel, *De amor y de sombra* (1984), also relates to writing in that it is the novelized re-counting of a true event she read in a journalistic article.

4. Rolf Carlé's interest in presenting the "official truth" about the guerrillas' efforts is evident in a number of situations. He is first depicted as an anxious young photographer, interested "en captar la imagen, aun a costa de cualquier riesgo." (202) Later he struggles with the idea of presenting the truth without revealing the whereabouts of the guerrillas (215 and 222).

5. Isabel Allende, personal interview, 5 January 1989.

6. Isabel Allende has explained her personal belief in the magical, transformational power of language in her essays: "La magia de las palabras," *Revista Iberoamericana* 132-133 (Julio-Diciembre 1985): 447-452 and also in *Los libros tienen sus propios espíritus*, in an essay by the same title, edited by Marcelo Coddou (Xalapa: Universidad Veracruzana, 1986): 15-20.

7. Allende's narrator is what Wayne C. Booth has called a dramatized narrator agent, someone "who produces some measurable effect on the course of events." *The Rhetoric of Fiction*, 1983 ed., (Chicago: U of Chicago P, 1961): 153-154.

8. The narrator's beliefs coincide precisely with Allende's own perspective on the power of language. See footnote #6 above for further information.

9. Isabel Allende often makes reference to the importance of beginning her writing on a blank white sheet of paper. Another such reference occurs on page 234 where she speaks of how she began to create on "un desierto blanco." She also commented on the necessity of this in her interview of 5 January 1989.

## Works Cited

Allende, Isabel. *Eva Luna*. Barcelona: Plaza y Janés, 1987.

——. Interview. 5 January 1989.

——. "La magia de las palabras." *Revista Iberoamericana* 132-133 (Julio-Diciembre) 1985: 447-452.

——. "Los libros tienen sus propios espíritus." *Los libros tienen sus propios espíritus*. Ed., Marcelo Coddou. Xalapa: Universidad Veracruzana, 1986: 15-20.

Booth, Wayne C. *The Rhetoric of Fiction*. 1983 ed. Chicago: U of Chicago P, 1961.

NORMA HELSPER

# Binding the Wounds of the Body Politic: Nation as Family in La casa de los espíritus

This essay will deal with a specific instance of what Kenneth Burke called the "stealing back and forth of symbols":

> The divine right of kings was first invoked by secular interests combating the theocrats. It held that God appointed the king, rather than the church authorities, to represent the secular interest of "the people". Later, when the church made peace with established monarchs, identifying its interest with the interests of the secular authorities, the church adopted the doctrine as its own. And subsequently the bourgeoisie repudiated the doctrine, in repudiating both monarch and state. It did so in the name of "rights," as the doctrine had originally been in the name of "rights." Among these "rights" was "freedom." And Marx in turn stole this bourgeois symbol for the proletariat. (229)

One of the concepts that has proven to be a popular one for "stealing back and forth" is that of the family. Perhaps because of the generally conservative nature of that institution, the Right has often been quick to claim the family as its own. In the introduction to their 1984 book *When*

From *Critical Approaches to Isabel Allende's Novels.* © 1991 by Peter Lang Publishers. Reprinted by permission.

*Biology Became Destiny: Women in Weimer and Nazi Germany*, Brithenthal et. al. remind us of this.

> A close look at the history addressed in this volume alerts us to the dangers signaled by well-financed, well-organized movements in command of the latest propaganda techniques that, then and now, mobilize around such code words as "pro-family"..., "patriotism," and "military strength." We want to stress that Nazism did not arrive full blown, with promises of war and gas chambers. It came slowly, step by step, draped in the prospective coloring of love for country, strong medicine to combat unemployment, and most importantly for our purposes, a pledge to restore the traditional family ... (Bridenthal xii)

During the years of the Popular Unity government in Chile (1970-1973), the Right also attempted to set itself up as the guardian of the family. For example, during the campaign preceding the elections won by Salvador Allende, rumors were circulated that a socialist government would usurp **patria potestad** or parental authority, taking children from their parents and sending them for indoctrination. (The same rumor had made hundreds of Cuban parents send their young children to the United States after the triumph of that revolution in 1959.) Here I will discuss how Chilean novelist Isabel Allende "steals back" the notion of family in her 1983 novel *La casa de los espíritus*.

The family is a powerful symbol in Western society. Analysts from Engels (in his 1884 work *The Origin of Family, Private Property and the State*) to contemporary feminists have identified the institution of the family as one which perpetuates the limiting of sex roles and women's oppression. The dominant conception of the family since the eighteenth century's industrial revolution is that which Christopher Lasch uses as the title of his history: *Haven in a Heartless World* (1977). This double identity of the family is not lost on Allende, and, in fact, the message of her book revolves around the institution's internal contradictions. In *La casa de los espíritus*, the traditional family as symbol is debunked and, simultaneously, the power of the family-as-image is reclaimed for the novelist's Utopian purpose. The hope which Allende holds out for the future of her country is based on one other than the model of an accepting, loving family.

The image of nation-as-family is most often utilized by ideologues who attempt to deny the existence or importance of class differences and sexual oppression.[1] This is not the case, however, of *La casa de los espíritus*, in which the traditional family is shown to be a respectable façade that hides the truth of rape, adultery, battering and domination. Isabel Allende implicitly criticizes the traditional family by associating it with the patriarch Esteban Trueba, who was "fanático, violento y anticuado, pero representaba mejor que nadie los valores de la familia, la tradición, la propiedad y el orden" (273). But the character Trueba also is made to set in motion what could be seen as a deconstruction of the tradition notion of "family." Because Trueba rapes a **campesina**, Pancha García, the traditional coveted place of the **primogénito**, the first born son, is filled by an illegitimate mestizo who never uses his father's last name. Trueba's legitimate children all rejected their "assigned" roles. His son Jaime, a physician, decides to use only his mother's family name when he finds that the name Trueba causes suspicion in his lower-class patients. Typically, the son of a **patrón** has his first sexual experience with a female servant, but in this case it is Trueba's daughter, Blanca, who chooses a **campesino**, Pedro Tercero García, for her lover. The enraged father goes after the young man with the purpose of killing him; Esteban García, Trueba's grandson by the **campesina** he raped, betrays Pedro Tercero's hiding place. But Trueba does not know García is his grandson and further denies him respect by refusing to pay him the promised reward.

By failing to give first to Pancha, and then to Esteban García, the recognition due human beings, let alone blood relatives, Trueba contributes to the creation of an inhuman monster. When grown, the young **campesino** comes to ask his **patrón** for a recommendation to the Chilean police academy. While waiting in the library, he comes close to sexually molesting Trueba's other, recognized grandchild, Alba:

> Se sentó en una de las butacas de cuero negro y poco a poco atrajo a la niña y la sentó en sus rodillas. Alba olía a Bayrum, una fragancia fresca y dulce que se mezclaba con su olor a natural de chiquilla transpirada. El muchacho acercó la nariz a su cuello y aspiró ese perfume desconocido de limpieza y bienestar, y sin saber por qué, se le llenaron los ojos de lágrimas. Sintió que odiaba a esa criatura casi tanto como odiaba al viejo Trueba. Ella encarnaba lo que él nunca tendría, lo que él nunca sería. (253)

The beast of class hatred later threatens to destroy Chilean society in general. In the exemplary case of the Trueba Del Valle family, Coronel Esteban García has a role in torturing Esteban Trueba's son, Jaime, and takes Alba as his special scapegoat, almost killing her. While his granddaughter is "disappeared," Esteban Trueba's contribution to creating her torture and

thereby almost destroying what he most loves in the world is brought home
to the reader. Senator Trueba is desperate when he goes to ask his old friend
Tránsito Soto for help:

> Tránsito ... puedo darle lo que me pida, cualquier cosa, con tal
> que encuentre a mi nieta Alba antes que un demente me siga
> mandando más dedos cortados ... discúlpeme que me ponga así,
> me tiemblan las manos, estoy muy nervioso, no puedo explicar lo
> que pasó, un paquete por correo y adentro sólo tres dedos
> humanos ... una broma macabra que me trae recuerdos, pero
> esos recuerdos nada tienen que ver con Alba, mi nieta ni siquiera
> había nacido entonces ... por favor, Tránsito ... soy un pobre
> viejo destrozado, apiádese y busque a mi nieta Alba antes que me
> la terminen de mandar en pedacitos por correo ... (368)

Trueba of course, is wrong in saying that the memories brought back to him
by the three human fingers he receives in the mail have nothing to do with
his granddaughter. The fingers that he remembers are those he cut from the
hand of Alba's father, Pedro Tercero García, in his rage over discovering that
the **campesino** and Trueba's daughter Blanca were lovers. The boy who
witnessed the event and who was later denied the reward promised him for
leading Trueba to Pedro's hideout was Trueba's illegitimate grandson
Esteban García. Now **Coronel** García, he, in effect, sends the message that
he will finish the job, started years earlier by the **patrón**, of destroying one
reminder of cross-class fraternizing.

Parallel to the legacy of cruelty, degradation, and revenge reviewed in
the preceding paragraphs, *La casa de los espíritus* posits another chain of events
which constitutes a Utopian image of hope for the salvation of both the
Trueba Del Valle family and for Chile. The novel picks up the story of this
positive chain with Esteban Trueba's marriage to Clara Del Valle. Trueba
starts forging his link of the negative chain with the rape of Pancha García,
his part in the positive chain begins with his tender love for his new wife
Clara. Although she disagrees with his world view and in many ways fails to
conform to a traditional woman's role, he loves her. This ability to love
someone very different from oneself is, in the final analysis, the major source
of hope for society's redemption.

The next generation's link of love is forged by Blanca Trueba, daughter
of Clara and Esteban, and Pedro Tercero García, the son of the peasant
foreman of their ranch. Their love is so forbidden and so strong that it is
associated with an earthquake:

> En un instante (Clara) comprendió la causa del color del aura de
> Blanca, sus ojeras, su desgano y su silencio, su somnolencia
> matinal y sus acuarelas vespertinas. En ese mismo momento
> comenzó el terremoto. (143)

Such a relationship across class lines "shakes the social edifice to its
foundations." In the construction of her story Allende makes sure to
highlight the interconnectedness of the generations. For example, the place
where Trueba's daughter and her friend first make love has special
significance: "Pedro Tercero la esperaba en el mismo sitio donde se habían
juntado el verano anterior y donde muchos años antes Esteban Trueba se
había apoderado de la humilde virginidad de Pancha García." (319)

The next link in the positive chain of events is Blanca and Pedro
Tercero's child Alba. Alba is a character who reverses the centrifugal
movement that the novel's characters experience up until her appearance on
the scene. Family members who no longer have or never had anything in
common share a love for Alba. But most important in the novel is the
relationship between grandfather and granddaughter. As Alma grows up, she
comes to have beliefs very different from those of her grandfather, but their
affection for each other survives. It is important to note here that they do not
simply "agree to disagree," nor do they diminish the scope of their
relationship by excluding certain topics from their conversational repertoire.
In one of the novel's sections narrated by Esteban, the ongoing dialogue with
his granddaughter is reflected.

> A veces yo iba al pueblo y volvía con un veterinario que revisaba
> a las vacas y a las gallinas y, de paso, echaba una mirada a los
> enfermos. No es cierto que yo partiera del principio de que si los
> conocimientos del veterinario alcanzaban para los animales,
> también servían para los pobres, como dice mi nieta cuando
> quiere ponerme furioso. (54)

She is loved by Trueba in spite of being the daughter of his enemy, just as she
will love her child, most probably engendered by a rapist. After her release
from the concentration camp, Alba writes:

> Me será muy difícil vengar a todos los que tienen que ser
> vengados, porque mi venganza no sería más que otra parte del
> mismo rito inexorable. Quiero pensar que mi oficio es la vida y
> que mi misión no es prolongar el odio, sino sólo llenar estas

páginas mientras espero el regreso de Miguel, mientras
entierro a mi abuelo que ahora descansa a mi lado en este cuarto,
mientras aguardo que lleguen tiempos mejores, gestando a la
criatura, que tengo en el vientre, hija de tantas violaciones, o tal
vez hija de Miguel, pero sobre todo hija mía. (379-380)

Alba also forms fraternal links with people who are not members of her
biological family: in the women's prison she cares for other inmates' children
as if they were her own and upon her release she is taken in and protected by
a stranger. By the novel's end, following the footsteps of her grandmother,
Alba has begun to forge a new model family which will include Chileans of
all social classes and political tendencies. This family is the Utopian image
which anchors the novel.

Alba embodies hope for the future, as her name implies: **Alba**, the
dawning of a new day, bringing with it another chance. In one of her typical
inversions, Allende places the victim of rape in the role of a pregnant Virgin
Mary. Since traditionally, especially in Spanish literature, sexual relations,
whether forced upon her or not, have always been the woman's fault, it can
be said that the awaited savior is a person denoted by two of the strongest
insults in the Spanish tongue: **hijo de puta, hijo de la chingada**. The novel
ends with Alba, and the reader, expecting the arrival of the child, an inverted
Christ figure in two ways. Rather than the child of any god, this one is of
unclear but doubtlessly human origin, conceived most probably in hate
rather than in love. And her mother writes, this child will be a girl. This
seems to suggest that hope will be embodied in a future in which "feminine"
values will have ascendancy over "masculine" ones.

As the preceding examples have illustrated, Allende finds hope in the
ability of people to love across social barriers. Another cause for optimism
proposed in the novel is the superior resilience of love in comparison to hate.
This latter emotion requires too much energy to maintain. When Trueba is
taken hostage by the **campesinos** on Las Tres Marías, Pedro Tercero, now a
government bureaucrat, comes to rescue his former **patrón** at Blanca's
request:

Era la primera vez que estaban frente a frente desde el día fatídico
en que Trueba le cobró la virginidad de su hija con un hachazo ...
Se observaron en silencio por largos segundos, pensando los dos
que el otro encarnaba lo más odioso en el mundo, pero sin
encontrar el fuego del antiguo odio en sus cora-zones. (318-319)

The other character who has trouble maintaining her hate is Alba.

> En la perrera escribí con el pensamiento que algún día tendría al coronel García vencido ante mí y podría vengar a todos los que tienen que ser vengados. Pero ahora dudo de mi odio … parece haberse diluído. (379)

Alba recognizes the possibility that the cycle of violence will continue:

> El día en que mi abuelo volteó entre los matorrales del río a su abuela, Pancha García, agregó otro eslabón en una cadena de hechos que debían cumplirse. Después el nieto de la mujer violada repite el gesto con la nieta del violador y dentro de cuarenta años, tal vez, mi nieto tumbe entre las matas del río a la suya y así, por los siglos venideros, en una historia inacabable de dolor, de sangre y de amor. (379)

Knowledge and understanding are proposed as the necessary elements in conquering fear and hate, because only with these tools can one work to see that the chain of terror is interrupted. Alba writes:

> Y ahora yo busco mi odio y no puedo encontrarlo. Siento que se apaga en la medida en que me explico la existencia del coronel García y de otros como él, que comprendo a mi abuelo y me entero de las cosas a través de los cuadernos de Clara … (379)

*La casa de los espíritus* is a novel of fantasy and of history. It recounts a sad chapter in Latin American history and simultaneously projects a Utopian vision into the future. Although its proposition is radical, the novel utilizes two of the most traditional images of Western culture: the family and the messianic child. Perhaps much of its power is derived from the use of these two ideas, which are deeply rooted in our collective psyche.

What Allende does with the family-as-symbol brings to mind another of Burke's ideas:

> Occasionally, when one makes a statement, his auditor will reprove him by observing that some Nazi ideologist has made a similar statement. No account is taken of the difference in the statement's function due to the difference of context in which it is used. This kind of "refutation" exemplifies to the fullest the

process of "being driven into a corner" whereby one despoils himself of an idea's serviceability simply because his opponent has misused it. (63-4)

Allende isn't about to be "driven into a corner." Rather than abandon the family, so laden with the positive idealized connotations of warmth, affection, safety and solidarity, Allende reconstitutes it. At least in her novel, "family" is inclusive rather than exclusive, since rich and poor, dark and light, left and right are shown to be "relatives." Ultimately, Esteban and Alba are able to bridge the gap of political differences because of their loving familial ties; and Alba, through her recognition that her torturer is also her kin, proposes the family as a model for her divided country: members of this family have oppressed, wounded, and tortured each other, but they are the same ones who must now heal one another. The family she posits is all of Chile.

## NOTE

1. See, for example, Hernán Vidal's analysis of an early play by Chilean playwright Egon Wolff, in "Una relectura del teatro democratacristiano inicial: Vodanovic y Wolff, el problema de nuestra ética colectivista," *Ideologies & Literature*, 2nd Series 1 (1985): 31-80.

## WORKS CITED

Allende, Isabel. *La casa de los espíritus*. 17th ed. Barcelona: Plaza & Janés, 1982.

Bridenthal, Renate, Atina Grossmann and Marion Kaplan. *When Biology Became Destiny: Women in Weimar and Nazi Germany*. New York: Monthly Review P, 1984.

Burke, Kenneth. *Attitudes Toward History*. vol. 1, New York: The New Republic, 1937. 2 vols.

Engels, Friedrich. *The Origin of the Family, Private Property and the State*. Trans. Ernest Untermann. Chicago: Charles Kerr, 1902.

Lasch, Christopher. *Haven in a Heartless World: The Family Besieged*. New York: Basic Books, 1977.

SUSAN DE CARVALHO

# Escrituras y Escritoras:
# The Artist-Protagonist of Isabel Allende

Isabel Allende has noted that *La casa de los espíritus* (1982) is the story of her family, or of a family similar to her own. She says that her grandmother was in fact clairvoyant and telekinetic, essentially similar to Clara. It follows, then, that Alba, who turns out to be the narrator, in many ways represents the author herself, the one who consolidates and disseminates the magically real family history. She is the heir to her grandmother's and mother's treasury of stories, which she combines with the equally tragic and fantastic level of her own experience, to produce written literature—to produce, in fact, *La casa de los espíritus*. Five years later, in *Eva Luna*, Allende presents us with another storyteller, this time seen completely from the first-person perspective. As does Alba Trueba (and Allende), Eva tells the stories that she learned, this time from her mother, but the stories are so intermingled with her own imagination and experience as to be completely her own.

All these women are storytellers. Clara del Valle and Consuelo, Eva Luna's mother, represent an important source for the style and content of the stories; Alba and Eva, and Isabel Allende, state that they write to record the history, to fix their roots. Clara and Consuelo tell stories, yet neither novel culminates with this phase of creation, but rather with the transformation of their stories into literature, a process which goes far beyond copying old notebooks. Alba is gradually led from a childhood of overflowing creativity

From *Discurso Literario* 10 (no. 1) (1992): 59-67. © 1992 by Discurso Literario. Reprinted by permission.

(first emerging in painting) to a life of political commitment. Although she writes down Blanca's stories as a child, and "anotaba tambié n las cosas que le parecían importantes," she does this "tal como lo hacía su abuela Clara," as a storyteller; she is not a literary artist until the end of the novel, after a complex process of maturation and awareness—a process which includes freedom and restriction, joy and despair, success and failure. This growth process towards literature is the primary focus of Eva Luna.

*Eva Luna*, then, is a novel of artistic self-exploration, a kind of Bildungsroman similar to Joyce's *Portrait of the Artist* or Lezama *Lima's Paradiso*. As in these novels, the episodes recounted are symbolic, important only in their effect on the narrator's own development. Eva Luna describes a process which clearly reflects Allende's own progess towards the publication of her first novel at the relatively late age of 38. Like Alba and Eva, the Chilean author was always a writer—of diaries, of journalism, of horoscopes and advice columns—but not of what is generally accepted as literature. The actual cause of this development, or the elements which compose the artist, are extremely difficult to define, for the artist herself and for literary critics. Yet her exploration of this mystery, begun in *Casa de los espíritus*, may be seen as the connecting thread of the episodic *Eva Luna*.

The childhood of Consuelo, Eva's mother, blends three cultural traditions into one. When found as an infant, "una cachorra desnuday cubierta de barro y excremento," she is an integral part of the jungle, yet she is not Indian but a redhead—a completely natural and ahistorical character, who maintains a real and magical perspective throughout her life: "pues quien ha abierto los ojos en el territorio más alucinante del mundo, pierde la capacidad de asombro." This acceptance of the marvelous and fantastic, as Alejo Carpentier noted in the forties, is a crucial aspect of modern Latin American fiction and, as we know, it is a constant in Allende's novels.

The second formative influence on Consuelo is that of the Mission, the Catholic tradition. In one respect this upbringing is seen as filled with repressive influences, an attempt to stifle the child's natural and overflowing creativity. As the narrator notes, "Dios era una presencia totalitaria," as the nuns try to bury the child's wild imagination under the weight of solemn European tradition: "Calla, insensata, calla y reza. Pídele al Señor que te ilumine." In spite of this attempt to "illuminate" the child by snuffing out her spirit, Catholicism also contributes to Consuelo's avid absorption of material for her fantasy world. As she would try to pray, "muy pronto se perdía en aventuras interminables donde los recuerdos de la selva alternaban con los personajes de la Historia Sagrada, cada uno con su cargamento de pasiones, venganzas, martirios y milagros." The only lasting effect of the repression, then, is to drive her fantasies into a completely inner world, "un tesoro discreto" which provides real consuelo both for her and for her daughter Eva, until the latter unlocks the treasure for her audiences.

The final element which Consuelo internalizes, to pass on to her daughter, is the European literary tradition. While working as a maid in the house of Professor Jones, she finds time to explore his labyrinthine library— the world's classics, but in no apparent order. Dates and backgrounds are not important; rather, the storyteller simply absorbs this heritage, which becomes inextricable from the tales that already populated her private world. Thus from three separate sources Consuelo, like Latin American literature itself, extracts and combines elements to form her own language and means of expression.

Consuelo, however, is not the central character of the novel; while contributing the entire base for Eva's creations, she does not go beyond her own inner fantasy world. The only person with whom she shares her stories is her daughter, who notes that without the stories, Consuelo is "silenciosa, capaz de disimularse entre los muebles, de perderse en el dibujo de la alfombra ... como si no existiera." She only exists, then, through her vivid but secret stories: "preservó intactas sus memorias de infancia ... retenía las anécdotas oídas al pasar y lo aprendido en sus lecturas, elaboraba la sustancia de sus propios sueños y con esos materiales fabricó un mundo para mí."

Thus Eva Luna learns from her mother to fantasize, to use her own private world as an escape, a space in which she has the power to create and control her own reality. This, however, is the initial storytelling phase, essential to literature but not solely responsible for it. Consuelo, like Clara, told stories for herself; it was left to the next generations to turn this richness outward, to create literature from the "tesoro discreto."

The next stage in this process for Eva is the discovery that her storytelling ability can win her affection and protection. At the age of 6 or 7, after her mother's death, Eva is sent to work for a mistress who considers her pensive silences "endemoniados," who washes her mouth with soap as punishment for talking to herself, who forbids her to daydream in front of a painting of the sea. Eva still escapes to the private world of her memories, in which her mother regularly appears; she also offers stories to the cook Elvira, her adopted grandmother, in exchange for nights in her bed or for admiration. The affection-starved child learns that she possesses a gift which sets her apart and can help her to create her own path; thus escapism is less necessary. Through her encounters with Elvira, Humberto Naranjo (who "no había oído en su vida alo que semejara remotamente a un cuento") and "la señora" of the brothel, Eva learns to communicate through her stories while gathering material for future tales. Notably, unlike the pícaros of the classical Spanish genre, Eva is not corrupted by her difficult and wandering life. In whatever situation she finds herself, there is someone who will listen to and appreciate her stories.

In the center of the novel occurs a crucial step in the literary apprenticeship of Eva Luna. Riad Halabí and the teacher Inés teach the adolescent Eva to read and, especially, to write. In *La casa de los espíritus*, this stage is taken for granted: Clara wrote since childhood, and Alba, "la condesa," never lacked for an education. Eva, however, learns to write at an age when she can be fully aware of the impact this new talent has on her creativity. After years of trying to retain an ocean of experiences and memories, even using verse forms to help her remember, she suddenly can record her thoughts and make them permanent. Allende—and Eva Luna herself—describe in detail the world of possibilities this opens:

> La escritura era lo mejor que me había ocurrido en toda mi existencia, estaba eufórica, leía en alta voz, andaba con el cuaderno bajo el brazo para usarlo a cada rato, anotaba pensamientos, nombres de flores, ruidos de pájaros, inventaba palabras. La posibilidad de escribir me permitió prescindir de las rimas para recordar y pude enredar los cuentos con múltiples personajes y aventuras.

At the same time, Eva Luna is happy for the first time, free from the degradation of her former positions: "Yo caminaba hablando alto, alegre, contenta de pertenecer a esa comunidad." She has less need to use her stories as escapism; this, combined with the ability to write, constitutes a significant development towards the creation of her literature.

Equally valuable is the young creator's ability to read. We have already seen the effect of literacy on Consuelo, who spent her spare time secretly devouring the Professor's books. Eva continues this process of literary acquisition, notably, with the tales of the *Arabian Nights*. She reads each story "no sé cuántas veces," internalizes them and then begins to alter them, making them her own, adding these new plots and characters to her own "tesoro discreto," which has become "un juego de infinitas posibilidades."

There is a significant juxtaposition of episodes here: while Eva learns to read, pronouncing the words aloud, her Turkish mistress Zulema listens intently to learn Spanish. One day, Zulema can suddenly speak fluently. This learning of a language parallels Eva's own exploration to find her literary language, her most effective means of self-expression.

Another symbol which underlines the importance of this phase of learning is the association of two gifts from Halabí: "la escritura y un certificado de existencia." Halabí bribes an official to forge a birth certificate for Eva, legitimizing her and giving her an identity; before this, according to Eva, "era como si no hubiera nacido." Writing performs a similar function of self-definition; writing is her "certificado de existencia."

Finally, near the end of this section, Eva describes her first writing experiences, the recording of her thoughts and actions in notebooks like those of Clara; she has progressed from being an introspective but immensely creative daydreamer to a very self-conscious constructor of a literary world:

> Pasaba parte de mi noche escribiendo y me gustaba tanto hacerlo, que se me iban las horas sin darme cuenta y a menudo me levantaba por la mañana con los ojos enrojecidos. Pero esas eran mis mejores horas. Sospechaba que nada existía verdaderamente, la realidad era una materia imprecisa y gelatinosa que mis sentidos captaban a medias ... yo podía tomar esa gelatina y moldearla para crear lo que deseara ... un mundo propio.

Significantly, this period of learning takes place in the tiny mountain town of Agua Santa, far from the sordid struggle for survival in the capital. The idyl ends, however, with the suicide of Zulema and the amorous experience with Halabí that marks Eva Luna's transition to womanhood.

Eva Luna is forced to return to the real world, and this confrontation with human tragedies and with love adds the final phase to her development from storyteller to artist. She lives with the androgynous Mimí, an astrologer who acts as a kind of guiding Muse; in fact, in one instance Eva refers to her as a "criatura mitológica." When Eva decides to take a factory job to support her now-crazy Godmother, Mimí urges her to study writing instead, to fulfill her destiny. The inevitability of Eva's course towards literature is very clear to the astrologer who, when Eva flees from the factory and the corrupt Colonel, consoles her thus: "—No hay mal que por bien no venga— sentenció Mimí al comprobar que la rueda de fortuna había dado medio giro para colocarme en el camino donde ella consideraba que siempre debía estar. —Ahora podrás escribir en serio."

Because she must earn a living, Eva cannot begin by writing poetry or novels; the only "art form" open to her is the formulaic telenovela. Often the submission of an artist to such an artificial art form as a means of support would represent a degradation, a surrendering of ideals. But Eva Luna, although writing television scripts, did not compromise the outpouring of her words onto paper, could not remember the genre's rules and restrictions, but rather is still guided by the memory of her mother: "yo andaba en plena selva dando alcance a una niña de cabellera roja. Seguí a ese ritmo sin acordarme de las recomendaciones recibidas."

During this initial "delirio" of her "universo recién nacido," Eva Luna learns that her path to self-realization lies through literary creation. The difference between her and other soap opera writers is made clear by the director Aravena's admission that her script violates all the rules; he is only producing it "porque no resistía la tentació n de escandalizar al país con esos adefesios y porque Mimí se lo había pedido."

The final contribution to the writer's literary formation appears in the form of her love for Huberto Naranjo and for Rolf Carlé. In all of the modern feminine characters of her novels—Alba (Casa), Irene (De amor y de sombra), Eva Luna—Isabel Allende links political commitment with romantic love. In all three novels, the protagonists initially involve themselves in the revolution only to help or protect their lovers; but soon their participation and level of commitment become very real. In the third novel, Eva Luna subtly alters her script, *Bolero*, using an acceptable medium to convey a subversive revolutionary message. Consistent with the trends of the post-boom generation, Allende clearly postulates as a constant in her literary production the overwhelming need to communicate the truth, both fantastic and horrible, to those who live a different reality.

Thus Eva arrives at her destiny, as an artist. Her literary production is not a simple talent or natural creativity; rather it is an irreducible fusion of a heritage of imagination, storytelling and a wonderful vision of reality, mixed with the effects of all other literature absorbed by the author, and finally, with the decision to use writing not as escapism but as a vehicle for truth. Eva Luna's *Bolero* is a very self-conscious attempt to communicate the protagonist's own world, which finally can no longer avoid its real historical circumstances. Its relationship to the novel *Eva Luna* is purposely made ambiguous; the reader suddenly doubts whether he is reading an autobiography or simply being told a story of intrigue and love. This added level, not present in *La casa de los espíritus*, reveals an awareness of the creative process far more developed than in the earlier novels and also creates a distance between reader and narrator. The self-awareness of the narrator is made clear in the surprising Epilogue, in which Eva Luna shows us that her earlier assertions about the creative power of her writing were not mere theories, but rather her practice: "Sospechaba que el final llegaría sólo con mi propia muerte y me atrajo la idea de ser yo también uno más de la historia y tener el poder de determinar mi fin o inventarme una vida." The open ending, in which Eva predicts that her love affair with Rolf will "desgastarse y deshacerse en hilachas," or perhaps will have a "final feliz," successfully fuses the planes of Eva's reality with her ambiguous fiction and with Allende's own presence in her literary creation. She too is "uno más de la historia," exploring through Eva Luna the mystery of her identity as an artist.

After reading the novel, one can return to Alba Trueba in *La casa de los espíritus* and see similar influences guiding her towards a similar literary destiny. She too begins with raw creativity and imagination, exemplified by her immense frescoes on the walls of her bedroom. She also inherits from her mother and grandmother a rich treasury of fantasy/history and by the age of six "había descubier to los libros mágicos de los baúles encantados de su legendario tío bisabuelo Marcos y había entrado de lleno en el mundo sin retorno de la fantasí a." While her learning to read and write occurs at a much earlier and therefore less self-aware age than Eva's, she also fails to make the transition from storyteller to novelist until faced with overwhelming personal and political tragedy. Like Eva, she is swept into politics through her love for Miguel, but her level of commitment is much more intense due to her nightmare of imprisonment. In fact, writing becomes her only anchor to life. She also has Muse-like figures who urge her towards this goal; Clara appears before her in the prison's dog pen to tell her that "la gracia no era morirse, puesto que eso llegaba de todos modos, sino sobrevivir, que era un milagro," and that her purpose in survival was to communicate truth through writing:

> ... para que el mundo se enterara del horror que ocurría paralelamente a la existencia apacible y ordenada de los que no querían saber, de los que podían tener la ilusión de una vida normal, de los que podían negar que iban a flote en una balsa sobre un mar de lamentos, ignorando, a pesar de todas las evidencias, que a pocas cuadras de su mundo feliz estaban los otros, los que sobreviven o mueren en el lado oscuro.

As Eva had Mimí to force a notebook upon her and urge her to write, so Alba follows the advice of Ana Díaz, who obtains notebooks even in the concentration camp; both guides see that writing has become a need and a means of survival for the women. Eva's writing carries her beyond the power of the lascivious Colonel, and when Alba next encounters Esteban García, she too is "más allá de su poder." For both women, literature becomes a means of confronting a complex reality, of dealing with it, and of finally overcoming or transcending it.

Thus Eva Luna and Alba Trueba may be seen to embody the diverse influences which brought Allende herself to become a novelist. However, the two novels are literary works and not a recipe for composing an artist. The author recognizes that uniting all of these sources and guides is some completely mysterious and unexplainable force, which she calls destino. Both novels end with that, with the writers' feeling of having begun to fill a role which had long been prepared for them. Eva Luna says of her first blank page:

> Creí que esa página me esperaba desde hace veintitantos añ os, que yo había vivido sólo para ese instante, y quise que a partir de ese momento mi único oficio fuera atrapar las historias suspendidas en el aire más delgado, para hacerlas mías.

The role of Mimí and astrology also demonstrate that writing, for Eva Luna, is not a career to earn a living, but rather a predestined fate. The role of the stars is equally present in *La casa de los espíritus*, in which Alba is surrounded from birth by favorable prognostications. In the end, she comes to terms with the horror of her prison experience by realizing that it is merely another piece that fits in the jigsaw puzzle of her own, and of a wider, "destino dibujado antes de mi nacimiento ... ninguna pincelada es inútil." Finally, in her own epilogue, Alba states that Clara filled her notebooks in order that Alba could one day turn them into literature: "Clara los escribió para que me sirvieran ahora para rescatar las cosas del pasado y sobrevivir a mi propio espanto."

By concluding the novels with an acceptance of destiny, Allende admits that, in fact, the forces which drive her and her characters to write are not completely explicable. Looking back on her life, she can explore and identify bases, influences, experiences of this reality, which moved her towards this destiny; but the actual making of an artist, for her, bridges the gap to another level of reality and thus remains a mystery.

RONIE-RICHELLE GARCÍA-JOHNSON

# The Struggle for Space:
# Feminism and Freedom

The temporal setting of the action in *The House of the Spirits* spans fifty years—from the early twenties to about 1974. Historically, and fictionally, within the novel, these were the years in which the women's movement began to gather strength, and then gain progress. While it is apparent that Allende has traced the development of women's struggle for freedom in her novel, some critics have suggested that Nivea, Clara, Blanca, and Alba are allegorical characters which epitomize women at various phases of Chilean social and political history. Michael Handelsman has proposed that Nivea symbolized the early suffragist movement, Clara, more personal statements of liberty, Blanca, the movement towards free and healthy passion, and Alba, the consolidation of these distinct forms of protest and their most recent successes. Marjorie Agosín asserts that the novel is "feminocéntrica." Patricia Hart argues that Clara and Blanca "indulge in passive behavior." Gabriela Mora has insisted that, while both male and female characters broke some stereotypes, Allende's female characters were not feminists. While the insightful arguments of Handelsman, Hart, Agosín and Mora lead to various conclusions, a spatial interpretation of the novel contributes to the idea that the Trueba women were proponents of their own independence.

A thorough and complex understanding of *The House of the Spirits* demands spatial interpretation, and thus a spatial examination of the

From *Revista Hispanica Moderna* 67 (no. 1) (June 1994): 184-193. © 1994 by Columbia University. Reprinted by permission.

treatment of women in the novel is imperative as well. There are treasures hidden in the spaces and rooms of Allende's novel, where the idea that bodies and structures are both houses, and that they are inseparable and essential, is fundamental. Careful examination reveals that, besides the bloody political battle between the military and the liberals, there is another war in the work. The battle of the sexes is cleverly manifested in the continuous struggle for space in the house; the main house in *The House of the Spirits* is a divided one. Allende's magnificent representation of the fight for dominance between men and women, the discordant coexistence of the male and female, is a prime example of the author's perception and presentation of a universal theme.

Allende utilized spatial symbolism to emphasize and parallel the actions of female characters as they sought to overcome the tyranny of patriarchy. In her novel, structures, and the spaces they contain, serve as metaphors for or symbols of social and political barriers. Rather than allowing these metaphorical or symbolic obstacles to determine their lives, the women of the Trueba family overcame them. Clara, Blanca, and Alba managed to defeat Esteban Trueba, who, with traditional notions of honor, of a woman's "place," and of sexuality, attempted to possess and confine these women. The Trueba women confronted Esteban in his own space, usurped his control of that area, expanded their lives into alternative spaces, or left Trueba's property altogether. Trueba and "his" women were contenders struggling to dominate the space they should have shared; by the end of the novel, Trueba found that he had lost the battle and the war.

Trueba's attitude towards women, "possessing" them, and keeping them within his own structures became apparent spatially in the beginning of the novel. After he learned of Rosa the Beautiful's death, he regretted not having married her sooner and he thought that, if he had known that she was to die, he would have "built her a palace studded with treasures from the ocean floor," "kidnapped her and locked her up," and only he "would have had the key." According to Trueba, his betrothed would have never been "stolen" from him by "death" if he had kept her to himself. Like many traditional fathers and husbands, Trueba regarded his women jealously and attempted to confine them as treasure in a chest to maintain their loyalty. So intense was Trueba's determination to keep his women with him that he prepared a tomb with a place for not only himself, but for his wife and his long-dead Rosa. No one, or thing, was going to "steal" his women from him again.

No structure, however, could keep Clara isolated and protected from the outside world. Clara had inherited her mother Nivea's determination to have her own way; she was a strong, willful woman. While Nivea enthusiastically promoted feminist causes, Clara quietly continued her own fight for freedom within her own home, the home that Trueba had built for her. Clara did not have to physically and permanently leave the structure of the house to escape the domination of her husband. She found freedom and battled Trueba with various spatial maneuvers. She existed, spiritually, in another space or dimension, and brought the outside world inside the space of the house to her. She manipulated the space within the house as she pleased and, when all other techniques failed, she locked herself up, in her own secluded space, out of Trueba's reach. This spatial analysis agrees with Agosín's interpretation; according to Agosín, Clara "inhabited her own space and her own imagination" and thus "evaded the presence of her spouse."

Clara had developed the habit of seeking alternative mental spaces in which to dwell as a child in her father's home. She would escape her immediate reality as she read a book, or imagined herself in far-away places. Her "magic" and her attempts to move articles about with the power of her mind distanced her from the "real" world. Once she was married, Clara maintained her secret, interior universe. As she prepared to give birth to her first child, she announced: "I think I'm going to levitate." Clara "meant that she wanted to rise to a level that would allow her to leave behind the discomfort and heaviness of pregnancy and the deep fatigue that had begun to seep into her bones. She entered one of her long periods of silence...." This last sentence is a key to Allende's use of pregnancy as a metaphor. Allende has said: "I need long periods of silence ... because the books build up inside of me little by little. It's like expecting a baby for some time." Clara was pregnant with more than a physical child, she was pregnant with love, creativity, and what would later be born as a text. This confirms Agosín's idea that Clara's silence was far from passive, it was a kind of writing. Whether Clara's silence is interpreted as a retreat, a refuge, as Agosín has termed it, or as a clever victory over the mundane, it is clear that she entered an alternative space, a "closed world free from any masculine insertion" as she "levitated" in silence.

Although, at the moment when Clara was preparing to give birth Trueba understood that this silence was a "last refuge," he later became distressed. He "wanted control over that undefined and luminous material that lay within her and that escaped him even in those moments when she appeared to be dying of pleasure." The patriarch "realized that Clara did not belong to him and that if she continued living in a world of apparitions ... she probably never would." Trueba could build a house to contain wife, and he could enter the space within her body, but he would never be allowed to enter the home she had built for herself inside her own head. Clara had defeated male domination.

Clara's magic and the happiness she found as she practiced it was attractive to artists, poets, and spiritualists. The "big house on the corner" became a gathering place for these marginal people as Clara invited them into the space of her home. Clara also opened her home to the unfortunates who needed food and shelter. By encouraging these people to enter the exterior world that represented her interior self, Clara let them into the space that was forbidden to Trueba. Not surprisingly, Trueba objected to the carnivalization of his home and the daily parade that marched through it. He insisted that the "big house on the corner" was not a thoroughfare and coldly ordered that the celebration of the everyday be stopped. Clara and her children, especially Nicolás, continued to live as they pleased, and to fill the space as they desired, while Trueba was out of town. Upon his return, the atmosphere of the house changed, and the party was over—temporarily. Trueba continually struggled to dominate the space of the house in the city and his family fought back with determined consistency.

As she found herself trapped in a particular space and time, and could not divorce Trueba, Clara had to manipulate her immediate area. She attempted to move objects with the power of her mind, and she redefined the limits of the structure Trueba had built for her in the "big house on the corner."

In response to Clara's imagination and the requirements of the moment, the noble, seigniorial architecture began sprouting all sorts of extra little rooms, staircases, turrets, and terraces. Each time a new guest arrived, the bricklayers would arrive and build another addition to the house. The big house on the corner soon came to resemble a labyrinth.

The use of the world labyrinth is telling, for it suggests a space that, rather than possessing a masculine, linear order, is as complex as the intuition of a woman. Trueba's perfect, logical space was transformed by a woman. Instead of allowing his space to enclose her, she opened it and recreated it to suit her.

The struggle for space came to a climax while Clara was still alive and surrounded by her eccentric friends and Trueba campaigned for the office of Senator of the Republic. Clara needed space for her continuous spiritual celebrations, and Trueba needed space for the operations of his political party.

The house filled with political propaganda and with the members of his party, who practically took it by storm, blending in with the hallway ghosts, the Rosicrucians, and the three Mora sisters. Clara's retinue was gradually pushed into the back rooms of the house ...

The house became a house divided as "an invisible border arose between the parts of the house occupied by Esteban Trueba and those occupied by his wife." As the house has traditionally represented the unification of its occupants, the "invisible" spatial division within the house is a symbol, not only of the Trueba's spliced relationship, but of the separation of the sexes.

Trueba believed that the spirituality that captivated his wife and her friends was for women only. Before Nicolás departed to India, he told him "I hope you return a man, because I'm fed up with all your eccentricities." He considered his other son, Jaime, to be eccentric as well, because he cared for the underprivileged and didn't want to join his father in business. Jaime, therefore, was not a "well-adjusted man." Other readers have noticed that with some special exceptions, such as Jaime, Pedro Tercero García, and the prostitute Tránsito Soto, the men in the novel operate with logical thinking while the women depend on their spiritual and emotional strength to survive. This presentation of men and women is based on beliefs which are prevalent in Latin America. The author of *The House of the Spirits* herself has stated that "at times science is less efficient than magic." As the "big house on the corner" in Allende's novel is a symbol for the family, the house naturally reflects the fact that the family, and the world, exists only because of the differences between two groups: women and men. It is not surprising that Allende chose to represent the schism spatially; as she spoke of her childhood, she noted that men and women were "segregated," and this implies a spatial understanding of the problem.

In the arena of the house in the city, Clara was victorious as she defended her independence. While the "facade of the house underwent no alterations" the most intimate interior of the house belonged to, was dominated by, and represented Clara. Even "the rear garden," once a perfect, strict emulation of "a French garden" became hers, "a tangled jungle in which every type of plant and flower had proliferated and where Clara's birds kept up a steady din, along with many generations of cats and dogs." The house belonged to Clara.

Campos discusses this conversion of space and, combining her ideas with those of Gastón Bachelard, concludes that the house "is Clara" ... the space of the "unconsciousness, of the Imagination, of the mother." Agosín states that Clara is the "soul" of the house on the corner. The validity of these ideas is confirmed with Allende's statement that the basement of the house was a womb. By manipulating the space of the house, it began to represent Clara, instead of Trueba. Gone was the house that Trueba had desired, planned, and built. His house was not a reflection of himself, as he had wanted, but of Clara, the family, and his relationship to them. One might venture as far to say that the house was female. With spatial symbols, Allende communicates the message that, although the patriarchy may seem to be in control, women and traditionally feminine spirits prevail behind the facade.

After Trueba slapped her and knocked her teeth out as she tried to defend her daughter, Clara's response to his physical violence was twofold. First, she refused to speak to him and then, she locked herself in her room. Clara's denial of access to the space of her room, of her body—the spaces which Trueba had violated—was a powerful weapon. Even more potent was her refusal to allow Trueba to enter her mental space; she would never verbally communicate with him again. Clara had once again defeated Trueba with his own space; he was the one who had built and decorated her room. While some have mistaken both of these manuevers for passivity, spatial analysis demonstrates that Clara's actions were far from passive, and thus provides evidence to support Agosín's assertions regarding feminine silence in the novel. Clara had refused the masculine body access to her feminine world, and she swore not to enter masculine verbal space. Trueba was, more than frustrated, defeated; he could not touch Clara's soul, let alone control it.

Blanca, Trueba's only daughter, continued the tradition of independence begun by her grandmother. Although she did not rally for women's suffrage, or practice magic like her mother to assert her freedom, Blanca defied her father. Trueba would have never sanctioned the love that Blanca had for the peasant leader Pedro Tercero García. The house that divided Blanca and Pedro Tercero García was the elaborate symbol of elite wealth and social grace; her home at The Three Marias sharply contrasted with the little hut in which her peasant lover lived. It would have been absurd for Pedro to cross into Trueba's space, to visit the big house, and it would have been scandalous for Blanca to debase herself by setting foot in the peasant's quarters. Nevertheless, Blanca asserted her freedom with her actions and by symbolically passing through space.

Instead of opening her window and waiting for her lover to climb over a wall and into her father's space, Blanca crossed the barriers of her father's home herself. She waited until her father was asleep, until the landscape was hidden in the darkness, to lock her bedroom door and leave her father's house and domination. She would slip out the window, climb down a trellis covered with flowers, and run in the darkness. She did not go to the peasant quarters to meet her lover—that space, technically, belonged to her father. Instead, she and Pedro Tercero García met far from the structures, the houses and the huts, which symbolized the tyranny imposed over both of them and found each other by the banks of the stream, which for them, represented the flow of life, freedom, and passion.

Trueba's characteristic reaction to Blanca's defiance was to violently regain his powerful authority over her. He beat her and forced her to marry the Count. When Blanca arrived at the big house the morning after her wedding to visit her mother, Trueba ordered her to return quickly to her husband. By leaving the hotel to go to her mother's house and space, Blanca was symbolically negating her marriage. Trueba sent Blanca away, out of his space. He could not tolerate the fact that his daughter had willfully negated his position by leaving his house in order to meet Pedro Tercero García. Trueba knew that, by leaving the protective space of his house, Blanca had escaped his masculine domination, and that she aspired to sexual freedom by inviting a man of her own choice to penetrate her physical space. While Blanca did obey her father and marry the Count, she did manage to keep a sacred space within her womb for the product of her union with Pedro: Alba. Later in the novel, Blanca subverted her father's dominion with the brazenly defiant act of bringing Pedro into Trueba's home.

While Clara didn't care to concern herself with the daily up-keep of the house, Blanca, and later, Alba, became devoted to its maintenance. They would feed the members of the household, keep the birds singing, the plants green, and do the gardening. During Trueba's absence, these women effectively ran the household. Bachelard discussed the idea that, while men build the external house, its is the women who, immersed in the day-to-day project of maintenance, make the house livable, or better—make it a home. "In the intimate harmony of walls and furniture, it may be said that we become conscious of a house that is built by women, since men only know how to build a house from the outside." In fact, as time passed, the women of the "big house on the corner" were responsible for the renovation and rebirth of the house. Bachelard is helpful with the concept of the renewal of the house as well: "housewifely care weaves the ties that unite a very ancient past to the new epoch." At the end of the novel it is Alba who convinces her father to renew the house and resurrect the garden, the symbol of freedom. Allende's message seems to be that with love and patience, women maintain their nations as well as their homes.

Alba's youth coincided with the late sixties and the early seventies, a time of sexual revolution. Despite the ideas of the youths, those of the older, empowered generations did not look favorably upon these developments. Trueba would never have consented to Alba having a pre-marital sexual relationship with anyone. He wouldn't have tolerated mere courtship if her suitor were someone like Miguel, a radical leftist. Like her mother, however, Alba did not let her grandfather's attitude stop her from loving the man of her choice. For, in Agosín's words, Alba was "the one destined to leave the benevolent space of the house on the corner" to join the struggle for social justice.

Alba did not run away from her home to live as she desired. Although at first she and Miguel would meet in his apartment, she found that the most comfortable solution was to bring Miguel into Trueba's home, where "in the labyrinth of the rear rooms, where no one ever went, they could make love undisturbed." The use of the word "labyrinth" reminds the reader that the house was still Clara's house, even though, after her death, it deteriorated for lack of her laughter. "One by one the lovers tried out all the abandoned rooms, and finally chose an improvised nest in the depths of the basement." Alba would lead Miguel in through the garden (the symbol of freedom) into the basement. It is spatially significant that the lovers went to the basement because their love, like the basement was "underground"—a secret.

The basement is, as the reader will remember, also a metaphor for the womb. Alba was leading Miguel to the most intimate of spaces, the space where life, (and text, in the cases of Clara and Alba,) is created. Their entrance into the basement was symbolic of sexual intercourse as well as of a more profound act of love. Alba and Miguel rearranged the space Trueba had created, as had her grandmother Clara, although they transformed the basement into a love nest. Alba and Miguel utilized the long-forgotten artifacts they found to turn their underground "nest" into an "nuptial chamber." Although they occupied the same space that Alba's grandparents had, Alba and Miguel shared a more fruitful love, and they did so by transforming the vestiges of an old world into a new "home."

Of all the actions of the women who had gone before her, Alba's spatial statement was by far the most assertive. Instead of preserving her intimate space with silence and magic, as Clara had, or leaving her "father's" home as Blanca had, Alba lived as she pleased in the space where she had grown up. This spatial relationship represents a confrontation with the patriarchy. Alba and Miguel's complicity as they recreated the basement, the history of the Truebas, to suit themselves, suggests that a new generation, women and men alike, would overcome that patriarchy. In Campos's words, they were the "salvation of the future."

The patriarchy, however, manipulated more than the freedom of the Trueba women. Just as Trueba attempted to control "his" women within the structures he had built for them, those with power in the country of which Allende wrote dominated the lives of workers, farmers, and every underprivileged citizen within the political structure. As Alba, and all the women of *The House of the Spirits* battled for their freedom as women, they struggled for political justice. The struggle for independence was not just a feminine one; it was a fight for the rights of all classes, creeds, and sexes. Clara had always been interested in the welfare of the poor. Blanca not only loved a leftist peasant, she hid this wanted man in her father's home after the Coup. Alba hid weapons for the resistance forces and her radical, guerrilla lover in her grandfather's home. She took food from the cupboards and sold furniture, including the portrait of her grandmother Clara, to feed the poor who were starving as a result of the Military's policies. Alba directly defied the government, and her grandfather, the symbol of conservatism, as she utilized Trueba's space and that which it contained. In *The House of the Spirits*, feminism and leftist liberalism were united in the struggle to preserve the Chilean home; feminine auras and the forces of freedom alike dwelt in the "house of the spirits."

CLAUDIA MARIE KOVACH

# Mask and Mirror: Isabel Allende's Mechanism for Justice in The House of the Spirits

> No one brings suit justly,
> no one goes to law honestly;
> They rely on empty pleas, they speak lies,
> conceiving mischief and begetting iniquity.
>
> (Isa. 59:4)

The prophet Isaiah thus envisions how the lack of truth, righteousness, and integrity in relationships brings the divisiveness of sin into the world. Injustice splinters the wholeness of creation, causing a disintegration of personal and interpersonal integrity. Novelist Isabel Allende echoes this cry when she tells an interviewer: "I feel terribly angry at the world. I think that the world is a crazy place, very unjust and unfair and violent, and I'm angry at that. I want to change the rules, change the world." Such a changing of the world requires, in religious terminology, a conversion, a method of promoting reconciliation. But reconciliation must begin with oneself, and Allende seems to realize this requirement. Suffering isolation from family and country after going into exile as a result of a military takeover, Allende felt the need to recapture her inner being. She turned to writing, that very significant social practice embraced by those seeking to express both the spiritual and social requirements of integrity and justice. Her own spiritual

From *Postcolonial Literature and the Biblical Call for Justice* (1994): 74-90. © 1994 by University Press of Mississippi. Reprinted by permission.

goals upon writing her first novel, *The House of the Spirits* (which began as a personal letter to her dying grandfather still back in Chile), centered on a recovery of identity, a reconstruction of self, a fostering of emotional, psychological, and spiritual integrity. By recovering and recounting her memories Allende gained the kind of wholeness that ontological liberationists cite as a first step toward the attainment of economic and social justice.

Although usually associated more readily with the current Latin American aesthetic of magic realism and with secular political fiction rather than with theological perspectives, Allende says that *The House of the Spirits* achieved a spiritual goal: "I felt that my roots had been recovered and that during that patient exercise of daily writing I had also recovered my own soul." Allende's statement implies her sensitivity to that insight found in Isaiah that connects social justice with personal integrity. An inner sense of worth and wholeness that comes from connection to and recognition of family and culture remains a basic prerequisite for achieving social justice. What Allende achieved in her own life by writing the novel is reflected in the novel as well, for it illuminates how reconciliation and mediation, particularly within the self, work together as necessary precursors to achieving biblical justice. Moreover, Allende's novel highlights through the women characters a particularly feminist focus that reflects biblical feminists' concern for recovering human integrity within the female person and by means of female intercession.

The first step to understanding the mechanism Allende uses in *The House of the Spirits* to set up a prophetic vision of female integrity and justice is to look at how the novel presents the role of memories. Achieving personal integrity in the face of experiences and social structures that have served to shatter, oppress, or repress identity cannot be accomplished by simple imperative. Integration requires an exploration of possibilities, a trying-on of alternatives, a viewing and reviewing of experiences. Continual reintegration by means of seeing memories from all angles, in both masked and mirrored ways, allows—as we shall see—for the reconciliation of self. This process establishes in *The House of the Spirits* a framework for conversion, a literal "turning toward," an instance of what Kierkegaard described as the ancient ideal of "recollection": "just as they [the Greeks] taught that all knowledge is a recollection, so will modern philosophy teach that the whole of life is a repetition." The life that Allende "re-peats" and "re-collects" throughout the novel by means of the women characters is her own and that of her family and country. Yet the novel points as well toward the possibilities of reconciliation inherent in all humanity; it speaks out for the conversion of oppressive social structures.

By writing, Allende breaks the oppression of her own silence and implicitly joins in the Latin American movement of concientizacion. This process of recovering the lost, of remembering what has been neglected, of reconstructing what has been left out, of reclaiming a forfeited heritage, is at the heart of a revolutionary liberation theology. This process of self-liberation "aims at breaking through the pervasive 'culture of silence,' that defines the oppressed condition, by an inner resurrection of soul that transforms a person from an object of conditions which determine his reality and consciousness to a subject of his own history and destiny." Perhaps more importantly, this movement prompts people to question the dominant power structure that forms the basis of their whole inherited tradition. The women of Allende 's novel both individually and together shatter the silence that sustains and contributes to oppression; they discover the power of repeated memories; they forge a new personal and cultural consciousness positing a chain of connection, love, and reconciliation. Forms of repetition in their lives help lead to self-liberation and to reconciliation beyond the self.

This radical recovery and reconstruction is at the center of Elisabeth Schüssler Fiorenza's ground-breaking *In Memory of Her*, a work that uses a combination of New Testament historiography and theology to define a "discipleship of equals": "Feminist biblical spirituality must be incarnated in a historical movement of women struggling for liberation. It must be lived in prophetic commitment, compassionate solidarity, consistent resistance, affirmative celebration, and in grassroots organizations of the ekklesia of women." This stance promotes unity and reconciliation; it provides a formula for justice that arises from relationships supported by repeated memories. Indeed, the very essence of solidarity for Fiorenza resides in the reclaiming of the lost: "to insist that women's history is an integral part of early Christian historiography [implies] the search for roots, for solidarity with our foresisters, and finally for the memory of their sufferings, struggles, and powers as women." Remembering this erased "her" takes the form of recollection, both as a kind of religious contemplation and as a recalling to mind of the temporarily forgotten. Solidarity is achieved by means of a recitation of memories, a repetition of the historical details that women share.

Such unity underpins the biblical call for justice, an appeal that centers on good and proper relationships—with God, with nature, and with other human beings. The personal, God-centered ideal seeks conversion, personal integrity, and self-discovery, what John S. Dunne calls "self-appropriation";

reverence for nature asks for responsible and ongoing stewardship of creation; social commitment reaches out beyond the self and penetrates both the macrocosm of political institutions and the microcosm of family life. Yet of all the relationships highlighted by Scripture, the first—personal peace and reconciliation with God (always for the Christian a product of the inner working of God's grace in one's life)—is perhaps the most important since it inspires attachment to the other two. As a result, the process of self-appropriation, the constant, repeated becoming of what one is, remains a prerequisite for this ideal and ultimately allows integration of all relationships into an harmonious whole, creating an experience of the shalom ideal described by Nicholas Wolterstorff. The act of self-discovery is a crucial step that leads to justice.

Primarily by means of the women characters of *The House of the Spirits*, Allende reconstitutes the biblical feminists' formula of solidarity by means of various kinds of repetition to achieve self-appropriation and shalom. The image of the mask (the irrational, the unconscious, the soul) and the image of the mirror (the rational, the conscious, the self) provide a mechanism for tracing the inner integrative conversion necessary for this rather complex but ideal form of justice. Allende's method is to create and re-create the images and themes of mirror and mask in a way that brings together the double-sided coin that unites the rational and the irrational, the objective and the subjective, the analytic and the intuitive. Repetition in its mirrored state and repetition in its masked form become for Allende a mechanism for complete reconciliation and justice.

*The House of the Spirits* reveals a world rife with injustice and peopled with individuals who lack the righteous integrity needed for such reconciliation. A family chronicle tracing several generations, the novel presents a concatenation of conflicting patriarchies that serve merely to spawn a chain of hatred and revenge. Personally, characters in the novel experience social alienation, spiritual perplexity, and psychological instability. Socially, the work depicts mistreatment of women, the abuse of tenant farmers, and the squalor of the city shantytowns. Politically, injustice reigns in the excesses of the conservative right, the extremes of the left-wing socialist reformers, and the violence of the deposing military dictatorship. Institutional religion stands as an oppressive purveyor of guilt and fear and a self-serving supporter of the status quo. Even nature adds its share of terror, destruction, and pain with the devastations of earthquakes and plagues.

Much of Allende's view of the world stems, of course, from her experience of injustice in her native Latin America. Exiled for sixteen years in Venezuela after the assassination in 1973 of her uncle, the former Chilean president Salvador Allende Gossens, Allende draws deeply upon her family history and the political upheaval in modern Chile. Yet she sides with Isaiah and the Psalmists who recognize the potential for divine and human justice, the hope for ultimate reconciliation for the faithful people of God: "Zion shall be redeemed by justice, and those in her who repent, by righteousness. But rebels and sinners shall be destroyed together, and those who forsake the LORD shall be consumed." Allende's hope is evidenced by her novelistic choices: she does not depict in *The House of the Spirits* merely an unjust, unfair, violent world. Like Isaiah, she denounces evil but also proclaims the potential for unity and equality; like the Psalmist, she demonstrates the possibilities for love in the world.

In recovering her own memories, Allende mirrors her own experiences and magically weaves a world in which women preserve their memories in various artistic forms, simultaneously breaking the silence of oppression and achieving solidarity. Clara's notebooks give witness to life; Blanca recounts the magic stories from her uncle Marcos's enchanted trunks; Alba cherishes the past in her own writing, succeeds in getting her grandfather to write his memories, and retrieves her grandmother's notebooks. Likewise, Rosa's fantastically embroidered tablecloth, Blanca's creches of imaginary animals, and Alba's amazing frescoes record the "wishes, memories, sorrows, and joys" of their lives. In every case, the recall of memories involves a constant and inexhaustible recurrence or repetition of shared actions, events, feelings that begin to carry out the program for community and remembering that Fiorenza advocates. Even the narrative structure of the novel itself reflects the goal of iterating personal memories in a way that mirrors the connection of the characters. The combination of Clara's notebooks (which span the whole period of her life), Alba's notes and experiences, and Esteban's reminiscences forges the essence of the three major personalities of the novel; the narration that shifts among these memories reflects these characters' close emotional and physical interrelation. Indeed, Clara's notebooks are organized according to events, not chronologically, to emphasize that the process of remembering in life often makes exact dates secondary to powerfully remembered personal experiences, events that can only be mirrored experientially rather than categorized systematically. Such repetition serves as a mirror of life and adds to the viewing and reviewing of self that eventually aids in the working out of conversion, redemption, reconciliation, and understanding. Repeated memories function as a mirror to bring into the open what is needed to realize emotional and spiritual integrity.

Another aspect of repetition appears in the image of the mask in which the action of concealing also serves, in a surreptitious way, to promote integration of the self and the soul. Early in the novel Nana tries to cure Clara's muteness by scaring her with innumerable costumes—much as one would try to cure a case of hiccups. In another instance where a type of healing is required, Férula is described as wearing an idol's mask when she returns from her agitated, detailed confession of what she witnessed as she peered through the partially opened door to Clara and Esteban's bedroom. Later, when she dies alone, having been expelled from the Trueba home by the wrathful Esteban, Férula is discovered decked out, masked, in finery found on the garbage dump. This masquerade shrouds her tortured soul yet speaks to the nature of the desires that her life of denial caused her to reject. Alba, too, knows the secret of the mask as she learns from her uncle Nicolas how to "conquer pain and other weaknesses of the flesh" by calling to mind countless examples of frightening, even macabre situations, or by inflicting physical pain so that she can learn to relax and let it pass through her. As a result, much later she does survive her ordeal of torture by masking reality and immersing herself in the task of retelling her story. In addition, the various establishments in which we meet the prostitute Transito Soto provide costumes that mask the truth of the situation and provide illusion for those for whom reality is unthinkable. The mask satisfies the inherent need for subconscious healing through the rehearsal of hidden, secret feelings. Only after the experience of such personal healing can the greater goal of reconciliation with the world and others successfully take place.

The narrative structure of the novel also adds another layer of mask. It contains an amalgam of first-person and third-person narratives, with Alba as the main compiler. The resulting shifts from the first person to the third, reflecting as well the "appropriation" of each person by each of the three narrators, keep the reader continually off balance in regard to point of view. The reader is made to experience at first hand a masking of voice, an (at least) intermittent veiling of person and reality. Moreover, the culling of event rather than chronology from Clara's notebooks may mirror many people's experience of life, but it also serves to incorporate a translucency that hides as much as it reveals. Reading the novel, then, becomes an experience of being transported into the sometimes hazy world of memories, the place where dreams, reminiscences, facts, guesses, wishes, and regrets intermingle.

Besides providing repeated thematic images, the juxtaposition of mask and mirror within the novel's narrative strategies begins to show how, in Jungian terms, the tensions between the irrational and the rational are evoked. Jung explains how elements sometimes found in dreams are not derived from the dreamer's personal experience but appear to be "aboriginal, innate, and inherited shapes of the human mind." Such irrational pieces, these "archetypes," are part of the so-called "collective unconscious," "the biological, prehistoric, and unconscious development of the mind in archaic man, whose psyche was still close to that of the animal." As human beings we all share this collective heritage, manifested in ritual, dream, and literature. Feminist archetypal critics note how repeated rituals, especially their modern manifestations in the form of novels, aid in the process of recovery and healing: "The novel performs the same role in women's lives as do the Eleusinian, dying-god, and witchcraft rituals—a restoration through remembering, crucial to our survival." Allende's juxtaposition of irrational mask and rational mirror in her novel serves to move her characters to these deeper levels of conscious and unconscious experience. As Allende also knows, recovering the lost requires the exercise of memory and the result is a reintegration of self that leads to personal integrity and the possibility of justice in the world. Creative expression, as in Allende's own exercise of it in *The House of the Spirits* and in the various examples of it in the lives of the female characters in the novel, provides an ideal landscape for repeating memories in their masked and mirrored forms in order to work out issues of identity and integrity.

Although, roughly speaking, the mask in *The House of the Spirits* symbolizes irrational myth and the mirror evokes rational, objective reality, the interrelationship of these elements is complex. Jung holds that the artist is peculiarly attuned to the unconscious, which manifests itself in visions within the imagination. Unlike Freud, however, Jung believed that such visions were not personal but transcended the artist's experience. Allende's mirror tends to repeat personal visions; her mask simultaneously rehearses mythical forms. Together, mask and mirror move the self and soul to a higher level of understanding so that justice may result. Accordingly, Aniela Jaffé explains the archetype that blends myth and reality as the psychological phenomenon, occurring equally with artists and medieval alchemists, of finding in objects a "secret soul," a "mysterious animation," a "spirit in the matter."

This archetypal interplay of mask and mirror, of irrational and rational, also derives in part from the action of magic realism in the novel, which illustrates Jaffé's discussion of the "secret soul" in objects. The source of much of current Latin American literary enchantment, magic realism can be traced to Europe during the period between the two world wars. Menton describes the movement as "longing for order, stability, reality, tranquility, and naive optimism" despite political, economic, and social tumult. It is not difficult to envision a similar psychological situation in Allende's Latin America where violent dictatorships, outrageous inflation, and unconscionable poverty are common. Because the goal of magic realism is to discover "the magic quality of everyday life and things," it contains both an ordered, stable, objective, representational treatment (mirror) and a mosaic-like, ghostly, mythological, visionary, playful presentation (mask). The first evokes the rational side of repetition, which consciously mirrors reality in an analytic, lineal, objective, abstract way. The second shows a masked, unconscious side of repetition that draws upon the intuitive, concrete, subjective truth. Allende's narrative technique of magic realism thus negotiates both mask and mirror, embodying a holistic vision of the world. It allows the individual conversion of character evident in the archetypal elements to begin the important move to the wider realm of social responsibility.

The distinctions between the two types of repetition that make up such mediation—irrational masking and rational mirroring—are not always clear; however, with Allende 's characters this vagueness becomes a virtue. Seen from another perspective, one might say that such repetitions are capable of drawing upon both sides of the brain. Indeed, findings in recent neuroscience indicate the importance of a linguistic theory that includes a consideration of language's dual tracks, roughly analogous to the action of the mask (right brain) and the mirror (left brain). As Brownstein notes, "it is likely that minds whose principal functions are managerial operate out of categorical imperatives, out of more heavily left-lateralized strategies, while the survival of women and other colonized people depends upon bilateral strategies, upon minds adept at negotiating difference." Allende's women seem to have this ability, and in *The House of the Spirits* this aesthetic forms a basis for the mediating mechanisms that allow justice through reconciliation.

Furthermore, to achieve reconciliation, neither mask nor mirror alone will suffice to mediate the discrepancies injustice propagates. The female approach in Allende's novel, especially that of the four women spanning generations, seems somehow to merge the two to create a kind of magical mediation—repetition with a difference. Accordingly, the novel gives insight into the mechanism of creative conversion and reconciliation; even the very names of the women repeat with a difference. Clara, Blanca, and Alba have names that indicate similar meaning: clarity of light, whiteness, brightness of dawn. The purity of the rose is hinted at in the name of Rosa. But for Allende's women, mediation requires an embrace of both the pain and the joy, the ugliness and the beauty, the evil and the good. Only then can an integrated wholeness serve as a reasonable expectation of justice.

Rosa, the first mediator in the female sodality of Allende's novel, embodies the contradictory elements necessary for this kind of integrity. Her name is indicative of clearness and purity, yet does it imply a red or white rose? Paradoxically, this ambiguity acts to unite rather than to separate the elements of reality and myth, the apparent and the hidden, the concrete and the abstract. For Rosa surprisingly holds a beauty that "struck fear in their hearts," an apparent contradiction that does much to explain her unique nature. Concrete beauty, which should please and attract, instead causes the opposite emotions of dread and intimidation. Both immediate family and potential suitors recognize this special quality of Rosa, and it marks her as an unforgettable being who in her very essence transcends the ordinary. She herself exists on a level beyond what most people experience and thus points to the possibility of another reality. Opinions and beliefs do not separate people in such a world where both mask and mirror are integrated. The possibility of justice thus exists in an environment where one can accept, in spite of the pain or insecurity they might bring, the shock and despair as well as the joy and the surprise of disparate elements.

Besides indicating paradox, both red and white images are important in symbolizing Rosa's mediating function. The red rose of martyrdom, of blood, adumbrates Rosa's early death and the guiding symbolism of her spiritual, saintly mediating presence throughout the generations of the del Valle and the Trueba families. Indeed, Rosa's perfection seems reflective as well of the stainless, matchless Blessed Virgin Mary, the "Rose of Sharon," the "rose without thorn," the mediatrix par excellence. Her simultaneous oneness with nature and otherworldliness even in death comes with a "scent of roses" as Nana, unsuspecting, brings her a morning breakfast tray. As Esteban Trueba stands watch over her coffin, he sees the beautiful "green fountain of her hair," an indication of her ephemeral nature, a magically real symbol of how her fair skin made her not only appear delicate, sickly, a somewhat unreal creature from the sea (half woman, half mermaid), but also signaled—as Nívea's premonition foretells—that Rosa was "a heavenly being, that she was not destined to last very long in the vulgar traffic of this world." Her death from accidental poisoning, rather than from frailness of constitution, is then another example of how expectations formed by the outer reality can be usurped by the play of forces beyond one's control. Rosa's impact on her family, especially the female members, comes in large part from this striking amalgamation of mask and mirror, of the unexpected and the expected, of the hidden and the revealed.

Rosa as mediator serves as the first touchstone in the family, especially as a basis for the process of self-appropriation that presupposes an ability to be reconciled with the Almighty. C. H. Dodd reviews "the problem of reconciling the immanence and the transcendence of God, which has its roots in primitive tension between the 'otherness' and the familiarity of the Divine." He describes the mediating use of angels, the Law, and "poetical or philosophical constructions in which the immanent Divine ... conceived as the Wisdom, or the Spirit, or the Word, of the transcendent God and these aspects of God are given a quasi-personal existence." Dodd sees these attempts at mediation as abstract, with the concrete manifestation emerging in the New Testament incarnation of the Word as Jesus Himself. Rosa mediates in a similar way by her ability to unite ephemeral otherworldliness with a very real sensual attractiveness. As angelic mediator, she can thus unite abstract and concrete, human and divine. Furthermore, she becomes a Christ-like symbol of mediation, a kind of scapegoat, in her death by innocently taking the poison intended for her father by his political enemies. But Severo del Valle's conscience is not cleansed by her death. On the contrary, he was "incapable of thinking that his daughter had died instead of him. He crumpled to the floor, moaning that he was the guilty one because of his ambition and bluster." She is a scapegoat, but an inadequate one. She can save her father from death (the action of the mirror), but she cannot redeem his conscience (the play of the mask). Rosa the Beautiful, the pure, becomes by her death enshrined in everyone's memory as the cause of the "shadow of suspended vengeance."

With these limitations, then, how does Rosa succeed as a mediator? Additional insights into mediating mechanisms can come from a look at René Girard's anthropological forays into the circumstances of mimetic desire as the mainspring of all human disorder and order. For Girard, identity or loss of difference stemming from the desire for identity can cause the disintegration of community structure: "The scapegoat victim provides an outlet for violence by unifying the entire community against him." Rosa operates instead in a more Christ-like capacity. Rather than forging community identity, Rosa unifies despite her inadequacy to relieve her father's suffering because identity is replaced by integrity. Instead of dissolving difference, Rosa embodies difference, the conflicting and competing elements of mask and mirror. The unification of community is thus not an artificial imposition of structure but a natural acceptance of heterogeneity. Christ's call to embrace one's enemies demands the embodiment of difference, the incongruency that Rosa represents in the family memory. She is the first in a line of women in *The House of the Spirits* who integrate mask and mirror in their lives symbolically and concretely. She displays her weaving of the rational and the irrational by embroidering "the largest tablecloth in the world" on which could be found concretely "a paradise of impossible creatures." An awareness of the destructive violence found within the desire for identity described by Girard should argue afresh for this alternative process, this integration of mask and mirror that Allende's women use to forge justice. With Rosa as the mediating scapegoat, the first step is taken in a self-appropriation, an action of becoming that includes both the dark, masked side and the reflective, mirrored part of experience. It is a process that unites positively rather than negatively and takes several generations to complete.

In a magical, spiritual way Rosa even becomes in death the mediator between her former fiancé, Esteban Trueba, and her sister Clara. Described by Esteban as "an apparition" that entered his life "like a distracted angel who stole my soul as she went by," Rosa is his first love and remains with him in dream and fantasy. It is memory of her, in fact, that leads him to seek a wife in the del Valle household: "He had gone to see the del Valle family to inquire if they might still have an unmarried daughter, because after so many years of absence and barbarism, he knew of nowhere else to begin to keep his promise to his mother of giving her legitimate grandchildren, and he concluded that if Severo and Nívea had accepted him as a prospective son-in-law in the days of Rosa the Beautiful, there was no reason they should refuse him, especially now that he was a rich man." After Clara's death Esteban builds "the most fitting, the most luxurious mausoleum in the world ... with statues made with angel wings" and plans to lie there one day between Clara and Rosa, thus finding support in life and death from the pair of sisters he loved so well and so long.

But Clara functions even more than Rosa as the mainstay of the family. Clara's clairvoyance often makes it seem that she too "lived in another world." Her reality is a "kaleidoscope of jumbled mirrors." Again, mediation occurs in a jumbled mosaic of the rational and the irrational, of the conscious and the unconscious, of the mirrored and the masked. By virtue of her clairvoyance, Clara has a special connection with nature. She is therefore quite sensitive to the contrasts between the life in the city and the life at Tres Marí as, the Trueba ancestral homestead where Esteban had made "progressive" improvements for which he prided himself. From the first, Clara recognizes the situation at Tres Marías to constitute "her mission in life": "She was not impressed by the brick houses, the school, and the abundant food, because her ability to see what was invisible immediately detected the workers' resentment, fear, and distrust; and the almost imperceptible noise that quieted them whenever she turned her head enabled her to guess certain things about her husband's character and past." She devotes herself to teaching the inhabitants of Tres Marías the basics of hygiene, literacy, and women's liberation. Only when she once again becomes pregnant does she revert to her "visionary tasks, speaking with apparitions and spending hours writing in her notebooks." By the act of writing, communicating her memories, she retains the mirror within the mask of the supernatural and secures a true mingling of the concrete and the abstract.

Clara's ability to combine mask and mirror becomes most apparent during her periods of silence in which she communicates only through writing. Once when fatigued with advanced pregnancy and long travel between Tres Marías and the city, Clara announces: "I think I'm going to elevate." "Not here," her husband replies, unsure whether mask or mirror would be presenting itself. He was [t]errified at the idea of Clara flying over the heads of the passengers along the track. But she wasn't talking about physical levitation; she meant she wanted to rise to a level that would allow her to leave behind the discomfort and heaviness of pregnancy and the deep fatigue that had begun to seep into her bones. She entered one of her long periods of silence—I think it lasted several months—during which she used her little slate, as she had in her days of muteness. This time I wasn't worried ... since I had come to understand that silence was my wife's last refuge, not a mental illness as Dr. Cuevas said it was."

Whether masking her physical discomfort as in this pregnancy, or masking her emotional pain as in her childhood response to Rosa's death, Clara still continues to mirror, to externalize her inner self through writing.

Despite her psychological distance during much of her time with her family, Clara nevertheless serves as a mediating force throughout the generations. Her self-appropriation takes Rosa's to the next stage of unifying the self and the soul, transforming her experiences of both mirror and mask into a source for communication. As a result, despite her apparent otherworldliness Clara can show compassion to the poor, a clear example of personal integrity that leads to justice. In fact, she includes an important "active" element to both sides of her personality in her compassionate helping of the peasants at Tres Marías and, when again in the spiritual realm, in writing her memories. Clara intuitively seems to know that when Genesis describes how "God created man in his own image" (1:27) the message is that human beings have an innate ability to reach out and find God in others. As a result, Clara's trip to the hacienda becomes an outreach as she improves both the physical and spiritual plight of the farm workers and contends with the results of earthquake and plague. Similarly, the active, concrete exercise of writing in her notebooks serves the purpose of externalizing her memories. She thus reaches out to her family through the chronicling of tangible events.

Even after Clara's death her notebooks, "which gave witness to life," give her granddaughter Alba the courage to transcend her ordeal at the hands of Colonel García. These notebooks also inspire Alba to convince her grandfather, the tough-skinned, violent *patrón* who started the chain of hatred and revenge, to write the story, the memories of their lives. Clara thus mediates primarily by uniting the mirror of memories and the mask of the visionary within the medium of her notebooks.

In the case of Clara's daughter Blanca, mediation takes place as a human defiance of social class in the quest for love and as a mystical connection to nature in her creative work in clay. The first form of mediation draws upon the mirror of concrete, uncompromised passion; the second appears within the mask of artistic self-expression. Indeed, when Blanca— this intended "white" one—is born, she shocks everyone with her hairy darkness and is described as appearing at birth as an "armadillo." Her double personality emerged even as a child:

> She was considered timid and morose. Only in the country, her skin tanned by the sun and her belly full of ripe fruit, running through the fields with Pedro Tercero, was she smiling and happy. Her mother said that that was the real Blanca, and that the other one, the one back in the city, was a Blanca in hibernation.... she showed not the slightest inclination for her mother's spiritualism or her father's fits of rage. The family jokingly said that she was the only normal person for many generations, and it was true she was a miracle of equilibrium and serenity.

Emblematic of the secret, hidden soul behind the evident, mirrored self, Blanca—despite her surface differences from other family members—retains in her artistic creations of imaginary animals the visionary ability of the beautiful Rosa who embroidered fantastic tablecloths and of Clara the Clairvoyant. She is especially important in the process of self-appropriation occurring in Allende's family of women because she mirrors the biblical message of reconciling love on all three levels of religious experience. Significantly, Blanca is first introduced to the process of pottery and the use of clay by Old Pedro García, her lover's grandfather, when he wishes to help her keep her hands busy and her mind off of her migraine headaches. Later, she shares this therapeutic gift of nature with mongoloid children, bringing them joy by teaching them how to mold the clay. Most importantly, through the power of human love, she transcends distinctions of class, essential to attaining justice in the world. Her devoted love for Pedro García Tercero, who was not of her own social class, adds the human side of Fiorenza's "praxis of agape" to the iterative yet incremental process of self-appropriation throughout the generations of women.

Alba, Blanca's daughter from her liaison, similarly contains the double action of self and soul. Her name, in fact, containing within it the idea of "white" and "dawn," also embraces the mediating connection that makes distinct definition unattainable, for it is impossible to determine exactly when night is completed and daybreak has arrived. In Spanish, the word can also mean "alb," the full-length white linen vestment with long sleeves that is gathered at the waist with a cincture and worn by a priest at Mass. Alba's mediating function is certainly priestlike in her ability to bring consolation to the tortured soul of her wrathful, vengeful, bitter old grandfather; indeed, she has always been the only one who could brighten the aging patriarch's life. Her visible legacy from her great-aunt Rosa, the first mediator, comes as distinctive "algae tones in her hair," a reality that cannot help but influence Esteban's feelings. Despite Alba's illegitimacy and the fact that her father is Esteban's bitter enemy, she becomes for Esteban "the only person I would ever have close to me the rest of my life." Wearing metonymically the masked vestments (hidden concrete outside garments) of the reconciler, Alba is likewise in the novel described as showing her mirrored soul (revealed abstract inside reality) when her transforming vision in the basement comes from a veritable "kaleidoscope of the mirror." Attributes of mask and mirror, inside and outside, abstract and concrete, soul and self, are finally merged in this woman who is able to transcend the hatred of several generations by piecing together the memories of many events, first in the torture chamber without paper or pen and later with the help of her grandfather Esteban's remembrances and of her grandmother Clara's notebooks. Because Alba has appropriated not only her own life experiences but also the souls of her women forebears, she forges community and can say that "now I seek my hatred and cannot seem to find it. I feel its flame going out as I come to understand the existence of Colonel Garcí a and the others like him, as I understand my grandfather and piece things together from Clara's notebooks, my mother's letters, the ledgers of Tres Marías, and the many other documents spread before me on the table." Alba realizes that not only through the repetition of life events through writing, thereby communicating the events, experiences, and "mission" of a person, a family, indeed of all human beings, but also through the repetition of the inner soul (which stage by stage brings one to be what one truly is) can the inimical, masked, dark side of the soul and clear-sighted self-integrity converge. This elimination of anger makes possible reconciliation and justice.

Alba's self-appropriation includes the appropriation of the qualities of her great-aunt Rosa, her grandmother Clara, and her mother Blanca, as well as her own experiences. She more than anyone else learns how to heed the biblical call for justice through a reconciliation with other people. Through her period of torture Alba mirrors the scapegoat experience of Rosa, but survives. At this level, Alba can finally dissolve the guilt, violence, and hate that Rosa's death could only augment in the family. Consequently, she can say: "It would be very difficult for me to avenge all those who should be avenged, because my revenge would be just another part of the same inexorable rite." She can indeed become an instrument of mediation by appropriating—a repetitive process—both the masked evils that terrorize her soul and the mirrored integrity of existence: "I want to think that my task is life and that my mission is not to prolong hatred but simply to fill these pages while I wait for Miguel, while I bury my grandfather, whose body lies beside me in this room, while I wait for better times to come, while I carry this child in my womb, the daughter of so many rapes or perhaps of Miguel, but above all, my own daughter." Alba thus recognizes the process of appropriation in the generations of the past and the future. Her integration includes the all-important task of communicating her memories and those of her family.

The reconciliation begun by Allende's women results from their being able somehow to see the integrated whole in its masked/mirrored manifestations of reality: distorted, gruesome, secret, magic, hidden. The process of writing, that is, mirroring, bearing "witness to life," allows an acceptance of responsibility for life, provides reverence for life, and finally brings reconciliation of all disruptive, excessive emotions. Justice ultimately comes from a blurring of the details that cause hate, revenge, jealousy. In engendering peace and forgiveness, acceptance of both mask and mirror recreates an integrated wholeness and regenerates that integrity in the world as justice.

Fiorenza notes that through the praxis of agape the women disciples of Jesus could exemplify true discipleship, a discipleship that indicts hate and the death-dealing powers of the world. This "discipleship of equals," one of service and love, is "continually recreated," for "[t]he true spiritual person is according to Paul one who walks in the Spirit, she who brings about this new world and family of God over and against the resistance and pull of all oppressive powers of this world's enslaving patriarchal structures." In *The House of the Spirits* Allende recreates in a way that integrates the totality for which justice strives. Her women recognize (intuitively if not cognitively) that in the end a personal experience of conversion (a literal "turning toward") is the key to true peace and justice. They learn that they must transcend suffering on the personal level before they can hope to apply this skill, sensitivity, and knowledge to the level of politics and society. In this sense and in the literal sense that she inhabits the world of her family memories—the spiritual reality of Rosa, Clara, and Blanca—Alba can be said to "walk in the Spirit." Her acts of gathering and communicating her memories in the form of the story preserving her "roots" reflect the identical process Allende herself goes through in writing *The House of the Spirits* and make her a kind of prophet promoting justice on the deepest levels. Fiorenza reminds us that the Gospel requires ekklesia, "a dynamic reality of Christian community. It is not a local or static term, it is not even a religious expression; it means the actual gathering of people." Can a work of fiction provide such a gathering? As it witnesses to an exploration of possibilities, a process of self-appropriation, a concrete reconstitution of memories, it can move toward Fiorenza's requirement of commitment, accountability, and solidarity in community that she finds to be "the hallmarks of our calling and struggle."

The concept of social class, especially, becomes insignificant in this feminine process of mosaic mediation reflecting a kaleidoscopic reality that engenders true reconciliation, a conversion that "converges" mask and mirror. Ironically, Esteban García does not realize that the woman he is torturing is his own cousin, through not only the patró n but also through the son of his grandmother's brother. Likewise, Alba's ignorance of the paternity of her unborn daughter—the result of multiple rapes—loses importance. Thus no longer do guilt, hate, or revenge control the interplay of relationships that knit human beings and their creator. Instead, redemption comes to Zion through a kaleidoscopic mirroring, a re-imagining and re-creation of integrity and justice.

PHILIP SWANSON

# Tyrants and Trash: Sex, Class and Culture in La casa de los espíritus

In an article published in *Ideologies and Literature*, Gabriela Mora gives Isabel Allende a sound drubbing on the grounds that the Chilean author reproposes in her fiction traditional negative female stereotypes and fails to equip her female characters with a serious political consciousness. Mora concludes—having spotted some unacceptable traces of individualism in the form of a few allusions to the idea of destiny—that, behind Allende's superficial revisionism, there lurk 'fundamentos más insidiosos que amarran a las gentes a creer en esencias e inmutabilidades'.[1] In other words, Isabel has committed the crime of liberal humanism, which, of course, if true, would put her in pretty bad odour with post-structuralist and feminist critics alike. Unfortunately, too, Allende's public persona does little to allay such fears. In a 1988 interview in the magazine *Mother Jones*, she gave a very bourgeois picture of the new-found idylicism of her life as a Californian housewife. She tells us how, having parted with her largely agreeable husband, she then fell head-over-heels with the handsome North American, William:

> And then somebody introduced us. William had read my
> second book, *Of Love and Shadow*, and he had liked it very much
> and he had wanted to meet me. And so we just looked at each other
> and fell in love immediately. In the first meeting.... Well, I think

From *Bulletin of Hispanic Studies LXXI* (no. 2) (April 1994): 217-237. © 1994 by Liverpool University Press. Reprinted by permission.

Frank Sinatra was singing 'Strangers in the Night' in the
restaurant and maybe that helped. And then we had a wonderful
pasta.

Soon she was packing her bags to rejoin him in the USA and did not return
home to Venezuela. The text of the interview is adorned by a photograph of
Isabel in a rather glamorous pose, twirling around with a colourful shawl in
the air (calling to mind the image of Beatriz Beltrán, the sharply satirized
middle-aged, middle-class, looks-and-fashion-conscious mother of the
protagonist of *De amor y de sombra*).[2] Add to this image her appropriation of
the conventions of popular and romantic fiction, the apparently wavering
ending of *La casa de los espíritus* and the repeated allegations of borrowing
from García Márquez, and we are left with an ideologically suspect standard-
bearer for women's fiction in Latin America.

The problem is that Isabel Allende's popular success has made her
(quite legitimately) a media figure. At the 1987 Hamburg Ibero-Americana
Festival, while her compatriot José Donoso—until the appearance of *La casa
de los espíritus* in 1982, the undisputed major modern Chilean novelist—was
giving a reading of the German translation of his *Casa de campo* in a cramped
bookshop in the peripheral suburb of Begedorf, Allende's fans were filling
the seats of the city's large theatre, the Deutsches Schauspielhaus. Not
surprisingly, the star treatment lavished upon her has tarnished her image in
certain academic circles. And, as far as feminist criticism is concerned, there
is little point—on a stylistic plane—in looking for manifestations of Irigaray's
'parler femme' or Cixous' 'écriture féminine', or in seeking stylistic parallels
with, say, the Brazilian Clarice Lispector's A *hora da estrela* or the African
American Toni Morrison's *Beloved*. Allende's style aims to be more
transparent. For her, writing is not 'about good literature but about telling a
story', it is 'un ancho canal de comunicación'.[3] Indeed, the effect of her work
is to invert the García Márquez model rather than imitate it. Despite the
Colombian's public political posture and despite Gerald Martin's efforts to
reduce his fiction to clear social messages,[4] *Cien años de soledad* remains
largely ineffective as a political novel precisely because of its ambiguous,
playful and magical nature. The magic of literature is somewhat different for
Allende: 'Eso tiene de maravilloso un libro', she says: 'establece un vínculo
entre quien lo escribe y quien lo lee. Es la magia de las palabras'. Putting it
plainly, she goes on:

Los escritores somos intérpretes de la realidad. Es cierto que
caminamos en el filo de los sueños, pero la ficción, aun la más

subjetiva, tiene un asidero en el mundo real. A los escritores de América Latina se les reprocha a veces que su literatura sea de denuncia. ¿Por qué no se limitan al arte y dejan de ocuparse de problemas irremediables?, les reclaman algunos. Creo que la respuesta está en que conocemos el poder de las palabras y estamos obligados a emplearlas para contribuir a un mejor destino de nuestra tierra.

Allende's aim is to provide 'una voz que habla por los que sufren y callan en nuestra tierra': in other words, to push the marginal into the mainstream. It is ironic that Luis Harss' landmark collection of conversations with Latin American writers from the 1960s is called *Into the Mainstream*. If this was to celebrate the Latin-American novel's coming of age, the only 'mainstream' into which most of its practitioners had entered was a rather narrow bourgeois or academic one. The strength of a novel like *La casa de los espíritus*, on the other hand, is that what it lacks in richness and multiplicity, it gains in sheer emotional and political power. And, as we shall see, a fundamental textual feature of the novel seems to be the displacement of the master discourse of the Boom in favour of a more directly politicized discourse of the post-Boom. This politicization includes sexual politics and brings us closer to a Kristevan model of marginality based on all 'that which is repressed in discourse and in the relations of production. Call it "woman" or "oppressed classes of society", it is the same struggle, and never the one without the other'.[5] Though Allende's early work may not betray the same 'jouissance' on a linguistic or stylistic level as Kristeva's French avant-garde texts, it does reveal an awareness of basic issues in the feminist debate and a degree of intellectual engagement with them. And if the allegedly ambivalent ending of *La casa de los espíritus* is a liberal form of Utopianism, this is not a million miles away from the position of a number of French feminist thinkers and is, in any case, combined with a harrowing exposé of real material oppression to act as a counterbalance. The complaints of Mora, then, if of a certain allure, are perhaps ultimately unjustified. Allende does not inhabit what has been called the 'rococo realm of the academy',[6] but does do the rounds of the American universities circuit: as a popular writer she does not need to satisfy Mora's criteria; as a serious one she rises to their challenge.

Jean Gilkison has argued that the portrayal of women in *De amor y de sombra* tends to undermine that novel's political impact.[7] Nonetheless, it seems plain that *La casa de los espíritus* at least attempts to establish a connection between the women's struggle and the class struggle. As Toril Moi has pointed out, marginalized groups like women and the working classes are actually central to the process of reproduction and the capitalist economy: 'it is precisely because the ruling order cannot maintain the *status quo* without the continual exploitation and oppression of these groups that it seeks to mask their central economic role by marginalizing them on the cultural, ideological and political levels'.[8] The main strategy in this programme of marginalization (and this is the principal argument of Moi's *Sexual/Textual Politics*) is the creation of an illusion of a unified individual and collective self, a given universal world order in which male, white, middle-class, heterosexual experience passes itself off as 'nature'. It is not surprising, therefore, that the discourse of the patriarch Esteban Trueba is replete with the language of order. One short, randomly-chosen sentence contains the words 'excentricidades', 'madurara', 'equilibrado' and 'sostén'.[9] In a typical elision, we are told that Trueba 'representaba mejor que nadie los valores de la familia, la tradición, la propiedad y el orden' (273). Thus bourgeois and capitalist values are made to appear synonomous with 'order'. With regard to women, Nívea's feminism is said to be 'en abierto desafío a la ley de Dios' (11), 'contra la naturaleza' and likely to produce 'una confusión y un desorden que puede terminar en un desastre' (65). This is exactly Trueba's view of the peasant and working classes. His 'teoría de los fuertes y los débiles' is 'la naturaleza', 'la realidad' and 'cómo es el mundo' (264). Indeed the oppression of women is repeatedly placed in a wider context of the oppression of the lower classes. For example, Pedro Segundo García's passive acceptance of his lot is seen in essentialist terms by Trueba as 'la timidez propia de la gente del campo' and, echoing the conventional role of the submissive woman with no independence or mobility, he speaks for all marginalized groups when he acknowledges to his master: 'Entendimos, patrón ... No tenemos donde ir, siempre hemos vivido aquí. Nos quedamos' (52). The parallel is continued into the graphic account of Trueba's violent rape of Pancha García. The vocabulary employed in the description of the rape ('fiereza', 'incrustándose', 'brutalidad', 'sangrientas') contrasts sharply with the young girl's total lack of resistance. Her passivity is not just a reflection of her position as a woman, but also her poverty and class status. Trueba's first words after the deed are: 'Desde mañana quiero que trabajes en la casa' (58). Her mother and grandmother had likewise been the enforced sexual and domestic servants of the 'casa patronal'. In this way the economy of ownership is mirrored in sexual relations and Trueba frequently talks of women in terms of property: as a sort of cattle (27), as a kind of consumer good to be purchased (37) or as something to be possessed totally (117). The link is reinforced by the dual perspective of Pedro Segundo García on Trueba and his wife Clara: 'La apreciaba tanto como odiaba a Esteban

Trueba' (149). The inference is that the women's and workers' struggles are an interconnected reaction against patriarchy. It is significant in this respect that, as the central female characters develop their own sense of identity as women, they achieve an increasing degree of solidarity with the underprivileged classes.

Of course, awareness is the first step towards resistance and, for this reason, one of the novel's principal tasks is to unmask the 'natural' as the learned. A young peasant grows up knowing 'su lugar en el mundo' (133), so that a relationship between the classes cannot take place 'porque esa posibilidad no estaba en el orden natural del mundo' (156). In fact, Pedro Segundo denies to his son the possiblity of social change for them: 'Siempre ha sido así, hijo. Usted no puede cambiar la ley de Dios' (147). Interestingly, Pedro Tercero grows up to invert the language of the natural order, arguing for 'leyes más justas y repúblicas como Dios manda' (154). The point is that 'nature' and 'order' are concepts appropriated by the dominant classes to preserve the prevailing hierarchy of power relations and that identity, therefore, is something which is socially constructed. As Simone de Beauvoir said of the 'second sex', 'One is not born a woman; one becomes one'.[10] The Nana hints at this harsh moulding into the values of the Symbolic Order when she claims that 'hay muchos niños que vuelan como las moscas, que adivinan los sueños y hablan con las ánimas, pero a todos se les pasa cuando pierden la inocencia' (15). She is herself a small but crucial figure in the novel's theory of identity. In a passage which recalls the depiction of the 'viejas', the old nursemaids and servants of Donoso's *El obsceno pájaro de la noche*, the Nana's life is summarized:

> Había nacido para acunar hijos ajenos, para usar la ropa que otros desechaban, para comer sus sobras, para vivir de sentimientos y tristezas prestadas, para envejecer bajo el techo de otros, para morir un día en su cuartucho del último patio, en una cama que no era suya y ser enterrada en una tumba común del Cementerio General. (114)

She is characterized (as a servant and woman) in terms of lack, absence, with no individual identity of her own. Like Humberto Peñaloza in Donoso's novel, she literally becomes 'nobody' as her identity is marginalized. Trueba's sister, Férula, is a similar case. Existing only to serve others (her mother, Trueba, Clara), she becomes sheer absence when, like Donoso's 'viejas', she is banished from her brother's house to a convent and supplements her own effective non-existence with a series of bizarre wigs and costumes (another possible borrowing from the 'disfraz'/'máscara' motif of *El obsceno pájaro de la noche*). In so far as the Nana is concerned, it is significant that she has no individualizing name, a feature shared with the string of peasant characters with names like Pedro García, Pedro Segundo García, Pedro Tercero García. These marginal characters are effectively reduced to the level of supplement to the greater reality that is socially created by the ruling classes, their vital supportive role neutralized by a process of false naturalization.

The obvious link between the Nana and *El obsceno pájaro de la noche* also brings to mind Donoso's Peta Ponce and the motif of the witch. The crushing of identity is based on fear of the potential power of those sectors whose centrality to the interests of the dominant group requires their marginalization. In Allende's novel, Esteban Trueba wants his house to be 'un reflejo de él', with 'un aspecto de orden y concierto, de pulcritud y civilización' (87), though under the influence of Clara it becomes 'un laberinto encantado imposible de limpiar, que desafiaba numerosas leyes urbanísticas y municipales' (88). This reflects Jerónimo de Azcoitía's desire, in Donoso's novel to replace any 'exuberancia natural' in his estate with 'estrictas formas geométricas'.[11] But Don Jerónimo's sense of order disintegrates as his wife Inés falls increasingly under the influence of the nursemaid and witch-figure Peta Ponce. Peta's residence lies at the edge of Jerónimo's symmetrical world in 'un desorden de construcciones utilitarias sin pretensión de belleza: el revés de la fachada', all of which 'hizo tastabillar [*sic*] su orden al reconocer en la Peta Ponce a una enemiga poderosa' (181, 183). Similarly, the edge of Esteban Trueba's country estate is the point where 'la casa perdía su señorial prestancia y empezaba el desorden de las perreras, los gallineros y los cuartos de los sirvientes' (40). Servant, woman or witch, then, are all terms which connote the possible rupture of a secure order. The creation of the notion of 'witch' is a means of exteriorizing and normalizing such a fear via a perverse form of sublimation and so weakening the threat by turning it into a negative, a taboo. All social structures grow, up to a point, out of a need to explain, to impose order (witches were essentially 'created' to explain otherwise inexplicable disasters) and, as Sharon Magnarelli observes, the real sin of witches was their alleged knowledge, that is recognition of the dark, chaotic side of life and hence embodiment of the threat to order.[12] So, in *La casa de los espíritus*, the priest, padre Restrepo, identifies the peculiarities of the child Clara with demonic possession, the phrase 'hasta ese día, no habían puesto nombre a las excentricidades de su hija menor' (14) hinting at the need to name, explain, naturalize and neutralize. She is later seen as 'una criatura algo estrafalaria' because she is 'poco apta para las responsabilidades matrimoniales y la vida doméstica' (83).

Dr Cuevas (the voice of science and reason) even diagnoses her silence (actually 'su último inviolable refugio') as 'una enfermedad mental' (105). Rosa, la Bella—echoing the hyperbole of Remedios la Bella's role as an extreme if unwitting *femme fatale in Cien años de soledad*—is also seen as threatening because of her beauty and femininity. She is twice referred to as a 'sirena' (12, 36) and we are told that 'su belleza atemorizaba' (28). Just as, following Magnarelli's line of thought, Eve is created from Adam's rib, so man projects his sexuality on to woman, seeing her as the provoker of his unruly desire. But the witch or the *femme fatale* is not the only manifestation of patriarchy's (ir)rationalization of a perceived danger. A link with politics is again apparent in the way Esteban Trueba turns any potential alteration of the ruling order into an example of the red peril of communism. At one stage he refers to 'la monstruosidad de que todos nacen con los mismos derechos' (65) and his ranting about 'commie subversives' and Soviet spies recalls the allegorical transformation, in the minds of the landowners, of the natives into 'antropófagos' (i.e. communists) in Donoso's *Casa de campo*. The child Wenceslao lays bare the true operation of the power structures and naturalizing processes at work here when he describes the cannibals/communists as 'una fantasía creada por los grandes con el fin de ejercer la represión mediante el terror, fantasía en que ellos mismos terminaron por creer' and 'una ficción con que los grandes pretenden dominarnos cultivando en nosotros ese miedo que ellos llaman orden'.[13]

A further feature of patriarchy is that, in its identification of itself with the natural order, it seeks to efface any trace of ideology in its own allegedly neutral position, assigning ideology to the extremes of 'cranky' theories like Marxism or feminism. It is no surprise, therefore, that Esteban Trueba's first-person discourse attempts to portray the landowner in liberal, common-sense terms. The 'yo' person signals a faith in an essential, unified self, a source of power and control, as opposed to the general passive mass of women and peasants whose lives he can mould 'con mi propia mano'. Indeed Trueba states clearly: 'Yo era como un padre para ellos' (53). He is the source and centre of everything and in his patriarchal role he can justify his power by casting himself in the role of father-provider. Hence he furnishes a comprehensive account of his programme of training, feeding, housing and caring for the health of his work-force, concluding that, 'Sí, he sido un buen patrón, de eso no hay duda' (55). Needless to say, this is, once again, a strategy designed exactly to perpetuate the marginalization of a group that is central to the landowner's needs. Education is a selective form of control: 'tenía la ambición de que todos los niños y adultos de las Tres Marías debían aprender a leer, escribir y sumar, aunque no era partidario de que adquirieran otros conocimientos, para que no se les llenara la cabeza con ideas inapropiadas a su estado y condición' (59). Feeding and health care are a means of ensuring that the peasants 'crecieran fuertes y sanos y pudieran trabajar desde pequeños' (59). Liberation here is actually a subtle form of repression: Pedro Segundo's potential for rebellion is disabled by his own recognition of his boss' achievements, leaving him with 'una mezcla de miedo y de rencorosa admiración' (61). What basically happens is that, like many women, the peasants internalize their perceived inferiority and accept their dependency as a natural state. In describing the positive changes he has personally introduced, Trueba comments of the peasants that: 'Eran gente buena y sencilla, no había revoltosos. También es cierto que eran muy pobres e ignorantes' (53-54). In other words, their naturally compliant nature is really a function of their deliberately generated ignorance, so that they become a blank page upon which the *patrón* can inscribe the hidden agenda of a seemingly quidditative order. As Trueba says, 'Fue necesario que yo llegara para que aquí hubiera orden, ley, trabajo ... Sin mí estarían perdidos. Si vamos al fondo de las cosas, no sirven ni para hacer los mandados, siempre lo he dicho: son como niños' (64).

In a specifically Latin American context, Trueba's world-view restates the basic values underlying the Spanish conquest and the emergence of the civilization-versus-barbarism ethic in the post-Independence subcontinent of the nineteenth century (and its survival into the twentieth). The Independence movement in general was, despite its liberationist rhetoric, largely aimed at furthering the interests of the well-off *criollo* classes, and, in many ways, the enlightened pursuit of 'civilization' by Sarmiento *et al* was an extension of this. Trueba clearly sees himself as bringing civilization to a backward countryside but, as *Cien años de soledad* has already shown, the civilization-versus-barbarism notion was a myth which was passed off as reality. Trueba's obsession with 'civilization' is reflected in his fascination with science and his favouring of European and North American customs and practices. His sister Férula incarnates a largely anti-countryside, anti-Latin American stance. She thinks that the child Blanca has 'malos modales' because 'parece un indio' (100), and she wants to 'vivir como cristiana', away from this 'purgatorio de incivilizados' (104). Inadvertently echoing the twin beliefs of biological determinism and scientific positivism, she feels trapped 'en una región inhumana, donde no funcionaban las leyes de Dios ni el progreso de la ciencia' (104). Yet Esteban's alternative 'civilization' is frequently mocked or subverted. The much-admired European Jean de Satigny—whose 'sentido práctico propio de los de su raza' is contrasted with 'aquellos bárbaros aborígenes' (191)—is actually involved in raping the country of its talent and natural treasures, is engaged in a plainly barbaric trade in chinchilla skins and turns out to be (in the novel's terms) a ridiculous dandy. Trueba's decision to visit a North American hospital 'porque había llegado a la prematura conclusión de que los doctores latinos eran todos unos charlatanes más cercanos al brujo aborigen que al científico' (216), has to be compared with old Pedro García's fixing of his master's broken bones in such a way that 'los médicos que lo revisaron después no podían creer que eso fuera posible' (145) (the old man—though he does not always get it right— similarly rids the estate of a plague of ants in the face of the helplessness of foreign modern technology). Trueba also wants to have his house built on the model of 'los nuevos palacetes de Europa y Norteamérica' (87), with a 'jardín versallesco' to offset the native tendency towards 'una selva enmarañada donde proliferaban variedades de plantas y flores ...' (200). However, it is said that Clara, the woman Trueba idolizes, 'creció como una planta salvaje, a pesar de las recomendaciones del doctor Cuevas, que había traído de Europa la novedad de los baños de agua fría y los golpes de electricidad para curar a los locos' (75). Clara's 'madness' (or 'barbarism') is, in fact, nothing more than the exuberance of a true Latin-American condition which should not be distorted by alien values, hence Nívea's readiness to 'amarla sin condiciones y aceptarla tal cual era' (74-75).

At the same time, woman, to Trueba's mind, is a key factor in the drive towards civilization. In the important third section of the second chapter, where he outlines his patriarchal philosophy, Trueba realizes that he himself is 'convirtiéndose en un bárbaro' (56). The solution comes to him when 'su sentido práctico le indicó que tenía que buscarse una mujer y, una vez tomada la decisión, la ansiedad que lo consumía se calmó y su rabia pareció aquietarse' (56). While this may seem to cast the woman in the typically gentle, feminine, supportive role, it does also show the falsehood of the male patriarchal notion of order, in the sense that Trueba depends on woman to overcome his own barbarism. So, union with a woman will be a positive development that will civilize him and his environs. Yet the irony is that he simply takes a woman: he rapes Pancha García. The episode, though upsetting, is a witty commentary on the civilization-versus-barbarism theme and its inherent contradictions. Significantly, however, it is the influence of Pancha which opens up Trueba to the more worthwhile aspects of 'civilization'. His commands turn into a 'súplica' and in his happiness with her:

> le mejoró por un tiempo el mal humor y comenzó a interesarse
> en sus inquilinos ... Se dio cuenta, por primera vez, que el peor

abandono no era el de las tierras y los animales, sino de los
habitantes de los Tres Marías, que habían vivido en el desamparo
desde la época en que su padre se jugó la dote y la herencia de su
madre. Decidió que era tiempo de llevar un poco de civilización
a ese rincón perdido entre la cordillera y el mar. (58-59)

Woman here is the source of positive action, but man thinks it is man. In
practice, the 'civilization' that Trueba brings is one which serves his own
purposes but which comes to be indistinguishable from the natural order of
things, the way of the world. By the end of the novel, though, he is finding
it difficult to 'seguir sosteniéndose en precaria estabilidad sobre un mundo
que se le hacía trizas ... Ya no tenía las ideas tan claras y se le había borrado
la frontera entre lo que le parecía bueno y lo que consideraba malo' (350). In
effect, the novel subverts the entire premise on which it superficially appears
to be based: in the end it is Esteban Trueba who is living in a fantasy world
rather than his supposedly eccentric wife Clara.

The evaluation of the alternative world of Clara and the other female
characters is a much thornier problem than the exposition of the gaps and
inconsistencies of the patriarchal discourse. Pointing out the errors is always
easier than providing the right answers, but then this has always been the
traditional role of literature. Isabel Allende here seems to oscillate between a
kind of female essentialism, a radical deconstruction of essentialism and a
more concrete political materialism. As an author rather than a systematic
thinker, she may end up with a cocktail of all three, but with an overall taste
that combines broadly consistent elements. This is, after all, a political work
written in a popular tone with the ultimate goal of touching an emotional
nerve and jolting the reader into a new awareness. The popular or mass-
market dimension means that there is little pretence of producing an open-
ended feminine[14] language of so-called 'other bisexuality' *à la* Cixous, nor
much evidence of the ruptures and breaks in symbolic language talked of by
Kristeva. None the less, some ideas associated with both thinkers can be
detected at what one imagines would be the more important level for Allende
of content.

Esteban Trueba can be identified with Cixous' 'Realm of the Proper',
while the female characters would be matched to the 'Realm of the Gift'.
Trueba, as an ambitious landowner, is clearly linked to property, self-
projection, hierarchy and so on. His driving fear of communism is a fear of
expropriation of land and power (or, for Cixous, the loss of the attribute or
castration). Women, needless to say, do not share this fear and can oppose
masculine culture (based on dominance) with the 'Realm of the Gift' (based

on giving and exchange). In the female characters of *La casa de los espíritus* such generosity is reflected in their sexuality and their charitable works, both of which, to different extents in differing cases, break down hierarchies and class divisions. The distinction is not unlike that of Annie Leclerc between desire and pleasure.[15] Trueba, for whom sexual and economic desire are much the same thing, always *wants* to own or possess an 'object', while the women's thought is based on pleasure or 'jouissance' (for instance, Blanca revelling in her housework or Clara in her world of spirits or all of the central women characters in their creative arts). This idea of female 'jouissance', though, suggests an essential feminine spirit, located in a sort of pre-Oedipal state. Indeed Allende's self-professed belief in a 'feminine solidarity' passed on from mother to daughter and excluding men[16] contains faint echoes of Cixous' notion of the mother as the origin of the source and voice in all female/feminine texts. Hence the bond between Nívea and Clara, 'estableciendo un vínculo tan fuerte, que se prolongó en las generaciones posteriores como una tradición familiar' (78) and repeated specifically in Clara's relationship with Blanca (117), Clara's own pregnancy in which she finds herself 'volcándose hacia el interior de sí misma, en un diálogo secreto y constante con la criatura' (93) and her belief in 'una memoria genética' (156) which allows mothers to pass on their 'locuras' (or special qualities) to their daughters. Hence too the evolving pattern of light imagery in the chain of names (Nívea-Clara-Blanca-Alba), implying that the world-view of each is informed and enriched by that inherited from the mother. This perhaps explains in part the use of water imagery in relation to women. The mermaid-like Rosa with her 'belleza de fondo de mar' (32) is like 'un habitante del agua' (12) and Trueba feels the urge to 'hundirme en sus aguas más profundas' (39). Clara, meantime, 'navegaba hábilmente por las agitadas aguas de la vida social y por las otras, sorprendentes, de su camino espiritual' (237). For Cixous, water is the essential feminine element, reflecting a closed womb-like world flowing through the female writer and keeping her in touch with the mother's voice.

Clara, living in her world of silence and spirits, is the most obvious example of this essentially feminine world. Her retreat into silence is a kind of retreat into the Semiotic or Imaginary unity with the mother, a challenge to the Symbolic Order (which, according to Lacan, is associated with the Law of the Father and is when language is acquired). Both instances of her self-immersion into silence involve solidarity with another woman and a rejection of masculine control. The first follows the symbolic 'rape' of Rosa by the representative of scientific knowledge, Dr Cuevas, in the form of her autopsy (described in a way connoting assumptions of male 'ownership' of the female body). The second comes after Trueba strikes her in response to her defence of Blanca's relationship with Pedro Tercero García. Clara's silent world undermines patriarchal binary thought, being a world where 'el tiempo no se marcaba con relojes ni calendarios ..., el pasado y el futuro eran parte de la misma cosa y la realidad del presente era un caleidoscopio de espejos desordenados donde todo podía ocurrir ..., donde no siempre funcionaban las leyes de la física o la lógica (78-79). The world of the spirits is an essentially female space where women meet to 'invocar a los espíritus e intercambiar cábalas y recetas de cocina' (115) and which excludes men, being 'una dimensión desconocida a la que él (Trueba) jamás podría llegar' (119). It relates also to a species of 'écriture féminine'. Clara's imaginative mind is set against Trueba's scientific rationalism: she loves to read, write and entertain poets, and when her husband removes all radios to keep the news from her, she simply discovers the truth through her intuitive powers (110-11). And though Allende's text makes no attempt to reproduce Clara's own style, it is made plain that the protagonist's 'cuadernos de anotar' are written in an experiential, non-chronological format (380), at one stage defying conventional logic (124). In Cixous' terms she is (perhaps) in the free space of the Lacanian Imaginary: 'the speaking/writing woman is in a space outside time (eternity), a space that allows no naming and no syntax'.[17]

There are a number of problems with this interpretation, however, and it would be highly reductive to rely too heavily on such a reading. For a start, it may seem inconsistent to oppose the patriarchal notion of a (false) natural order with a theory of an essential feminine nature (or, for that matter, an essentialist view of the innocent peasant or native Latin American). Having said that, at the level of an exposé of the workings of patriarchy, the text is not necessarily anti-essentialist in any strict sense: in many ways it seems simply to be arguing that 'true nature' (which is unruly) has been replaced by a counterfeit nature (which is ruly but artificial). This opens the way to a simplified version of the Kristevan concept of 'bisexuality' (though, of course, Kristeva herself is no essentialist). From this point of view, the promotion of the female sex ('stage two' feminism) should give way to a more generalized weakening of gender divisions and dissolution of binary distinctions ('stage three' feminism). Though this does not lead to any real semiotic theory of writing in Allende, the deconstruction of rigid binary oppositions (right/wrong, appropriate/inappropriate, sane/mad, mine/yours and so on) does involve a reinterpretation of societal structures in a way which binds the question of woman's position to wider political or ideological questions. So, Clara's spiritualism is not purely and essentially feminine: it is said, for instance, (albeit in a comic context), that Marcos 'tenía la teoría de que esta condición estaba presente en todos los seres humanos, especialmente en los de su familia, y que si no funcionaba con eficiencia era sólo por falta de entrenamiento' (21). All human beings have the potential to dissolve or at least loosen up the binary divisions that separate them. This is the significance of the hybrid figures that are portrayed in Rosa's sewing, Blanca's pottery and Alba's painting. In a similar way, Blanca's fairy tales tell of 'un príncipe que durmió cien años, ... doncellas que peleaban cuerpo a cuerpo con los dragones, ... un lobo perdido en el bosque a quien una niña destripó sin razón alguna' (269). This also aids an understanding of the roles of the male children Jaime and Nicolás, sometimes thought to be poorly integrated into the text. They are equally marginal and anti-stereotypical. Despite being trained in the traditional art of upper-class manhood (117), the initially more conventional Nicolás becomes an outrageous-looking member of an Eastern religious group and Jaime abandons sexual and social norms by becoming 'un sentimental incorregible', a timid bookworm, a socialist and a friend of Pedro Tercero García (168).[18] As Allende herself has said, 'men and women are not really so different' but are 'mutilated' by social 'education' and 'rigid roles'.[19] These characters represent a plea for the slackening of those rigid class and gender roles. And this is really the key to the entire narrative structure of the novel. Esteban Trueba's first-person narrative is mixed in with a third-person narrative by a female narrator. Sandra Boschetto has commented that 'la mediación metatextual será un intento por parte de la autora de reconciliar oposiciones, de fundir diferencias para crear una sola realidad totalizadora e incluyente, texto en blanco'.[20] This is perhaps the nearest the novel gets to textual 'bisexuality' as it were. But more meaningfully, Trueba's first-person narration regularly refers to the variant viewpoints of 'mi nieta', while the third-person perspective intervenes. Thus the novel revolves around a dialectic between Trueba and Alba, inaugurating a *rapprochement* between previously opposite sexes, age groups and sociopolitical loyalties. And hence the centrality of Trueba. Though some see it as a weakness to have a male character as the structural back-bone of a feminist novel, his centrality is the centrality of patriarchal binary logic which is in opposition with the 'bisexuality' of the other members of his family. Yet the 'bisexual' role invades and subverts the patriarchal pole. Trueba, as we shall see, undergoes a learning process and by the end of the novel he has moved towards Alba's position. And if Alba's epilogue seems a rather corny plea for mutual love, the basis of her appeal lies in the desired erasure of binary conflict which gives the text much of its cohesion.

While all this may seem rather utopian, the learning process does also enjoy a more concrete, material manifestation in *La casa de los espíritus*. Early on in the novel, Rosa's idealized, romanticized view of the young Trueba's exploits in the gold mines is said to be totally at odds with the harsh reality he has to face (13). This is an early hint at the potentially suspect nature of a 'feminine' world-view which does not take account of material factors. From this perspective, Clara's silence and spiritualism needs to be re-interpreted. The two occasions she goes silent (discussed earlier) are, in fact, quite different. The first is ostensibly a traumatic reaction to the shock of Rosa's autopsy: it is a retreat from reality and into 'un universo inventado para ella, protegida de las inclemencias de la vida, donde se confundían la verdad prosaica de las cosas materiales con la verdad tumultuosa de los sueños' (78-79). This is paralleled by her spiritualism up to and in adult life, described as 'su tendencia a evadir la realidad y perderse en el ensueño' (123). The second silence, however, disrupts this pattern. It is not so much a retreat as an act of rebellion. The crucial changes come in the fifth and sixth chapters. The earthquake wakes her up from 'una larga infancia ... sin obligaciones', exposing her 'necesidades básicas, que antes había ignorado' and making her spiritualism seem irrelevant (148). She becomes a working woman instead of 'un ángel vestido de blanco' (155). This change is heralded by the freeing of the birds and the disappearance of the spirits:

> Abrieron una por una las jaulas de los pájaros y el cielo se llenó de caturras, canarios, jilgueros y cristofués, que revolotearon enceguecidos por la libertad y finalmente emprendieron el vuelo en todas direcciones. Blanca notó que en todos esos afanes, no apareció fantasma alguno detrás de las cortinas, no llegó ningún Rosacruz advertido por su sexto sentido, ni poeta hambriento llamado por la necesidad. Su madre parecía haberse convertido en una señora común y silvestre.
> —Usted ha cambiado mucho mamá—observó Blanca.
> —No soy yo, hija. Es el mundo que ha cambiado—respondió Clara. (151)

This may be a symbolic liberation of a material feminist and class consciousness. She travels alone for the first time, realizes that 'ya no contaba con su marido, con Férula o con Nana' (148) and initiates her clearly significant friendship with the peasant Pedro Segundo García, to whom she is said to move closer as she now drifts away from the patriarchal Trueba (159-60). The final break with Trueba comes when he hits her following her open denunciation of his sexism, classism and hypocrisy. The blow sends her reeling into the arms of Pedro Segundo García and she never speaks to Trueba again: a conscious decision to reject patriarchal values and an acknowledgement of the material reality of class struggle.

In fact, the evolution of the feminism of all the main female protagonists is inextricably bound up with a similarly developing progressiveness and consciousness of material issues. Taking them chronologically, Nívea is a suffragette, but one who wears a fur coat and classy shoes to preach equality to a group of comfortless workers and discusses her campaign over tea and pastries in the Plaza de Armas (77-78). Her daughter, Clara, recognizes that it should be more than just a question of trying to 'tranquilizarnos la conciencia' and that the poor 'no necesitan caridad, sino justicia' (247); she defies her husband, spurns fashion and jewellery and has a friendship with a peasant. Her daughter, Blanca, continues her mother's charitable works, stands up to her father's authority, raises an illegitimate child and—going a stage further than Clara—has a lasting affair with Pedro Tercero García, a peasant leader, revolutionary singer and member of a Marxist government.[21] Finally, her daughter, Alba, joins the student political movement, has a relationship with a guerrilla leader and ends up a victim of torture. She becomes the most fully integrated with the interlinked class, political and women's struggles. She finds solidarity with fellow prisoner, the working-class Ana Díaz, whose non-individualizing name associates her with the masses at large. As it happens, Ana used to distrust Alba because she was a 'burguesa'. Alba's 'education' is now complete, therefore, and is symbolically crowned by her positive encounter with ordinary women in a prison camp and, later, in a shanty town. And so, importantly, she puts Clara's non-chronological notes into order and writes a coherent history of her family (263). The material world, perceived through a feminist and politically aware perspective, has displaced the 'feminine' world of the spirits.

The relationship of Alba's text to Clara's text brings us back to the question of style and tone. It has been argued elsewhere that from, roughly, the late 1960s/early 1970s the Latin-American novel began to experience a shift away from complex, even tortuous narrative forms towards more popular forms, often (though not always) relatively straightforward and more directly political: a shift as it were from the Boom to a post-Boom.[22] The new novel had acquired an official air, lapsing into stereotype and a kind of heavy neo-classicism. The re-evaluation of popular culture (meaning, broadly speaking, mass culture rather than indigenism) by writers like Puig, Cabrera Infante, the later Donoso and Vargas Llosa brought a refreshing wind of change. Puig notes a connection between the previous valuation of popular culture and the valuation of women. Women, he says, especially in the Hispanic world, are rather like 'géneros menores': 'se goza con ellas pero nadie se las respeta'.[23] Hence in Allende's novel, which is firmly aimed at a wide market embracing a sizable middle-brow audience, the transition from spiritualism to materialism, from Clara's less penetrable text to Alba's accessible text, there is a re-enactment of the shift from Boom to post-Boom in a way which establishes a parallel between emancipation and narrative form. This is something of an inversion of the (by this stage) conventional view that formal textual disruption is revolutionary in political terms because it challenges the bourgeois, capitalist or patriarchal order. As Antonio Skármeta—one of the figures closely associated with the post-Boom—has said of the new novel (in a way applicable perhaps also to certain aspects of Cixous' and Kristeva's theories of writing): 'Creo que la literatura del boom ha hecho más por cubrir que descubrir'.[24] There is certainly ambiguity and even inconsistency in *La casa de los espíritus*, but those who accuse Allende of ideological impurity or masculinist aesthetics miss the point of this wish to translate notions of a feminine essence or consciousness into the more concrete and broadly-based arena of social and political reality, to address serious and difficult questions but simultaneously communicate with a larger public.

At this point, the question of the relationship of *La casa de los espíritus* to *Cien años de soledad* becomes unavoidable. The similarities are obvious: in both novels Latin-American history is explored via a lengthy family saga punctuated by bizarre or fantastic occurrences; the style (in its use of time and display of so-called 'magical realism') is alike in some ways; and there are some specific parallels such as those between Rosa la Bella and Remedios la Bella or tío Marcos' obsession with progress and inventions and that of several members of the Buendía family. But the most crucial point of contact is that between Alba's work with her mother's 'cuadernos de anotar' and that of various Buendías with Melquíades' parchments. There are key differences here, though. Clara's scripts are quite dissimilar to those of Melquíades. His are deliberately obscure (they are written in Sanskrit, verse and secret code) and are notoriously difficult to decipher. Clara's are certainly non-chronological. However, this is justified on the grounds that they represent an intuitive feminine space which merely needs to be channelled into a more material direction: Alba's task is, therefore, simply one of ordering and rendering useful an eminently decipherable text. Though Martin makes the claim that 'nothing, surely, could be clearer' for his feasible but highly reductive reading of Aureliano's cracking of the code of Melquíades' manuscripts as a political awakening,[25] it seems an inescapable conclusion that this ending is much less satisfactory in concrete sociopolitical terms than the position in which Alba finds herself *vis-á-vis* Clara's notebooks. Why are Aureliano and Macondo destroyed at this point of realization? Is the text he deciphers the same as the one we are reading? Is he discovering his own fictionality and, if so, what can the novel say to us about reality? If the novel is a reflection on history and reality, why is it so dependent on a 'magical' world-view for its appeal? And why is that view both celebrated and undermined?[26] *Cien años de soledad* is redolent with possibilities and associations, but, for that very reason, maintains an inevitably ambivalent relation to reality. Allende's novel, on the other hand, is, for Peter Earle, a 'celebration of reality'.[27] It refers, pretty unequivocally, to a specific (Chilean) reality instead of taking refuge in a quasi-allegorical unreality. Indeed it appears explicitly to reject the García Márquez approach. Clara, we are told, 'no era partidaria de repetir los nombres en la familia, porque eso siembra confusión en los cuadernos de anotar la vida' (233)—a clear swipe at the obfuscation of García Márquez with his litany of José Arcadios and Aurelianos. And Alba sifts through her mother and grandmother's correspondence in order to preserve the facts, 'salvándolos de la nebulosa de los hechos improbables' (219)—a criticism of an excessive tendency towards fantasy.

　　　This position is supported by a narrative structure which appears to overturn the magical element. The magical strand is converted into a realist strand, as has already been seen in relation to the evolution of Clara as a character, a process summed up in Alba's allusion to 'un mundo mágico que se acabó' (78). The book is made up of fifteen chapters (including the epilogue). The middle chapter, the eighth, 'El conde', is clearly a kind of pivotal interlude: it takes place in a different geographical location, is marginal to the mainstream of the action, and is the only chapter not to be divided into a series of sub-sections. After this chapter, the symmetrical centre of the novel, there is a marked structural shift. Chapter Nine starts with the birth of Alba and ends with the death of Clara: the world of magic is over and a grim new realism is ushered in. The change in the house of the spirits will be sharp: 'Alba sabía que su abuela era el alma de la gran casa de la esquina. Los demás lo supieron más tarde, cuando Clara murió y la casa perdió las flores, los amigos transeúntes y los espíritus juguetones y entró de lleno en la época del estropicio' (250). The chapter ends with Jaime's diagnosis 'Mamá ya se fue' and the next one starts immediately with the title 'La época del estropicio', explaining that 'la muerte de Clara' means that 'los tiempos cambiaron', giving way to 'deterioro' and 'ruina' (262). Significantly, the next chapter is called 'El despertar'. The remainder of the book is an only tokenly veiled account of the election of Allende, the Pinochet coup and the appalling aftermath. The final chapter before the epilogue is 'La hora de la verdad'. Alba now comes face to face with a horrific reality (torture and repression). Material change will now be all important.

This structural pattern does not really mean the negation of Clara's position by that of Alba. Clara's spiritualism, on one level, simply represents happy times which are destroyed by natural and political cataclysms. The world of the spirits, in other words, is the sort of ideal place the world should be. In the meantime, the positive force of Clara's spiritualism needs to be harnessed on a practical and political level. Yet if Clara is associated with magic, Esteban Trueba is equally living in a fantasy: the fantasy of a patriarchal natural order. But his fantasy world is also subverted by reality in the form of the arrest of Alba: he realizes 'al fin que había llegado la hora de la verdad, después de casi noventa años de vivir bajo su propia ley' (353). The title of Allende's second novel, *De amor y de sombra*, could be a gloss on the first. Structurally 'amor' is overthrown by 'sombra' but there has always been a shadow hanging over love, and even now love survives despite the shadow: if people can learn (Alba) and change (Trueba), then perhaps one day 'sombra' will be overthrown by 'amor'.

The interplay between love and shadow and between magic and reality suggests a final feature of the structural pattern of *La casa de los espíritus*: the relationship of the circle and the straight line. It is a commonplace in García Márquez criticism to talk of the circular structure of *Cien años de soledad*.[28] But circularity and progressive politics are strange bedfellows. In *La casa de los espíritus* there is a narrator in the present trying to recuperate the past and reconstruct a link through to the present: this implies both a straight line and a learning process. This is reflected in turn in the evolution in the feminism and politics of the central line of female characters discussed earlier. Alba's name is 'el último de una cadena de palabras luminosas que quieren decir lo mismo' (234), but the chain Nívea-Clara-Blanca-Alba indicates a progression in the positive image of whiteness, culminating in Alba, a kind of new dawn or new hope amidst the darkness and despair. Yet this is set against a series of instances or images of circularity. For example, despite Clara's distaste for the duplication of names, there are some classic García Márquez-style repetitions, such as Férula's assumption of the role of the Nana and the recurrent children's games with the books from tío Marcos' trunk (91). More specifically, the novel sets up a pattern of circularity in which a victim becomes a victimizer. Férula sacrifices her life to look after her mother, while her brother Esteban Trueba enjoys a freedom of which she is envious: before long she is manipulating and victimizing her brother (45-47, 92), though she, of course, becomes his victim too. Trueba's greed and arrogance has its roots in his poverty as a child or youth (48, 201): emblematic of this is the humiliating episode of the 'café vienés' at the Hotel Francés, which scars him for life (45-46). Victimizing others, Trueba ensures the repetition of the circle. Esteban García, a kind of Frankenstein's monster, resents the wealth and power of the grandfather who created his bastard father and dreams of revenge (170). Alba, who 'encarnaba lo que nunca tendría, lo que él nunca sería (253), is in turn raped by him. This raises another central circular or repeated motif of *Cien años de soledad*, incest. Though incest can be identified with solitude and non-solidarity in García Márquez, it is often celebrated in a bawdy, earthy way as, for example, with the final couple Aureliano Babilonia and Amaranta Ursula. Here there is nothing marvellous about incest: it is an unequivocal image of a distorted society. So, circularity and repetition in the style of García Márquez are associated with negative and destructive forces, while the straight line of female development is positive and progressive. This may be the function of the del Valle family's tree. In a repetitious 'rito de iniciación', all the male members of the family wanting to start wearing long trousers had to climb the tree to prove their worth—until cousin Jerónimo falls and is killed and Nívea intervenes and orders that the tree be cut down. Rodrigo Cánovas has identified the tree with the family tree.[29] Yet this is the point at which the circular male ritual is stopped and a female dynasty begins. In the same chapter Clara decides to speak again, announcing her marriage. The only offspring of this marriage to produce a child will be the female, Blanca; her daughter is pregnant at the end of the novel. Thus a productive female line displaces a circle of sterile male activity, culminating in Blanca and Alba's role in the disintegration of a hitherto hermetic integrated phallic male self as their experience forces the patriarch Trueba out of his false circle and into the world of 'verdad'. Once more, this ties to the level of class and politics. The moving turning-point of Trueba's embrace with Pedro Tercero García (a positive development) follows the more-or-less exact (though inverted) repetition of a dialogue between them that had taken place some time earlier: the circular trap has been punctured (345, 319). The peasant names, Pedro García, Pedro Segundo García and Pedro Tercero García, echo the reduplication of names in *Cien años de soledad*, suggesting they are caught in a hopeless circle of oppression. But their names contain the seeds of numerical progress (Segundo, Tercero), linking them to the forward-moving chain. As Allende herself has commented, 'nada es un callejón sin salida, es que siempre al final hay una respuesta, hay una salida, hay una solución'.[30]

The epilogue of the novel may now seem more acceptable. Even if there is an element of fudge and some toying with the buzz notions of the new novel, Mora's judgement that it represents 'una postura conservadora'[31] is somewhat harsh. True, the final pages do talk of repetition and predetermination: 'Sospecho que todo lo ocurrido no es fortuito, sino que corresponde a un destino dibujado antes de mi nacimiento y Esteban García es parte de ese dibujo ...' (379). But surely this is a reference to the Frankenstein idea—that oppressive patriarchal systems will inevitably breed their own monsters which will one day turn around and bite. Trueba and the system he represents have brought disaster upon themselves. However, Alba realizes that this apparently cyclic pattern, this 'trazo tosco y torcido', has a hidden meaning, that 'ninguna pincelada es inútil' and that, when the 'rompecabezas' is deciphered, 'el resultado sería armonioso' (379). Putting it simply, people can learn from the past and there is hope. It is equally true that the last line of the novel takes us back to the first. Yet this does not close the text in a vicious circle of inevitability. The last line is from Clara's diaries, from which Alba has learned a positive lesson. If directed along proper avenues, writing can overcome confused, circular patterns and help us to 'ver las cosas en su dimensión real y ... burlar a la mala memoria' (379). In other words, the last sentence underlines Alba's vital political function as a mainstream testimonial writer: she will retrace the family history in an accessible form so that people can learn from it. Alba's role in the 'rompecabezas' is to replace the stifling circle of a false order with the straight line of learning and truth:

> Clara ... le sugirió, además, que escribiera un testimonio que algún día podría servir para sacar a la luz el terrible secreto que estaba viviendo, para que el mundo se enterara del horror que ocurría paralelamente a la existencia apacible y ordenada de los que no querían saber, de los que podían tener la ilusión de una vida normal, de los que podían negar que iban a flòte en una balsa sobre un mar de lamentos, ignorando, a pesar de todas las evidencias, que a pocas cuadras de su mundo feliz estaban los otros, los que sobreviven o mueren en el lado oscuro. (362-63)

This, also, is the role of Isabel Allende. Popular culture can, without doubt, be exploited as an agent of oppression, but it can also be liberating. Its value, when used appropriately, is that it can distil relatively complex concepts into a readily-digestible form: essentially, the process that has been described here. Thus, when old Férula, ticking off Trueba for his ostentation, comes out with the sort of naive-sounding hackneyed cliché conventionally thought typical of her social-sexual role, she is actually crystallizing the argument of the novel and an important historical truth: 'tanto despilfarro era seguramente pecado mortal y Dios iba a castigar a todos por gastar en chabacanerías de nuevo rico lo que estaría mejor empleado ayudando a los pobres' (87). Similarly, a simple song by Pedro Tercero García about chickens and foxes (in which the once-timid chickens get together to scare off the sly fox) has a far greater political impact than the more recondite messages of the Socialist Party 'panfletos' that he tirelessly distributes (157). So, those academics who mistrust Isabel Allende because of the mainstreamism of her work are effectively mirroring the sentiments of Esteban Trueba with his loathing of 'la música popular' (203) and his prohibition of radios that transmit 'canciones subversivas' and 'comedias y folletines' (274). The supposedly trashy world of women, peasants and popular culture can be seen to challenge the official tyrannies of patriarchy, capitalism and cultural supremacism. Thus the various theoretical positons rehearsed in *La casa de los espíritus* are condensed into a concise but simple philosophy of love in the closing pages. Alba says: 'Me será muy difícil vengar a todos los que tienen que ser vengados, porque mi venganza no sería más que otra parte del mismo rito inexorable. Quiero pensar que mi oficio es la vida y que mi misión no es prolongar el odio, sino sólo llenar estas páginas ...' (379). She has set herself free from aimless circularities (social, political, sexual and artistic) and chosen to use her writing to communicate a clear and powerful message of love. This will be the most effective way of trashing the tyrants.

## NOTES

1. Gabriela Mora, 'Las novelas de Isabel Allende y el papel de la mujer como ciudadana', *Ideologies and Literature*, II, 1 (1987), 53-61, at p. 60.

2. Douglas Foster, 'Isabel Allende Unveiled', *Mother Jones*, XIII (1988), No. 10, 42-46. It should be pointed out that, since this article was written, there have been a number of developments in Isabel Allende's public and personal life, amongst them the tragic loss of her daughter.

3. Linda Levine and Jo Anne Engelbert, 'The World is Full of Stories', *Review*, XXXIV (1980), 18-20, at p. 20; Isabel Allende, 'La magia de las

palabras', *Revista Iberoamericana*, LI (1985), 447-52, at p. 451: the remaining quotations in this paragraph come from the same page.

4.  Gerald Martin, *Journeys through the Labyrinth: Latin American Fiction in the Twentieth Century* (London: Verso, 1989), 218-35.

5.  Julia Kristeva, 'La femme, ce n'est jamais ça', *Tel Quel*, LIX (1974), 19-24, at p. 24, quoted in Toril Moi, *Sexual/Textual Politics: Feminist Literary Theory* (London: Routledge, 1990), 164. The theoretical positions outlined in this essay are largely drawn from Moi's excellent survey. The main references are to Hélène Cixous and Julia Kristeva, particularly, in the latter case, *La Révolution du langage poétique* (Paris: Seuil, 1974), in which she examines avant-garde and modernist writers.

6.  Gene H. Bell-Villada, *García Márquez: The Man and His Work* (Chapel Hill: Univ. of North Carolina Press, 1990), 208.

7.  Jean Gilkison, 'The Appropriation of the Conventions of Romance in Isabel Allende's *De amor y de sombra*'. Paper given at the conference of the Association of Hispanists of Great Britain and Ireland, Belfast, 1991. I am grateful to Dr Gilkison for providing me with a copy of her entertaining and persuasively-argued paper.

8.  See Moi, *op. cit.*, 171.

9.  Isabel Allende, *La casa de los espíritus* (Barcelona: Plaza y Janés, 18th ed., 1985), 203.

10.  See Moi, *op. cit.*, 92.

11.  José Donoso, *El obsceno pájaro de la noche* (Barcelona: Seix Barral, 6th ed., 1979), 230.

12.  'José Donoso's *El obsceno pájaro de la noche*: Witches Everywhere and Nowhere', in Sharon Magnarelli, *The Lost Rib: Female Characters in the Spanish-American Novel* (London: Associated University Presses, 1985), 147-68. The general comments on witches here draw on Magnarelli's stimulating analysis.

13.  José Donoso, *Casa de campo* (Barcelona: Seix Barral, 3rd ed., 1980), 34, 130.

14.  The French word, 'féminin' translates as 'female' and 'feminine'. Usage here will vary according to context. Broadly speaking, 'feminine' is preferred to 'female' where possible essential qualities of the sex are being considered. The adjective 'masculine' poses a similar problem.

15.  Annie Leclerc, extract from *Parole de femme* (Paris: Grasset, 1974), in *French Feminist Thought: A Reader*, ed. Toril Moi (Oxford: Basil Blackwell, 1987), 73-79. I am grateful to Dr Jean Andrews for bringing this item to my attention.

16. See Levine and Engelbert, *art. cit.*, 18.

17. See Moi, *op. cit.*, 114.

18. Mario A. Rojas, in '*La casa de los espíritus*, de Isabel Allende: un caleidoscopio de espejos desordenados', *Revista Iberoamericana*, LI (1985), 917-25, usefully discusses the tendency to 'obliterar las rígidas dicotomías que polarizan la diferenciación genérica' (921). In particular, he notes hints of androgyny in the portrayal of Jaime and other characters (216). Similar points could be made about the later Nicolás.

19. See Levine and Engelbert, *art. cit.*, 19.

20. Sandra M. Boschetto, 'Dialéctica metatextual y sexual en *La casa de los espíritus* de Isabel Allende', *Hispania*, LXXII (1989), No. 3, 526-32, at p. 530. Unfortunately, the overall argument of Boschetto's well-written article is the familiar and, in this case, irrelevant one that the text is merely a 'signo representando otros signos, significantes apuntando a otros significantes' (562).

21. There are obvious shades of Víctor Jara here, though he died in the repression that followed the coup. Mora complains that Pedro Tercero García's escape to and success in Canada devalues his political significance (*art. cit.*, 57).

22. For a fuller discussion of the post-Boom see my 'Conclusion: After the Boom', in *Landmarks in Modern Latin American Fiction*, ed. Philip Swanson (London: Routledge, 1990), 222-45.

23. M. Osorio, 'Entrevista con Manuel Puig', *Cuadernos para el Diálogo*, CCXXXI (1977), 51-53, at p. 52. Puig does not, however, in my view, always expound a coherent view of popular culture or reconcile it adequately with politics or the aesthetics of the new novel. See my 'Sailing Away on a Boat to Nowhere: *El beso de la mujer araña* and *Kiss of the Spider Woman*, from Novel to Film', in *Essays on Hispanic Themes in Honour of Edward C. Riley*, eds. Jennifer Lowe and Philip Swanson (Edinburgh: Univ. of Edinburgh, 1989), 331-59.

24. Verónica Cortínez, 'Polifonía: entrevista a Isabel Allende y Antonio Skármeta', *Revista Chilena de Literatura*, XXXII (1988), 79-89, at p. 80.

25. See Martin, *op. cit.*, 231.

26. For a fuller discussion of these questions see my *Cómo leer a Gabriel García Márquez* (Madrid: Júcar, 1991).

27. Peter G. Earle, 'Literature as Survival: Allende's *The House of the Spirits*', *Contemporary Literature*, XXVIII (1987), No. 4, 543-54, at pp. 543-44.

28. Of course, not all critics would reduce *Cien años de soledad* to a circular structure. See my survey of the various critical positions in *Cómo leer a Gabriel García Márquez*.

29. Rodrigo Cánovas, 'Los espíritus literarios y políticos de Isabel Allende', *Revista Chilena de Literatura*, XXXII (1988), 119-29, at p. 122.

30. See Cortínez, *art. cit.*, 81. A slightly less convincing case of the circle-v-straight line is that of Tránsito Soto. Marjorie Agosín, in 'Isabel Allende: *La casa de los espíritus*', Revista Interamericana de Bibliografía, XXXV (1985), 448-58, has argued that Clara uses her femininity as a means of self-advancement when she turns silence (traditional feminine coyness and passivity) into a weapon and act of defiance (450 *ff*). In a similar way, Tránsito Soto uses her female sexuality to progress from small-town whore to wealthy star turn of a top brothel in the capital. This linear development is matched by a circular inversion. Trueba lends her the money to start her off on her, he thinks, laughable ambition, but he ends up begging her to help him free Alba. The right-wing senator is now out of favour with the dictatorship, while she (a former member of a co-operative) is in a position of influence with the government. Trueba's full-circle turnabout may represent the inevitable come-uppance of an unjust system, but the prostitute remains a dubious symbol of emancipation.

31. See Mora, *art. cit.*, 55.

LYNNE DIAMOND-NIGH

# Eva Luna: *Writing as History*

In the beginning was the Word. And in the end. The opening lines of Isabel
Allende's *Eva Luna* (1989) place us squarely in a world created and structured
by the written word: "My name is Eva, which means 'life,' according to a
book of names my mother consulted." Indeed, the entire first chapter of that
novel functions to displace our center of reference from the real world to the
world of the Book where the life of the imagination is privileged. The
epigraph to Allende's work comes from the paradigmatic *Arabian Nights*, in
which Scheherezade's story-telling keeps her from a certain and undeserved
death, setting up a primary theme of salvation through fabulation.
Fabulation is here redemption of the collective, for Scheherezade's fables
save not only herself but all women, thus putting an end, by nonviolent
means, to the death sentence enacted upon the harem/population. The
importance of this becomes more evident when we reflect upon the novel
and the cultural context from which Isabel Allende writes.

The lack of connection between writing and political activism has been
one of the major charges levelled at the self-reflexive literature characteristic
of the Boom that immediately preceded Allende's work. Although her
literature is not innovative in the formal way that high modern Boom
literature was, she very clearly believes in the revolutionary possibilities of
literature to create and remake life and the impossibility of an authentic

From *Studies in Twentieth Century Literature* 19 (no. 1) (Winter 1995): 29-42. ©1995 by *Studies
in Twentieth Century Literature*. Reprinted by permission.

literature that is not intimately connected with reality. In *Eva Luna* and in *The House of the Spirits* (1985) as well, she shows that writing has a sacred, transcendental quality, which is explored in the creation and resurrection myths and stories that appear in those novels. Eva describes her mother and the legacy she passes on:

> Words are free, she used to say, and she appropriated them; they were all hers. She sowed in my mind the idea that reality is not only what we see on the surface; it has a magical dimension as well and, if we so desire, it is legitimate to enhance it and color it to make our journey through life less trying.

Allende's language here reflects the commodification/impoverishment of reality in a world ruled by economic and political repression as a counterpoint to one lightened by the liberating potential of words. But if instead fiction is not integrated into reality, the opposite occurs, as with Zulema, Riad Halabí's wife: "My stories did not make her happy; they merely filled her head with romantic ideas, and led her to dream of impossible escapades and borrowed heroes, distancing her totally from reality." Eva tells the Minister of Defense that her ideas come from "things that are happening and things that happened before I was born...." What she doesn't say is that Bolero, her telenovela, which he is questioning, is the story of her (made) life.

Clearly, then, because fiction is so intimately entwined with life, it is a priori political. Rolf Carlé, the documentary cinéaste, and his mentor and boss, Señor Aravena, debate this concept numerous times in the book, even though they genuinely agree that art can change history; it is for that reason that they run the risk of arrest, torture, and even death.

At the very end of the book Rolf and Eva merge the personal and the political when they agree to tell the story of the guerrillas' escape from Santa María through an episode in her telenovela, a story in which they both had participated and which Rolf had filmed. This device, quite common in Chile and other similar political regimes, ensures the diffusion of the truth that censors will not allow on the regular news channels.

This Bildungsroman of Eva's professional development as a writer reflects—in a somewhat fragmented manner—important developments in Latin American literary history. While reading this novel I felt that her personal quest was paralleled by an aesthetic quest, manifested in the trying on and taking off of various genres, literary movements and myths characteristic of Latin America; she even goes so far as to explicitly allude to specific authors and their individual works. Although some of these are simply lightheartedly parodied, others are reworked and reinterpreted in the light of the feminist enterprise of the past twenty-five years. *Eva Luna* transgresses fundamentally because it has an intellectually strong, sexual, nurturing, very feminine protagonist, setting up an initial rupture with the dichotomy so clearly demarcated by Octavio Paz between "the mother and the whore."

Four primary categories suggest themselves: myth and the mythic consciousness; magical realism; Boom writers; and then a miscellaneous grouping that subsumes a host of other significant literatures and literary themes: the picaresque, the neo-romantic, novels of the dictators, the ever-present conflict between civilization and barbarism, and testimonial literature. As the novel's contact with soap operas and radio serials is so evident, this article will not address that connection.

The critic Wolfgang Karrer has suggested the importance of the creation myth in chapter one of this novel. I would like to suggest that two other chapters, six and ten, also participate in a creation myth, and that all three of these are linked by the idea of creation through words. Chapter one gives us the physical creation of the first woman, Eva/Eve, chapter six her re-creation as an erotic being, and chapter ten a further incarnation as a politically committed writer.

In "Transformation and Transvestism in *Eva Luna*," Karrer suggests that the "opening story of Consuelo and the Indian gardener, dying and resurrecting under Consuelo's love making, carries overtones of a creation myth. Man and woman, Indian and Spanish races (in a neat gender inversion of the Pocahontas/Malinche myth), death and life, moon and 'Sándolo Sol' ... snake and life essence, all fuse to create *Eva Luna*." From the beginning, then, traditionally masculine frameworks of separation and hierarchy are deconstructed and converted to traditionally feminine ones of wholeness and fusion, a changeover that the critic Z. Nelly Martínez has read as a political act in Allende's *The House of the Spirits* (1991). Karrer also suggests that Eva fulfills the archetypal code described by Della Grisa (1985) which:

> begins both with the title and her name. It determines her miraculous creation, the heroic liberation from mother to father figures, it provides friendly helpers and magical gifts, and leads to her magical transformation from domestic prisoner to liberator of prisoners.... But instead of reflecting Latin American history in this circular myth ... Allende chooses to thoroughly feminize it. It is *Eva Luna* who rescues Rolf Carlé from the dragon of his past, who brings the treasure to Mimí, helps to free the prisoners and take the good news to the people. Her individuation owes more

to mother, "grandmother" Elvira, and "sister" Mimí than to male help from Huberto Naranjo or even Riad Halabí.

It is Halabí, however, who gives birth to the second Eva in chapter six. He rescues her and brings her to Agua Santa where she says that "for the first time in my life, I was free to come and go; until then I had always been confined behind walls or forced to wander lost in a hostile city." He teaches her to read and write; he gives her the emotional and financial security and leisure to do so; just as important, he provides her with a birth certificate, the only proof of her existence in the world. Like Scheherezade with the sultan in the *Arabian Nights*, he brings her to life as an erotic being, as an embodiment of the life-force Eros. Most interestingly, however, he does not become her lover until the night before she leaves, as a result of her metamorphosis and not as its cause. Thus, it is as nurturer and guide (a "helper" in Della Grisa's terminology) that he functions. And the agency of this instruction is through none other than that book which reigns over all of *Eva Luna*, the *Arabian Nights*, "in which I immersed myself so deeply I completely lost sight of reality. Eroticism and fantasy blew into my life with the force of a typhoon, erasing all limitations and turning the known order of things upside down." Z. Nelly Martínez, in the aforementioned article, describes Allende's concept of Eros and its connection to writing and the feminine artist:

> Also useful here is Michel Foucault's opposition between ars erotica and scientia sexualis, an opposition that brings attention to the repressive power of Western sexuality and to the liberating power of Eros. Thus Foucault equates (Western) knowledge with (patriarchal) might and sees art as expressive of Eros and hence as a liberating force. Free and creative. Eros is evidently subversive and hence demonic in the Western imagination.

And thus it functions, for Eva is wrongly accused of Halabí's wife's death, arrested, tortured and driven out of town by people who cannot understand the nature of her relationship with Halabí, but instead interpret it as a clandestine sexual liaison that causes Zulema's death.

Eva's last birth, as committed writer, is one that fuses both her erotic and intellectual being and brings together her personal relationship with Rolf and her source of inspiration in the collective unconscious:

> I awakened early. It was a soft and slightly rainy Wednesday, not very different from others in my life, but I treasure that Wednesday as a special day, one that belonged only to me. I took a clean white sheet of paper—like a sheet freshly ironed for making love—and rolled it into the carriage.... I believed that that page ha[d] been waiting for me for more than twenty years, that I had lived only for that instant.... I wrote my name, and immediately the words began to flow, one thing linked to another and another.... I could see an order to the stories stored in my genetic memory since before my birth, and the many others I had been writing for years in my notebooks.

When we examine the language used here and the language used later to describe Eva and Rolf, we see that both evoke the same suggestion of eternity and destiny:

> He strode forward and kissed me exactly as it happens in romantic novels, exactly as I had been wanting him to do for a century, and exactly as I had been describing moments before in a scene between the protagonists of my Bolero. Once we were close, I was able unobtrusively to drink in the smell of the man, recognizing, at long last, the scent of the other half of my being. I understood then why from the first I thought I had known him before.

What is just as interesting here, it seems to me, is the plenitude of existence that Eva experiences when she writes, the complete fulfillment of herself as a unique being: the day that belongs only to her and the fact that the mere inscription of her name calls forth her creations.

Naming: in the mythic consciousness the use of a name is a sacred ritual, calling what had previously been unnamed into existence, creating a destiny if given to a person. It is intimate, private and personal and speaks to the very core of a person's being. When Eva returns to the Indians at the end of the novel, she asks the name of one of them whom she was sure she had previously known, "but El Negro had explained that it would be discourteous to ask. For these Indians, he said, to name is to touch the heart; they consider it offensive to call a stranger by name or to be named by him...." With this sense of the sacred replacing the patriarchal appropriation signaled by a child's taking of the name of the father, Eva's name creates her destiny and marks her as a part of a larger community:

Her name will be Eva, so she will love life. "And her last name?" "None. Her father's name isn't important." "Everybody needs a last name. Only a dog can run around with one name." "Her father belonged to the Luna tribe, the Children of the Moon. Let it be Luna, then. *Eva Luna....*"

Consuelo, too, is marked by her name: time and time again after her death Eva calls on her for strength, courage and guidance, and she even becomes a visible presence in much the same way as Eva's characters who will invade her house and make a hurricane of chaos for Elvira to clean. Eva herself notes her mother's destiny when she says that "she realized that the moment had come for her to justify the name Consuelo and console this man in his misfortune." But Consuelo is not only defined by her name; she also embodies Jung's collective unconscious, always present, never forgetting: "She placed at my feet the treasures of the Orient, the moon, and beyond.... she retained all the anecdotes she had heard and those she had learned in her readings. She manufactured the substance of her own dreams, and from those materials constructed a world for me." We saw that this collective memory was part of the wellspring pouring from Eva's writing of her name, and we later see that she in turn passes it on to Rolf: "she understood that in her desire to please him she had given him her own memory: she no longer knew what was hers or how much now belonged to him; their pasts had been woven into a single strand."

The sense of time as being eternal and undifferentiated, flowing in a circular movement that subverts the Western idea of progress, evolution, sequence and non-connection, is explicitly elaborated in the first chapter of Genesis. Mircea Eliade, in his *Cosmos and History* (1959) characterizes it as sacred time, "in illo tempore." In the Mission where Consuelo was raised, "time is bent and distances deceive the human eye, persuading the traveler to wander in circles"; it is a Garden of Eden where "she roamed outdoors, sniffing the flora and the fauna, her mind filled with images, smells, colors, and myths borne on the river current." This cyclical, repetitive, mythic time sense dominates the narrative, fusing the beginning and end of the novel, when Eva returns to the Indians (her origins) in the jungle close to Agua Santa and takes part in an act of political commitment that makes her part of a collective. Riad Halabí's gift of the belly dance, only to be performed for the man Eva loves, is a mirror of the tooth-shaped gold nugget given by El Portugués to Consuelo, who would wear it "until she met someone she would give it to as a gift of love."

The belief in the unity of all things, this fusion and change, the nondiscrimination between seeming opposites, also characterize the mythic world-view. Gender differences disappear and the animate/inanimate dichotomy as nature is invested with mystery, potential and life. Masculine and feminine principles metamorphose and meld, producing "mythological beings" more complete than either of the two genders: this may be the only way we can understand Mimí's puzzling decision not to take the step of having a vagina constructed, one that would finally complete her sex change. I would like to suggest that Riad Halabí embodies a feminine principle: he gives birth to Eva's second incarnation, thus fusing the father and mother into one. Highlighting the beginning of chapter six are words which seem somewhat disorienting when applied to a man: "Riad Halabí was one of those persons who are undone by their own compassion." Although he has been a successful businessman, most of what we know of him focuses on his sensitivity, gentleness, and emotional life, a focus most usually reserved for feminine characters. And in a foreshadowing of the end of the book he incarnates a woman:

> Sometimes he covered the lower half of his face with a dishcloth, in the manner of an odalisque's veil, and danced for me, clumsily, arms uplifted, belly gyrating wildly. So it was, amid shouts of laughter, that I learned the belly dance. "It is a sacred dance—you will dance it only for the man you love most in your life," Riad Halabí told me.

We can view Eva's time with Riad as an apprenticeship for her relationship with Rolf, who also embodies mythic and feminine principles of wholeness and fusion. This we have already seen in his enactment of the myth that lovers are one soul split and thrown to separate parts of the earth, from which they must make their way back to each other to form a complete being. Throughout the novel, Eva's and Rolf's geographical, social, professional and personal orbits come ever closer. Emotions, not the intellect, rule Rolf's life: "He denied his emotions but at any unguarded time was demolished by them."

On the other hand we have Huberto Naranjo who, despite his apparently revolutionary ideas, will never allow revolution in gender roles and relations, which makes a permanent relationship with Eva impossible: "For Naranjo and others like him, 'the people' seemed to be composed exclusively of men; we women should contribute to the struggle but were excluded from decision-making and power. His revolution would not change my fate in any fundamental way...."

Allende here deconstructs the Western idea of transvestism/travesty with its emphasis on unnaturalness and evil, separation and otherness, and uses the mythic consciousness of Latin American history to change its polarity to plenitude and wholeness. On a smaller scale, this idea obtains throughout the novel, as prostitutes and transvestites become major commercial and social successes, delinquents and street roughs guerrilla heroes, and the picaresque adventure a romantic melodrama. Rupert's faith in cross-breeding to create the strongest and best breeds, the madrina's Siamese twins of different races and the use of the word "she" to refer back to the usually masculine "person," are examples in miniature.

Eva's experience of the mythic world unfolds in the first part of the novel, most specifically in the Genesis portion of the first chapter. Her stories form part of literary oral tradition. She learns the art of storytelling from her mother, learns to use her stories as tools of barter, survival, escape and emotional comfort, but it is not until chapter six, the exact mid-point of the novel, which takes place in Agua Santa, that she gains the skills of reading and writing.

Allende's acknowledgment of magical realism occurs both as specific references and in the creation of the microcosm of magical realism, La Colonia, where Eva's masculine counterpart, Rolf Carlé, grows up. There are clear allusions to the two foundational figures of magical realism in Latin America, Jorge Luis Borges and Alejo Carpentier. Carpenter's idea of "lo real maravilloso" is echoed by Eva the first time she goes to La Colonia and says, "I had the feeling that I was in a world so new that sound had not yet been created." Borges' idea of the simultaneity of times and spaces, most explicit in his short story, "El Aleph," (1948) is reflected in Eva's description of the garden in the Mission:

> The world was bounded by the iron railings of the garden. Within them, time was ruled by caprice; in half an hour I could make six trips around the globe, and a moonbeam in the patio would fill my thoughts for a week.... Space expanded and con- tracted according to my will: the cubby beneath the stairs contained an entire planetary system, but the sky seen through the attic skylight was nothing more than a pale circle of glass.

There seems to be no irony or parody in these descriptions, which is not the case in the extended meditation on La Colonia, which represents magical realism imposed from the outside. It is a fairytale village, a transplanted Austrian homeland marked by self-isolation and imposition, a place where no one speaks Spanish, and where many of the children have defects because of inbreeding, another reference, perhaps, to the Nazi policy of the "pure race" suggested by the concentration camp episode; a colony in Allende's damning terms. It is basically sterile, unreal, "preserved in a bubble where time had stopped and geography was illusory.... For Rolf it was like walking into a movie." Aravena urges him to leave:

> You can't stay in La Colonia forever, he said. It's fine for a neurotic like myself to come here and fortify my body and get the poisons out of my system, but no normal young man should live in this stage set. Rolf Carlé was familiar with the works of Shakespeare, Molière and Calderón de la Barca, but he had never been in a theater and could not see its relationship with the village.

It seems significant that the three authors cited are not Latin American, but represent the three most important colonial powers, England, France and Spain. Rolf's knowledge of literature, then, has no connection with the world that surrounds him. Elzbieta Sklodowska suggests in an article on Miguel Barnet that "this perception ... resembles the construction of the so-called magic realist narrative in that it frames the 'other' as fantastically exotic. What we get instead of difference is awkwardness." Magical realism, then, in the context of La Colonia, is not indigenous but an overlay that represents the desire by outsiders to marginalize Latin America.

The authentically "magic" is Agua Santa. The road/threshold to and from it passes by the Palace of the Poor, which materializes and etherizes as a hallucinatory apparition. It is a microcosm of the *Arabian Nights*, dominated by the guiding force of the Arabian Riad Halabí. The differences between Agua Santa and La Colonia focus on the dichotomy between integration and domination: although not Hispanic, Riad integrates himself into the life of the community and becomes its guiding force in commerce, village improvements and education. He brings Eva there; the Indians come from the jungle every week and join them. The only person who does not become part of the community is his wife, Zulema, who ends up committing suicide. It is there that Eva discovers three magic forces in her life, reading, writing, and the erotic, while it is significant that no creation takes place in La Colonia. In Agua Santa, it is only when the forces of repression take over that everything changes, including the townspeople, and Eva is forced to leave.

No discussion of magical realism or the Boom can possibly take place without discussing Gabriel García Márquez and *One Hundred Years of Solitude* (1970); it seemed at one point that no scholarship on Isabel Allende could take place either, particularly none on *The House of the Spirits*, without that same discussion. In *Eva Luna*, Allende parodies this obsession (and cites herself intratextually) through Mimí: "Ever since she had seen a line of people outside a bookstore waiting to have their books signed by a thickly mustached Colombian writer on a triumphal tour, she had showered me with notebooks, pencils and dictionaries. That's a good career, Eva. You don't have to get up too early and three's no one to order you around...." Nonetheless, the marks of García Márquez remain evident: prolepses, levitations, fairies that appear in the surreal clarity of dusk, notebooks that encapsulate life, the military that tries to annihilate history, "wiping out entire tribes and erasing every trace of their passage on earth," a clear reference to the end of *One Hundred Years*. It is, then, not the influence of García Márquez to which Allende objects, but his patriarchal appropriation of all following writing and literature, whether explicitly fostered by him, by scholars, or by readers.

Other writers of the Latin American Boom, Isabel Allende's direct literary predecessors, can be read in *Eva Luna*. Several of the borrowings/allusions come from protagonists in major new novels: Alejandra of Ernesto Sá bato's *On Heroes and Tombs* (1981) finds her way into Eva's soap opera *Bolero*; the transvestite La Manuela in José Donoso's *Hell has no Limits* (1972) is completely reinterpreted as Melesio/Mimí; Jorge Amado's *Gabriela: Clove and Cinnamon* (1962) resonates in Rolf's two cousins with their "natural aroma of cinnamon, clove, vanilla and lemon." The narrative structure of an interlocking soap opera narrative with an autofiction has a precedent in Mario Vargas Llosa's *Aunt Julia and the Scriptwriter* (1982), and Alejo Carpentier's *Lost Steps* (1956) is mirrored in Eva's return to her Indian origins in the jungle: while there, she "re-gains" her life by resuming the menstrual periods that had ceased after Zulema's suicide but, like the protagonist in Carpentier's novel, she cannot stay and returns to her life in the city.

It could be argued that these are mere coincidences and show more of this writer's flights of fancy than any authorial intention. I would like to counter with the idea that the specular quality of the *Arabian Nights* profoundly informs this work, that *Eva Luna* explicitly is a coming to terms with the literary currents and movements of Latin American history, the closest of which, in chronological terms, is the Boom, and that the allusive interplay and resonating structure I have just mentioned is a way of forming an intertextual web that unites all of Latin American literature, a device which is totally compatible with the feminist ideology of fusion and integration I have been mentioning throughout this piece.

Chapters three and five clearly embrace that paradigmatic Spanish form of literature, the picaresque, which Pilar V. Rotella defines in "Allende's *Eva Luna* and the Picaresque Tradition" as "that of an unheroic protagonist caught up in a chaotic world, enduring a series of adventures and encounters that make him both a victim of the world and its exploiter." Along with first-person point of view and episodic structure, "picaresque narratives often remain open-ended and often laced with interpolated tales...." Allende reinterprets this genre in significant ways, most particularly the use of a feminine *pícara* (not without literary precedent but unusual), and the changeover of Eva from a picaresque character to a genuine heroine, one who risks her life and uses her narrative gifts for the service of others. With the changeover in the protagonist, the novel itself changes modalities, a transformation that Rotella aptly describes: "*Eva Luna's* and her friends' efforts to create a better world by destroying at least one bastion of political oppression and, especially, her own surrender to—supposedly—extra-ordinary love and lasting happiness, lead toward the idealized vision of romance." The romance modality, too, undergoes important changes in the hands of Eva and Allende, as it remains firmly planted in reality. One of the characteristics of Eva's stories is the elimination of characters polarized into villains and heroes/heroines. The traditional romance/soap opera ending of "happily ever after" is replaced by a more realistic ending, one which she suggests is more suited to her morbid temperament. It is also one which is often more feminist in its overtones and, as such, is not at all pleasing to Huberto Naranjo. The ending of *Eva Luna* itself is ambiguous, with the traditional happy ending suggested as only one of several equal possibilities.

The romance polarized characterization is mirrored in the polarized thematics of the regional novel, which has often been implicitly subtitled "civilization and barbarism." The first story Eva tells Rolf and Aravena begins thus: "Times were hard in the south. Not in the south of this country, but the south of the world, where seasons are reversed and winter does not occur at Christmastime as it does in civilized nations, but in the middle of the year, as in barbaric lands...." This allusion is not only to the internal geography of Latin American literary history but to the same spirits that see Latin America as a barbaric/exotic land, framing it in the same way as do the magical realist narratives we have already discussed.

Literature of the dictators, with a long history in Latin America and a more recent flowering in the 1980s, at which time many of the major Boom writers penned such works, is also cited in *Eva Luna*: the figure of El Benefactor who could not be buried because the people would not believe that "the tyrant's immortality was only a myth," shows in a humorous way the logical consequences of the mythification of a person, a mythification which is too often used for repressive ends. But Allende here, as she does in the ending of *The House of the Spirits*, suggests that there is a way out: in *The House of the Spirits*, Alba breaks the evolutionary pattern of crime, oppression and revenge by deciding not to hate her torturers; in *Eva Luna*, the Minister of Defense, who knows all about her, her contacts with the guerrillas, and her use of Bolero to disseminate the truth, does not arrest her but requests her mediation to reach an agreement with them.

The reverse side of this literature, what we have come to call testimonial, embodies one of the primary themes of *Eva Luna*, memory, and the resurrection of lost and never-heard voices. From the beginning of this novel, memory takes its place as a life-sustaining force: Consuelo tells Eva that she never will die if Eva continues to remember her; Eva writes from the "genetic memory" which has been passed on to her by her mother; she re-creates her own and others' memories so that they become positive rather than negative remembrances; she passes on to and fuses her memories with Rolf until they are one. Allende's long, allusive meditations on Latin American literary history ensure that this history, too, will remain alive. In the novel, Eva tries to avoid telling about Zulema and her lover, Kamal, but comes to the following conclusion: "My first thought was that if we kept silent, it would be as if nothing had happened—what is not voiced scarcely exists; silence would gradually erase everything, and the memory would fade." Without memory, without voice, without stories, life ceases.

CATHERINE R. PERRICONE

# *Genre and Metarealism in Allende's* Paula

Isabel Allende's latest book, *Paula* (1994), can be called a "metarealistic narrative" for the way it transcends the designation of "memoir" and appropriates multiple generic discourses anchored in reality: history, biography, elegy, confession, autobiography, *Bildungsroman*, and testimonial. The literary framework of the narrative is paradigmatic of the reality Allende presents because of the essential relationship these genres have to reality. Stated another way, the generic forms themselves exemplify reality owing to their essential foundation in the real. Yet, at the same time, the book approaches the novelesque in the Bakhtinian sense. Likewise the fictional element associated with the novel surfaces in the employment of magical realism, the *leyenda*, and even the injection of a *cuento de hadas*. As Barbara Mujica observes, "sections of the book read like a novel, at times exhibiting an almost surrealist atmosphere" (41).

To explain the use here of the term "metarealism" it is useful to recall that, in its origins, realism represented an attempt first associated with nineteenth-century writers to give an "objective" or truthful view of the reality of their social milieu. Realistic authors undertook "a description, distinguished by its precision and thoroughness, of the hidden inner mechanisms that animate and explain ... movements of the social community as a whole and of its individual members ... (Gold 11). Readers will

From *Hispania* 81 (no. 1) (March 1998): 42-49. © 1998 by American Association of Teachers of Spanish and Portuguese, Inc. Reprinted by permission.

immediately see how this essential description of realism contrasts with the various forms of the literary tendency which have appeared over the years and its diverse critical interpretations. Yet this succinct definition provides a basis for a discussion of a new kind of realism found in Allende's *Paula*, since the work illustrates another phase of realism's evolution in a changing world.[1]

The proposed concept of "metarealism" is analogous to the definition of metafiction as "fiction about fiction—that is, fiction that includes within itself a commentary on its own narrative and/or linguistic identity" (Hutcheon 1). "Metarealism" can be defined as "reality about reality," that is, reality which incorporates within itself a commentary on its own *verisimilitude* and *accuracy* or *veracity*. The structural "reality" composed of the multigeneric discourses previously mentioned becomes, then, a physical and spatial commentary on the verisimilitude and accuracy or veracity of the narrative. This explains why in *Paula* Allende uses so many "realistic" discursive modes to face the reality of her daughter's death, the catalyst for the work.

The term of realism has been associated with the novel, so it follows that Allende's metarealistic narrative may resemble a novel. In fact, early in the text, Allende demonstrates one of the processes described by Bakhtin as crucial to a novel: the creative authorial intention by which the writer appropriates diverse and stratified languages, each with its own voice, view, intention, and direction, "to [her] own semantic and expressive intention" (294). Pursuant to this, Allende writes "Me vuelco en estas páginas en un intento irracional de vencer mi terror, se me ocurre que si doy forma a esta devastación podré ayudarte [Paula] y ayudarme, el meticuloso ejericio de la escritura puede ser nuestra salvación" (17).

Although the author is dealing with actual people, her work is fictional in the sense that the people and events she describes now possess an acquired "reality" as characters or events in a literary work. Conceptually, their invented reality results in entities separate from the actual models upon which they were based. Allende's (re)invention of these people and incidents in a fictional mode (giving form to "esta devastación" [17]) was a cathartic effort to help her understand the tragedy of her daughter's death. Simultaneously, it was indicative of her attempt to restore order not only to her own life but also to Paula's through the rigorous process of writing. Furthermore, this intentionality on the part of the author exemplifies the very nature of the fictional prose which Bakhtin describes as the novel: its plasticity and constantly changing nature vis-à-vis a developing reality, in this instance a reality set in motion through personal life events.

If *Paula* therefore resembles a novelistic genre, it will be possible to examine its "multiplicity of social voices" (Bakhtin 263) within the context of its multigeneric discourse. The title of the work, *Paula*, suggests a biography of Allende's daughter of the same name. Taking Paula's illness as a starting point, Allende recounts the life of her daughter through a series of flashbacks until the time of her death from a rare disease called porphyria.[2] The narrative is structured around the two stages of Paula's illness: "Primera Parte: Diciembre 1991–Mayo 1992," when Paula lies comatose in a hospital in Madrid, and "Segunda Parte: Mayo-Diciembre 1992," when Paula, whose health has now irrevocably deteriorated, is with Allende and her second husband William (Willie) in San Francisco, California. An epilogue entitled "Navidad 1992" describes Paula's death on December 6, 1992. While the first words of the narrative clearly indicate that the story *belongs* to Paula: "Escucha, Paula, voy a contarte una historia, para que cuando despiertes no estés tan perdida" (11)—it is not solely *her* story or biography. Rather it is a narrative, originally intended to apprise her daughter of the family history, including the author's personal life. Thus, at this juncture *Paula* partakes of two genres: biography and history. The title of the work also implies that *Paula* is an elegy. In various sections of the novel, Allende praises the extraordinary qualities of her daughter, as in the two examples which follow. In the first she describes how Paula had spent the last week of her normal life: "Acababas de regresar de un retiro espiritual con las monjas del colegio en el cual trabajas, cuarenta horas a la semana como voluntaria ayudando a niños sin recursos…" (27). In the second, in a tone reminiscent of Federico García Lorca's elegy to Ignacio Sánchez Mejías, she writes: "¡Ah, la gracia tuya, Paula! Tu aire suave, tu intensidad impredecible, tu feroz disciplina intelectual, tu generosidad, tu alocada ternura…(90).[3]

Consequently, it is possible to view *Paula* as historical for its account of family history, biographical for the author's interpretive comments on her daughter's twenty-eight year life, and elegiac for the laudatory descriptions of Paula's character and personality.

The next discursive voice in *Paula* is the autobiographical account or memoir in which Allende narrates events from her own childhood in the 1940s, her teenage years, her journalistic and television careers both before and after her marriage, the birth of her two children—Paula and Nicolás, the role she played in the dangerous era after Pinochet became President of Chile when she was helping the regime's political enemies, her exile in Caracas, her extramarital affairs, her divorce from her husband Michael, the genesis and flowering of her literary career, and her second marriage to a San Francisco lawyer. Unquestionably autobiographical in nature, the narrative is simultaneously an adaptation of a *Bildungsroman* as it demonstrates the evolution of Allende's character through the years until her fiftieth birthday. But yet another language, in the Bakhtinian sense of the word, injects itself into the narrative: the confession. In this confessional mode Isabel Allende appears compelled to reveal the intimate details of her life, perhaps as a means towards making amends for any perceived failings of the past or to expunge the guilt she experiences for enjoying good health while her young daughter lies dying.

In addition, therefore, to the historical, biographical, autobiographical, and elegiac elements, a unique convergence of other discursive voices emerges through Allende's reliance upon a form distinguished by its relationship to a *Bildungsroman* and a confessional literary work. Working within the parameters of these generic modes, Allende is able to confront a situation which, as it immobilizes her daughter, causes the author to stop and take stock of her own life. The validity of this assessment can be found in Allende's moving lamentation to her brother Juan:

> —No lo sé. ¡Si pudiera entregarle mi vida y morir en su lugar! Estoy perdida, no sé quién soy, trato de recordar quién era yo antes, pero sólo encuentro disfraces, máscaras, proyecciones, imágenes confusas de una mujer que no reconozco. ¿Soy la feminista que creía ser, o soy esa joven frívola que aparecía en televisón con plumas de avestruz en el trasero? ¿La madre obsesiva, la esposa infiel, la aventurera temeraria o la mujer cobarde? ¿Soy la que asilaba perseguidos políticos o la que escapó porque no pudo soportar el miedo? Demasiadas contradicciones...—(352)[4]

At the same time, the entire narrative is testimonial. Allende was caught, in both her professional and private life, between a traditional patriarchal culture and an evolving society exemplified in the new feminist movement of the 1960s. Like other narrators of testimonial literature, Allende was both a protagonist and a witness to social and political events about which she felt compelled to write in order to address political corruption and repression in some way.[5] Allende was a staunch supporter of the socialist government of President Salvador Allende (which opposing factions considered communistic), and was actively involved in trying to assist the victims of the subsequent dictatorship of General Augusto Pinochet.

Although others have used a multigeneric approach, Allende brings to this literary orientation a special concept of reality, her unique objectivity, deriving from her many years as a journalist and scriptwriter for her own television shows. In these capacities she conducted interviews and investigative reports in order to present the "reality" of the times. She had experience, therefore, in giving—or at least attempting to present—accurate accounts of events. Yet on one occasion when she was attempting to interview Pablo Neruda, he exclaimed:

> —¡[Entrevistarme a] mí? ¡Jamás permitiría que me sometiera a semejante prueba! se rió—. Usted debe ser la peor periodista de este país, hija. Es incapaz de ser objetiva, se pone al centro de todo, y sospecho que miente bastante y cuando no tiene una noticia, la in-venta. ¿Por qué no se dedica a escribir novelas mejor? En la literatura esos defectos son virtudes. (202)

While the question naturally arises from this quotation as to whether Allende is a reliable narrator, it is also significant to ask why she would include Neruda's comment in this particular book. I suggest that in her quest to find her own identity, an essential part of the autobiographical segments of *Paula*, she is trying to defend her career as a writer. If, after all, a literary giant indicated her capacity for writing fiction, she must be in the right profession. Indeed her literary career is a reality occupying a central place in her life and in the work at hand which she describes as "…una larga introspección, es un viaje hacia las cavernas más oscuras de la conciencia, una lenta meditación" (17). Conversely, she may have suddenly realized that she was exposing the most intimate details of her life and wanted to project the vision of an unreliable narrator or, as Neruda suggested, to portray herself as one who was indeed inventing "facts." In actuality, this questioning which might arise as to the author's veracity only adds to the narrative's verisimilitude by creating a sense of doubt, an obviously human condition.

Among the many examples which could be presented, one which particularly demonstrates how Allende's literary experience and talent necessarily impact upon the way she views and presents reality is found on the very first page of *Paula* where she states she is going to relate her family's history:

> La *leyenda* familiar comienza a principios del siglo pasado, cuando un fornido marinero vasco desembarcó en las costas de Chile, con

la cabeza perdida en proyectos de grandeza y protegido por el relicario de su madre colgado al cuello, pero para qué ir tan atrás, basta decir que su descendencia fue una estirpe de mujeres impetuosas y hombres de brazos firmes para el trabajo y corazón sentimental. (11; italics mine)

*Paula* therefore contains a very special kind of history, a metahistorical narrative, a *leyenda* which goes beyond mere facts to suggest the kinds of lives these familial ancestors were going to lead, and, as the narrative unfolds, how contemporary protagonists express themselves in thought and action.[6] In this history/legend she exposes truth or reality in a philosophical sense, rather than attempting to write a historical account based solely on visible facts.

Allende's reality is a combination or intertwining of life and art, and readers familiar with her novels and short stories delight in seeing how she either specifically describes the source of her fiction or includes episodes from her life and those of her relatives or friends, who can be recognized as the bases for characters and plots in *La casa de los espíritus, De amor y de sombra, Eva Luna, El plan infinito,* and *Cuentos de Eva Luna.*[7] Especially significant as an aspect of *Paula's* metareality is the fact that Allende not only explains her intentionality and directionality but also refers to the contemporaneous act of writing the work as her daughter's illness progresses towards its inexorable end. Thus the evolving reality of a daughter's life and impending death and the simultaneity of the author's artistic direction of multigeneric voices result in a discrete literary work. Consequently, readers experience a unique view of reality: the portrayal of the lives of real people within a narrative which is real not only in its concrete existence of words on a page, but also by virtue of the fact that the author attests to its evolving reality within the pages of the text. Consequently life and art are simultaneously evolving in the artistic and realistic expression of self-awareness. As Allende states in the interview she granted to Barbara Mujica, art is a *sustaining* force. She began writing during the year Paula was dying and continued to do so during the first year of mourning. Writing was the author's way of separating the never-changing days, of allowing time to pass: "It was like by writing the day, the day happened" (38). This significantly puts into question Hayden White's statement that "[w]e do not *live* stories, even if we give our lives meaning by retrospectively casting them in the form of stories" (401). Allende did not "retrospectively cast" this story; it was precisely this recounting of past events *in the context of an event in progress* which made the very act of writing a "lived" story. Viewed from this perspective, *Paula* is a metarealistic narrative in its function as a *reality* (the genre) about *reality* (human life).

There are other examples to demonstrate why this can be called a metarealistic work. Responding to those who might argue that *Paula* merely continues Allende's extensive use of actual people and events as sources for a fictional account, I suggest that this narrative is significantly different. First, while in her novels and short stories prior to this work readers may be aware of the source of the "reality" Allende is presenting (in a number of interviews, Allende has elaborated on the persons and events inspiring her fiction),[8] there is no doubt as to the source of *Paula's* characters and plot. Readers learn in the brief foreword that:

> En diciembre de 1991 mi hija Paula cayó enferma de gravedad y poco después entró en coma. Estas páginas fueron escritas durante horas interminables en los pasillos de un hospital de Madrid y en un cuarto de hotel, donde viví varios meses. También junto a su cama, en nuestra casa de California, en el verano y el otoño de 1992. [iii]

Secondly, the narrative utilizes new temporal perspectives, in comparison with the novelist's prior works, which metonymically express the intimate relationship between past and present. For example, the present time of the narrative is the period between December 1991 and 1992 as far as its creation is concerned, a time frame which also corresponds to the limits of *Paula's* illness. The initial framework, therefore, devolves upon the present. However, Allende also narrates the past, but, as she does so, she is most concerned with her daughter, as the inspirational theme of the text as well as its intended reader. As a result, she frequently addresses Paula directly in the present tense, creating thereby a triple dialogue between past and present, between herself and her daughter—and significantly for my thesis— between the real present embracing Paula's illness and a metareal present time surrounding the act of writing *Paula*. This triple communication is effected by Allende's (the real and invented author's) use of the first person in Part 1 of the narrative, whereby she creates her metareal voice, and by her employment of "tú" to indicate the beloved daughter to whom the story is directed. In Part 2, Allende continues her narration in the first person, but now speaks of Paula in the third person: "Ya no escribo para que cuando mi hija despierte no esté tan perdida, porque no despertará. Estas páginas *no tienen destinatario*, Paula nunca podrá leerlas…(227; emphasis mine).

Concerning the "non-directionality" of the second part of the narrative, signified by changes in the personal marker from *tú* to *ella*, at first it seems to be solely a sign of the futility of Allende's continuing efforts to speak with her comatose daughter. Even the *yo-tú* relationship of the first part of the novel had at best been a sign of that hoped-for communication at some future date when Paula would have recovered from her illness. However, Allende's switch to the third person with respect to Paula signals remarkable changes regarding communication between mother and daughter. In an unspecified number of instances, Allende's daughter has begun to appear to her. Regarding the last appearance, the novelist writes that her daughter came to her ... "de nuevo anoche" (hence the inference that she has appeared before): "[L]a sentí entrar a mi pieza con su paso liviano y su gracia conmovedora, como era antes de los ultrajes de la enfermedad, en camisa de dormir y zapatillas" (348).

It is, however, the daughter who conducts a lengthy dialogue (dialogic insofar as there is a speaker and a listener) initiated by the words, "Escucha, mamá, despierta, no quiero que pienses que sueñes" (348). In a phrase mimetic of Allende's initial address to her daughter—"Escucha, Paula, voy a contarte una historia" (11)—Paula tells her mother that she needs her help to die, not by physical but rather by psychological means. It is her mother, she says, who keeps her from leaving this life, since she is the only one who does not accept the fact that she will never return to what she was before. She recalls some of the happy times she and her mother had shared, as well as the brief contentment she and her husband (Ernesto) had experienced. As Paula is reiterating her plea for release—"...que no me retengas más" (350)—the novelist's husband (Willie) exclaims: "¡Despierta, estás llorando dormida! ... Despierta, despierta, es una pesadilla..." (350). Allende's response is indicative of her special approach to reality. Shoving her husband away when he turns on the light, she states: "Paula me sonríe y me hace una señal de adiós con la mano antes de alejarse por el pasillo con su camisa blanca flotando como alas y sus pies descalzos rozando apenas la alfombra. *Junto a mi cama quedan sus zapatillas de piel de conejo* (350; emphasis mine).

The second example whereby Paula communicates in another way is in a letter which she had written on her honeymoon with the directive that it should be read after her death. It is a missive that transforms the work into an even more poignant metareality. Without knowing it, Paula was "writing her own story," as evinced by the following excerpt: "'*No quiero permanecer atrapada en mi cuerpo* [a premonition of comatose state that preceded her death]. *Liberada de él podré acompañar de más cerca a los que amo, aunque estén en los cuatro extremos del planeta*'" (355). Continuing her letter, Paula describes how she wishes to be cremated and her ashes scattered "en la naturaleza" (355). After explaining the disposition of her savings account—to be used for food or education for children—she reiterates her love for her husband. She then asks that her parents, her brother (Nicolás), and her grandparents remember her. Finally, she writes: "*"No me olviden y ¡alegren esas caras! Acuérdense que los espíritus ayudamos, acompañamos y protegemos mejor a quienes están contentos. Los amo mucho. Paula"*" (356).

Both these examples raise questions as well as illuminate Allende's special approach to reality. Is Paula's conversation with her mother solely an example of magical realism, a narrative discourse that partially characterized Allende's first novel, *La casa de los espíritus?* Are readers correct in assuming that Paula actually wrote a letter that anticipated her untimely death?[9]

Whether the vision of her daughter was a dream, a figment of her imagination, or even a genuine parapsychological event, its magical realist quality serves to further illustrate the metareality of this novel wherein a stylistic device intimately associated with human lives produces a visible expression of the reality of a mother suffering the death of a child. Similarly the prescient letter becomes a visible sign of dual realities: one whereby people have been known to predict the circumstances of their death, and the other, exemplifying a mother's attempt to cope with Paula's illness and death.[10]

*Paula* is more than the sum of its various discursive voices. Through Allende's seamless blending of her own artistic authorial voice with the previously described discursive voices, she has created a unique work, a "metarealistic narrative" with a strong relationship to the novelesque. Using Bakhtin's theory of the novel as a point of departure for my theory on the originality of the Chilean writer's latest book, I have proposed that all of the generic modes utilized by the author are paradigmatic of the author's intentionality. First, the very structures of these narrative forms have provided the framework for the order Allende wished to restore both for herself and her daughter. Secondly, the multigeneric voices' inherent predisposition towards the narration of the human condition essentially reflect the story Allende recounted in the context of a personal tragedy. Paraphrasing again Hutcheon's previously cited definition of metafiction (cited above), this metarealistic narrative is *reality* about *reality*, that is *reality* that includes within itself a commentary on its own *verisimilitude* or *accuracy*. The author has created this unique discursive mode in the way she has utilized an especially dialogic body of generic forms recognized as authentic expressions of human experience to relate a reality which intricately combined art with actual events.

Although Isabel Allende has exposed herself in the very personal nature of this narrative, it is appropriate to add that, in a sense, it was Paula who co-authored the book, not only because she inspired it, but because of the even more intimate relationship into which mother and daughter were subsumed. In the concluding section of the epilogue, Allende wrote: "...soy Paula y también soy yo misma, soy nada y todo lo demás en esta vida y otras vidas, inmortal" (366). Allende feels totally united with her daughter, who has passed into eternity. Allende is the author/mother to whom Paula owes both her real and metarealistic existence, and also her immortality. Conversely, Paula's life and immortality are signs of Allende's real and metarealistic modes of existence; "Paula," as the real person and the metareal entity, has redirected Allende's life in art and in reality.

Paula has been the inspiration for this metarealistic narrative, and based on Isabel Allende's final words to her daughter, she will now join the ranks of those first "spirits" who helped her write *La casa de los espíritus*: "Adiós, Paula, mujer,/Bienvenida, Paula, espíritu" (366).

## NOTES

1. Recent books by Gold and Herman discuss the issue of realism.

2. According to the *Merck Manual*, there are various forms of this disease. The particular kind that Allende's daughter suffered appears to have been Erythropoietic Uroporphyria and Günther's Disease and is a "recessively transmitted hereditary disorder characterized by severe cutaneous lesions on exposed areas of the body, hemolytic anemia, and large amounts of uroporphyrin in the urine" (Berkow and Fletcher 992). Both Paula's father and her brother were diagnosed as having the genetic disorder, as Allende writes in this work and is quoted as saying (Mujica 38).

3. One might mention other examples of the elegiac form, such as Jorge Manrique's famous "Coplas por la muerte de su padre." The *tú* of Allende's lament corresponds more to the intense personal tone of the last portion of "Llanto por Ignacio Sánchez Mejías" entitled "Alma ausente."

4. This is a succinct summary of her life from adolescence up to the present time of the novel. The cryptic reference to the "joven frívola ... con plumas de avestruz" refers to an episode of investigative reporting during which Allende interviewed for a job as a dancer to find out about the exploitation of young women for a nude dance review (195–99).

5. The description of testimonial literature used here is a synthesis of definitions appearing in Gugelberger, specifically those by John Beverley, Marc Zimmerman, and George Yúdice. The use of the testimonial has characterized much of Allende's work, as explained by Moody 39–43; Otero treats a related subject (61–67).

6. One could argue that this might be one of the most effective ways to write history. Pure facts often obscure the basic humanity of humankind's story and fail to emphasize the spiritual and mythical qualities of a person's or a people's odyssey through time. Hayden White treats this question. Specifically germane to the discussion at hand is the "fictive element" he finds in historical accounts, a statement widely criticized by fellow historians.

7. For example, besides referring to all of her works by their titles, she writes that "La Meme," her grandmother was the inspiration for "...el personaje que más amo de todo los que aparecen en mis libros Clara, clarísima, clarividente, en *La casa de los espíritus* (36–37). She includes episodes about the family's dog named "Pelvina López-Pun," which undoubtedly inspired "Barrabás" in *La casa* ... (65). The author's description of events after Pinochet's military coup relate to her novel *De amor y de sombra* (219–52), as well as her subsequently naming specific sources for her characters in *De amor...*; for example, she mentions a friend named Francisco, who served as a model for the protagonist of the same name. Two of her friends at the magazine where she worked inspired the character of Irene; and Gustavo Morante was based on a Chilean military officer she knew. Allende's statement regarding "Eva Luna" is also revealing: "Eva Luna dice al final de mi tercer libro *cuando escribo cuento la vida como me gustaría que fuera, como una novela*" (287, emphasis in the original). The examples proliferate throughout *Paula* with respect to the plot and characters of her novels and short stories (*Cuentos de Eva Luna*).

8. Allende has given numerous interviews, among them Linda Levine and Jo Anne Englebert, "The World Is Full of Stories," *Latin American Literature and Arts*, 34 (1985): 18–20; Michael Moody, "Una conversación con Isabel Allende," *Chasqui: Revista de Literatura Latinoamericana* 16.2–3 (1987): 51–58; Douglas Foster, "Isabel Allende Unveiled," *Mother Jones* 13.10 (1988) 42–46; Inés Dölz-Blackburn, "Interview with Isabel Allende," *Confluencia Revista Hispánica de Cultura y Literatura* 6.1 (1990): 93–104; Edith Dimo Gary, "Entrevista con Isabel Allende," *Alba de América*, 8.14–15 (1990): 331–43; and Jacqueline Cruz et al, "Entrevista a Isabel Allende," *Mester* 20.2 (1991) 127–34.

9. According to Mujica (41), as well as a speech given by Allende on February 20, 1997 at a symposium on Latin American Women Writers at Agnes Scott College (Decatur, Georgia), which I attended, Paula did in fact write the letter.

10. In her attempt to comprehend the tragedy of her daughter's death, Allende used another discursive voice within the context of the work, one which is paradigmatic of Paula's story: the fairy tale. Allende relates this fairy tale to "don Manuel," a patient in the room with her daughter. In it she tells of a princess who had been showered with gifts by her fairy godmothers but who, at the same time, had been cursed by an evil sorcerer who had placed "una bomba de tiempo en su cuerpo, antes que su madre pudiera impedirlo" (61). Everyone had forgotten about it until the daughter was twenty-eight years of age at which time, the bomb exploded and "la muchacha se sumió en un sueño tan profundo como la muerte" (61). Like the traditional fairy tale it is a fictional account containing an essential truth.

## WORKS CITED

Allende, Isabel. *La casa de los espíritus*. Barcelona: Plaza & Janés, 1982.

———. *Cuentos de Eva Luna*. Buenos Aires: Sudamericana, 1990.

———. *De amor y de sombra*. Barcelona: Plaza & Janés, 1984.

———. *Eva Luna*. Mexico City: Edivisión, 1988.

———. *Paula*. Barcelona, Plaza & Janés, 1994.

———. *El plan infinito*. Buenos Aires: Sudamericana, 1991.

Bakhtin, M.M. *The Dialogic Imagination: Four Essays*. Trans. Caryl Emerson and M. Holquist. Ed. Michael Holquist. Austin and London: U of Texas P, 1981.

Berkow, Robert, and Andrew J. Fletcher, eds. *The Merck Manual of Diagnosis and Therapy*. Rahway, NJ: Merck, Sharp & Dohme Research Laboratories, 1987.

Cruz, Jacqueline, et al. "Entrevista a Isabel Allende." *Mester* 20.2 (1991): 127–43.

Dölz-Blackburn, Inés. "Interview with Isabel Allende," *Confluencia: Revista Hispánica de Cultura y Literatura* 6.1 (1990): 93–104.

Foster, Douglas. *Mother Jones* 13.10 (1988): 42–46.

Gary, Edith Dimo. "Entrevista con Isabel Allende." *Alba de América* 8.14–15 (1990): 331–43.

Gold, Hazel. *The Reframing of Realism: Galdós and the Discourses of the Nineteenth-Century Spanish Novel*. Durham and London: Duke UP, 1993.

Gugelberger, Georg M., ed. *The Real Thing: Testimonial Discourse and Latin America*. Durham and London: Duke UP, 1996.

Herman, Luc. *Concept of Realism*. Columbia, SC: Camden House, 1996.

Hutcheon, Linda. *Narcissistic Narrative: The Metafictional Paradox*. Waterloo, Ontario, Canada: Wilfred Laurier UP, 1980.

Levine, Linda and Jo Anne Engelbert. "The World is Full of Stories." *Latin American Literature and Arts* 34 (1985): 18–20.

Moody, Michael. "Una conversación con Isabel Allende." *Chasqui: Revista de Literatura Latinoamericana* 16.2–3 (1987): 51–58.

———. "Isabel Allende and the Testimonial Novel." *Confluencia: Revista Hispánica de Cultura y Literature* 2.1 (1986): 39–43.

Mujica, Barbara, "The Life Force of Language." *Americas* 47.6 (1995): 36–43.

Otero, José. "La historia como ficción en *Eva Luna* de Isabel Allende." *Confluencia: Revista Hispánica de Cultura y Literatura* 6.1 (1990): 61–67.

White, Hayden, "The Historical Text as Literary Artifact." *Tropics of Discourse*. Baltimore and London: John Hopkins UP, 1978. 81–100.

CAROLYN PINET

# Choosing Barrabás: Dog as Text & Text as Dog in Isabel Allende's La casa de los espíritus

## TEXT AS PUZZLE

In the beginning of *La casa de los espíritus*, the child Clara writes herself and her magical dog into being in the only sentence that is quoted directly from her notebooks, "Barrabás llegó a la familia por vía marítima" (9) by her granddaughter, Alba, fifty years later. Already a text exists within a text: Alba's, and hers within another text: Allende's. *La casa de los espíritus* is a gathering of texts.[1] Alba makes this clear at the end of the story in the Epilogue when she says that she and her grandfather have pieced the story together from "los cuadernos de Clara, las cartas de mi madre, los libros de administración de las Tres Marías y tantos otros documentos ..." (379), that is, so many fragments that she assembled to make a whole and in order to find meaning.

Text as puzzle is an apt starting point for Allende's method of plotting narratives. Characters tell stories, image stories and write stories throughout the novel. How are we to take these stories? Do they compete with one another in any way? Does Allende privilege one form of story over others? Further, how does she deal with the "master narrative," the official story imposed by the Chilean church and state?

From *Hispanófila* 123 (May 1998): 55–65. © 1998 by University of North Carolina. Reprinted by permission.

*La casa de los espíritus* is first a history of a family in Chile and includes very
specific historical events, particularly those dealing with the rise and fall of
Salvador Allende and the coming to power of General Pinochet.
Contemporary historiographers generally recognize that history cannot give
us a conclusive version of "what happened." It comes to us through
documents of various kinds; also through oral retelling. We do not have
direct access to the events themselves. Consequently we have to recognize
that history is a shifting set of narratives. Roland Barthes has said, "Historical
discourse does not follow the real—rather it only signifies it" (Finke 23).[2]
What we traditionally called hard "historical fact" is often what remained
after a kind of pruning or even suppression of competing versions of reality.
How does a novelist, then, deal with this competition of discourses in order
to write a narrative and bring order out of chaos? Michel Serre has suggested
that the linear representation of historical narrative does not take in the
complexity of events. He further asserts that competing discourses cause the
"noise" of the text.[3] Therefore, a narrative about the past must emerge as
distinct from background noise, that is from details that are judged marginal
or irrelevant. The feminist critic, Laurie Finke, argues however that "noise"
must be central to any narrative that attempts to encompass the complexity
of past events. Her goal in criticism is to "fore-ground that which has been
defined as noise and then marginalized or excluded as nonmeaningful, to
make complex that which has traditionally been considered as 'true' or
'factual'" (25). This is a very fruitful approach to a consideration of Allende's
novel which is an attempt to conjure up the past in a variety of ways with an
array of materials. Her novel begins with reminiscence, a form of
remembering which has been dismissed by many historiographers (who
prefer numbers and graphs) as a subjective and unreliable way to record
events. After mentioning the mythical dog Barrabás, who came to the child
Clara from the sea, Allende has Alba continue:

> Ya entonces tenía el hábito de escribir las cosas importantes y más
> tarde, cuando se quedó muda, escribía también las trivialidades,
> sin sospechar que cincuenta años después, sus cuadernos me
> servirían para rescatar la memoria del pasado y para sobrevivir a
> mi propio espanto. (9)

Is Barrabás important or just a trivial detail in a reminiscence text? He comes
to Clara on the Thursday of Holy Week (9). He is released from a cage to
her as Barrabas, the thief and murderer was released to the people by Pilate.
He remains with her throughout her childhood until the day of her formal

bethrothal to an older man when he is mysteriously butchered and consigned to oblivion just as the original Barrabás was mentioned and then forgotten by the apostolic text that recounts the story of Jesus. Yet Allende's circular narrative begins and ends with Barrabás. Her story is linear and, in some respects, quite conventional; it is only later that Alba sees that the linear is transcended and Barrabás reinstated in the last line of the book (380). From the beginning of the novel Allende shows herself to be conscious of the problems of a writer who is trying to reclaim her past, of the shifting narratives and interpretations, of the stòries jostling for recognition, of the topsy-turvy nature of interpretation which may or may not privilege the "important" over the "trivial."[4] What is more, as a woman not only on the margins of her own society but exiled from it, she must conjure a text into being: a text which reflects the ambiguities of her position as woman and writer both within and outside the mostly male Chilean tradition. Barrabás, then, I propose, is a cypher for the text that attempts to represent "noise" as competing narratives; also to make the marginal central and to reinstate the "trivial" (background) as foreground.

Doris Meyer, in her article "Parenting the Text: Female Creativity and Dialogic Relationships in Isabel Allende's *La casa de los espíritus*," discussed lucidly the way in which the double-voiced discourse—the collaborative story of Alba and her grandfather Trueba—"subverts the historical stereotypes" of the past (Meyer 361) while at the same time using and exploring them. As she asserts, Allende effectively "parents" her text, thinking back through both the mothers and fathers.[5] I will further explore the various ways she does this through Finke's expanded concept of "noise." "Noise," she points out, is invariably feminine. An attempt to give "noise" a place involves putting it into a female discourse. Further Finke asserts that, in order to subvert the official discourse, women have routinely practiced poaching: that is, they have used "any method at hand to wrest their own meaning from patriarchal cultural practices designed to keep them in their places" (Finke 25).[6] Consequently, a study of Allende's narrative puzzle is a study of a series of strategies she uses to raise questions about the "official story" and so-called "definitive interpretations."

## POACHING AND THE MASTER NARRATIVE

Allende makes it clear from the start that the official story, that of church and state, is to be challenged. In an apocalyptic passage Clara, the young child, enters the space where women are supposed to be covered and silent (St. Paul) and commits a double blasphemy when she questions the Jesuit priest,

Father Restrepo's fire-and-brimstone tirade: "–¡Pst! ¡Padre Restrepo! Si el cuento del infierno fuera pura mentira, nos chingamos todos ... (14)". The disingenuous child confronts this bastion of patriarchy head-on and is consigned to the devil, "¡Soberbia endemoniada!" (14). How will she survive in a patriarchal, conservative Chile? How will she plot herself?

Allende endows Clara with special powers from early on: she is clairvoyant. Her gifts of prophecy are encouraged and developed by her magical Uncle Marcos who is similarly endowed and who figures in her life as a heroic adventurer/inventor/magician/storyteller. Marcos represents that stage in the history and mythology of the New World when it was being "discovered" by European explorers and chroniclers. Both he and Clara move between the oral and written word in a continuous ebb-and-flow, between Marcos's magic books, his tales of his adventures told to Clara and the messages that Clara would whisper to Marcos that he in turn would transmit to the ear of a client seeking a fortune, but embellished with words of his own. Allende records the free flow of "information" and its ambiguities and the sense of power the child derives from the spoken and written word in relation to the future as well as to the past. She also shows (as García Márquez did in *Cien años de soledad*) that from early on the marvellous was always an integral part of the real. Clara, absorbing this; will pass on an invaluable legacy through the daughters: she will "poach" from the Latin American story what was always hers. Barrabás, the magical dog, will be part of that legacy.

Clara's sister Rosa poaches in a different way because she is relatively silent. However, she is equally inspired by the magical and the marvellous and reproduces this inspiration in a series of beasts on an endless tablecloth (12-13). Again one thinks of the early chronicles and medieval pictures of fantastic and fabulous creatures. What is more interesting is that Rosa does not merely reproduce these images but creates and improvises her own: "Comenzó con perros, gatos y mariposas, pero pronto la fantasía se apoderó de su labor y fue apareciendo un paraíso de bestias imposibles que nacían de su aguja ..." (13). In this way she is like Clara who also improvises when she prophesies. But Rosa and her plot are obliterated by the political enemies of her father who poison her by mistake. The brutal patriarchal political plot annihilates the magical daughter. Rosa's "story" then survives as noise in the historical and linear story of Chile's political history. Allende retrieves her story and at the same time shows that it is at best irrelevant to the powerful oligarchy. At worst it is dangerous: magical women have always been perceived as plotting evil.

Clara, traumatized by Rosa's death, which she had predicted, chooses nine years of silence. Several critics have shown that this is a very fertile silence.[7] In fact during these years she tries out all kinds of plots for herself in rehearsal for later life. She reads voraciously both magic books and party documents. She expands her power over dreams and prophecies, giving readings and interpretations which she writes down. She also writes in her notebooks that bear witness to life. Here she records "important events and trivialities" and the story her mother Nivea tells her about the family. One might say Clara is learning her art and craft of adulthood survival. Certainly she makes no distinction between the "real" and the "magical" in her appetite for knowledge. Her other great childhood loss is the death of her Uncle Marcos but she is compensated for this by her beloved Barrabás who turns up in his place. Barrabás, mostly dog, is in fact a fabulous hybrid animal of indeterminate origin, a relative to one of Rosa's mythical creatures embroidered on the tablecloth: "La gente lo creía una cruza de perro con yegua, suponía que podían aparecerle alas, cuernos y un aliento sulfuroso de dragón, como las bestias que bordaba Rosa en su interminable mantel" (25).

Barrabás is destined to die rather as Rosa did: mysteriously and suddenly. He dies at the moment Clara is betrothed to her future husband, Esteban Trueba, whom she intends to marry without love. If that is not enough Trueba has him split down the middle and made into a rug. Clara faints in horror and the hide is removed and shoved into a corner of the basement with the magic books of Uncle Marcos where "... se defendió de las polillas y del abandono con una tenacidad digna de mejor causa, hasta que otras generaciones lo rescataron" (91). This is not the last of Barrabás, as Allende indicates. For the moment the "noise" of Barrabás is suppressed, but Allende (and Alba) will return to celebrate him. Barrabás turns out not merely to be the trivial plaything of Clara's childhood or an amusing invention of hers and her uncle. He must die to be reborn, recovered and retold because he is the last piece placed in order to make the puzzle whole and comprehensible.

## THE PLOT THICKENS

Clara's daughter, Blanca, commits the unpardonable sin of falling in love with a peasant, Pedro Tercero, who becomes a revolutionary. What is more, she actively contributes to his education by taking him the magical books of Uncle Marcos which he devours whole. But it is from old Pedro, Pedro Tercero's grandfather, that the two hear the most potent story of all, that of the Fox and the Hens, which reverses the traditional story of the oppressed by having the hens gang up on the Fox and chase him out (128). The written magical stories of Uncle Marcos serve to educate Pedro Tercero to literacy, but the oral tale of the Fox and the Hens is the one story he believes will change his history and that of his oppressed class. Pedro Tercero has not yet left his village and come into contact with another powerful story, that of Karl Marx in his *Communist Manifesto*, but the tale circulating in the village vividly anticipates it and, in addition, possesses the hallucinatory quality of the oral re-telling. Allende demonstrates the potential power of an oppressed group of people through their own tradition and voice. She also shows how the sign may shift in a story according to who claims the voice, thus threatening the official power structure. Blanca can be said to poach this concept. In fact Blanca is a genius at appropriating earlier texts and using them to her advantage. She does it all her life when she fashions her own extraordinary creatures out of clay after the manner of Rosa's tablecloth (156). Clara puts this down to a genetic memory at work in the women of the family which saves these creative activities from oblivion. Blanca also retells Uncle Marcos's magic stories to her daughter Alba. In this case she "forgets" the originals and transforms and inverts these stories as a matter of course, assigning all the heroic actions to the female characters. Alba is inspired to write them down to preserve them (269). In this way the earlier stories are reinterpreted and passed on in their new form. Blanca has in her own way rescued "noise," having learned this from her mother, her lover and his grandfather; she presides over "parented texts."

## THE HOUSE AS TEXT

The huge, pretentious house that Esteban Trueba builds for Clara is a metaphor for how women have poached in order to reclaim their space. The house is traditionally where Latin American women hold sway. Yet at first Clara has no interest in it, although later she becomes its mainstay. Trueba constructs the house as a reflection of himself and his prestige; it is meant to symbolize the beauty and order of western civilization as conceived by the ruling oligarchy who in their false snobbery imitated the style of Europe and North America. However, later Clara changes and improves on this house/text and transforms it into an "enchanted labyrinth." She makes the house more "feminine" and "Chilean" in her own way and in her own time. In this house Alba, her granddaughter, learns to read and write through newspapers and the magic books that survive in the basement. Here she constructs her world through games and painting, assembling her own possible texts while in touch with the magical components of the family's past, including Barrabás (239-40). She paints a fresco which resembles her Aunt's tablecloth and her mother's clay creatures (240). The house, while suggesting the space of a text, itself contains texts like a Chinese box puzzle. Eventually, Alba paints a large pink heart in the last empty space on the fresco and says goodbye to childhood (283). What texts do we abandon, then, in "growing up"? In particular we must ask this about Clara.

## CLARA: THE LONG CHILDHOOD

In many respects Clara refuses to grow up. The movement of her life is an ebb and flow between being a detached, ethereal creature of the spirits and a practical pragmatic woman who is a survivor of earthly calamities. The late portrait of her in a rocking-chair suspended above the floor suggests the movement back and forth between different dimensions and roles in her life. It has been suggested that Clara is forced to "grow up" as her spirit world is overtaken by the realities of the political climate and history. Does Allende kill Clara off with this is mind? Yet after her death the house goes into a decline and the text and texture of Trueba's family life deteriorates. But Clara's room remains intact and it is here the notebooks survive, although out of order (263).

Chile is in ferment. The messages of Karl Marx on the one hand and of the entrenched oligarchy on the other are polarizing the country into opposing camps. But; says a spokesperson for the oligarchy, Marxism won't make it on Chilean soil; it doesn't allow for the magical side of things (272). He is wrong in the short term, right in the long.

As history appears to overtake myth, ghosts wander through the house. Yet while the history of Chile builds to a series of galvanizing events, the house retains its ability to undergo further metamorphoses. While the old magical attraction of the place survives in the basement where Alba conducts her love affair, history—the political events of the 60s and 70s—starts to seep in. Salvador Allende comes to power in Chile in 1973, the first Marxist president ever to be legally elected. The initial euphoria is replaced by disaster when the country is further polarized between left and right. At this point Allende does not pretend to concur with the "official story" later put out by a military dictatorship and a censored press. On the contrary, she tells the story of how Allende's government was essentially sabotaged by the Chilean oligarchy in collaboration with the U.S. government of Nixon and

Kissinger. Clearly, the "growing up" that takes place in the house has to do with a choice of text: the best one to convey the story of contemporary Chile when the novel's characters are inexorably drawn into the master narrative. However, this does not necessarily mean that other textual possibilities have been permanently abandoned.

The house becomes a battleground as the family fights over its space. The political joins forces with the personal and Allende has us witness the tensions between ideologies and generations. Esteban Trueba hides arms there for the right; Alba and her Uncle Jaime cart them off and bury them. Blanca hoards provisions as the shortage of goods grows; Alba gives them away to the needy. Blanca sequesters her lover, Pedro Tercero, in a room in the house. Alba uses the abandoned wing to hide political refugees of the left and then gets them out of the country. Gradually space becomes assigned differently (346-47): the house is taken over by Alba and by Clara's ghost while Trueba is marooned and isolated in three rooms. Thus, what had essentially become Clara's before her death is poached back by her and her granddaughter and reclaimed. Alba, who has been catapulted into political activism, uses the traditionally domestic space for political purposes. Of course she is punished for it. She is the "bad girl" who oversteps the margins of class and gender and violates the "master text."[8] Her "noise" is the worst kind, so she is taken away as a dangerous political prisoner to submit to the sadism and revenge of Esteban García, the illegitimate grandson of her grandfather.

What we can say about the above scenario is that the house, in its space, harbors both linear history and myth and that "foreground" and "background" are constantly in competition. First Clara's ghost and memory are marginalized as noise, as is Alba's childhood, even her clandestine love-affair, while the chronology of history takes over the foreground. However, by the end of the book, the house is again full of magic and Clara walks freely through all the rooms.

## MORE NOISE: RETURN OF BARRABÁS

Alba is forced to live through a revenge plot because she is caught in the "master narrative." When she is on the verge of death her grandmother, Clara, appears to her and suggests a new text. As the critic Gerald Martin points out, this text is to be a testimony so that, to paraphrase Clara's words to Alba, people who would like to would not be able to deny what had happened during the Terror and after in Chile.[9] At that time Alba exists in a topsy-turvey world where ordinary words have lost their familiar meaning (355). She must restore sanity to herself and the world through writing in her mind. In the concentration camp, inspired by Clara and by the women who want their stories told too, who sing with her to survive, she starts by singing and then by telling all their stories. Ana Díaz, a woman in the movement, who had earlier put down upper class bourgeoise woman, is the one who places a notebook and pencil in her hand. For a time in the camp she is both telling and writing stories. On her return to the house and reunion with her grandfather, he urges her to write the story the reader is reading so that if she has to leave the country she can always take her roots with her (378). Their collaboration crosses generations, gender and the barrier between history and myth. It also involves a transformation.

If noise is feminine, then Allende re-instates the feminine in new ways by poaching from the "master narrative" and by adding to it and transmuting it. That is, she tells a chronological narrative which is constantly interrupted and refracted by "noise," by plots that challenge the revenge story and by the possibility of a text that will remake the future as well as the past: Alba's future and the future of Chile. With her apparently conventional text she actually proposes an alternative story or stories.

At the end of the novel Barrabás is re-instated. Alba and Trueba rescue him from the basement, "soberbio en su indefinible constitución biológica" (371), and put him down as a rug upstairs in Clara's room. Barrabás reappears to show us he is indestructible and immortal; he is the cypher that survives as "noise" and, having been assigned for years to the background, he is restored to the foreground. He is the key to the revenge story and to its alternatives. He had originally been taken into the house as a substitute for Marcos, the magician, and had been killed in a bloody and gratuitous act of violence. Somehow he has survived. As Allende has commented, the magical side of Chile is impossible to kill. Barrabás is both Chile's history and beyond Chile's history. His "indefinible constitución biológica" denotes a text that seeks to create an ambiguous and indefinable reality.

Allende chooses to begin and end her text, that of the novel, with Clara's words about Barrabás. What is curious about this choice is that a few years after Allende's novel appeared, General Pinochet, Chile's dictator of fifteen years, stood before the people on October 25, 1988, and asked them to choose between him and Barrabas: "Don't forget that in the history of the world, there was a plebiscite, in which Christ and Barrabas were being judged, and the people chose Barrabas."[10] In his mind, Pinochet was asking the people to choose between himself (the chosen Savior, a Christ figure) and Barrabas (the anti-Christ, murderer and thief). He attempted to assume power over the official story by a gross distortion in giving himself the role of "protector of democracy," whereas of course Barrabas (the opposition in Chile) represented all that threatened "democracy": the "Evil Empire," "communism," etc. But the Chilean people refused to go along with this manichean version of reality or to concur with Pinochet's "master narrative." They elected "Barrabas" in the guise of the Christian Democrat Patricio Aylwin, whom they believed would guarantee an orderly and legal return to civilian government. A majority of Chilean women cast the "No" vote against Pinochet in the plebiscite of 1988.[11]

Isabel Allende has commented that the Pinochet Dictatorship was an aberration for Chile and that it could not endure. The polarization caused by the master narrative had produced a situation that was, to her, inconceivable. Alba and Esteban perceive this as they piece together the puzzle: the revenge story will not do as a master text, not for the right or the left. At the end of the novel Clara's spirit permeates the house; it informs and inhabits a space where dualities and polarities are erased. Thus also with Barrabás's return meaning is wrested from the past to inform and shape present and future. The dog emerges from the mechanical, linear narrative as beginning and end in the timeless circle of Allende's making; yet the circle is open because he is both the last piece and the first, within and beyond the text and patriarchal system, just as Allende herself is. His is the trivial, magical tale that is finally endowed with significance amid the laughter of the cosmos. The "noise" of Barrabás is the "noise" of the dispossessed in Chile who finally find a voice, of the women who will survive no matter who governs and the power of the dialogic text that is actually the place of many voices and many stories which are constantly being revised, restated, and restored. As we read Clara's words quoted by the pregnant Alba, telling of the dog's arrival and the last piece of the puzzle falls into place, we experience the paradox and irony of text and anti-texts in retelling and prophecy and we glimpse the possibility of a new beginning.

## NOTES

1.  Isabel Allende commented in a 1989 interview: "The novel is a magic trunk where everything fits: poetry, essays, testimonies, fantasies, documentaries, everything! Through it we can give fictional order to chaos and find a key to the labyrinth of history" (16).

2.  I am indebted to Laurie Finke's analysis of Roland Barthes and Michel Serre in her book, *Feminist Theory, Women's Writing*, where she

demonstrates how French contemporary criticism may be adapted to include both the historical moment and a feminist perspective.

3.  Laurie Finke discussed Michel Serre's theory of "noise" and Alice Jardine's use of the term "alterity" to show how "noise" is invariably feminine. A critical approach to a novel such as Allende's will therefore involve "an exploration of the cultural and historical specificity of oppression, resistance, co-optation and subversion which marks writing by and about women" (26).

4.  Isabel Allende commented in 1991 that the novel is a "gigantic tapestry in which everything is mixed in together and some things are topsy-turvy" (29).

5.  Doris Meyer draws on a comprehensive list of European and American critics (notably Jean Franco and Elaine Showalter) to examine the blending of two narrative voices, that of Alba and her grandfather Trueba in Allende's "metatext." She shows clearly how, in this process, that which is marginalized becomes foregrounded when she comments "the muted voice (Alba) has become the dominant one in the novel" (361).

6.  Laurie Finke's concept of "poaching" is an extremely useful one in assessing the writing of a novelist who has to confront the power of the patriarchal voice in a Latin American dictatorship such as that of Chile 1973-1990.

7.  Sandra Boschetto and Doris Meyer, to name two.

8.  Alba is only one example of this phenomenon. Argentinian women, filmed for the *Americas* series (PBS) after the Dirty War, who had been raped and tortured, commented that they were perceived as "bad" and deserving of punishment because they had broken all the rules and acted "against nature" as women.

9.  Gerald Martin discussed the importance of writing as testimony for Allende in a 1989 book on Latin American fiction (353).

10. This is a translation of part of a speech which appeared in the Chilean newspaper, *La Época*, October 26, 1988.

11. This is documented by Peter Winn in his book, *Americas* and by Tina Rosenberg in her essay on Chile in *Children of Cain*.

## Works Cited

Allende, Isabel. *La casa de los espíritus*. Barcelona: Plaza and Janes, 1982.

―――. *Interviews With Latin American Writers*. Marie-Lise Gazarián Gautier. Dalkey Archive P, 1989. 7-24.

―――. *Women Writers of Latin America*. Magdalena García Pinto. U of Texas P, 1991, 23-42.

Boschetto, Sandra M. "Dialéctica metatextual y sexual en *La casa de los espíritus de Isabel Allende*." *Hispania* 72 (1989): 526-32.

Constable, Pamela and Arturo Valenzuela. *A Nation of Enemies. Chile Under Pinochet*. New York: W. W. Norton & Co., 1993. 296.

Finke, Laurie A. *Feminist Theory, Women's Writing*. Eds. Shari Benstock and Celeste Schenck. Ithaca and London: Cornell UP, 1992.

Franco, Jean. *Plotting Women. Gender and Representation in Mexico*. New York: Columbia UP, 1989.

Martin, Gerald. *Journeys through the Labyrinth. Latin American Fiction in the Twentieth Century*. New York and London: Verso, 1989. 351-55.

Meyer, Doris. "'Parenting the Text': Female Creativity and Dialogic Relationships in Isabel Allende's *La casa de los espíritus*." *Hispania* 73 (1990): 360-65.

Rosenberg, Tina. *Children of Cain. Violence and the Violent in Latin America*. New York: Viking Penguin, 1992, 333-87.

Winn, Peter. *Americas*. New York: Pantheon Books, 1992. 313-45.

CAROLINE BENNETT

# The Other and the Other-Worldly: The Function of Magic in Isabel Allende's La casa de los espíritus

Latin American fiction in the magical realist style, despite its authors' expressed desire to find a voice for oppressed people, frequently adopts a patriarchal tone, ignoring the role of women in society. The popular Chilean novelist, Isabel Allende, attempts to redress the balance by exploring women's colonization and repression by patriarchy, and the means by which they endeavour to resist the oppressive, dominant ideologies in which they are inscribed. Allende's best-known novel, *La casa de los espíritus*, charts the lives of four female generations of the upper-class del Valle family, starting with Nívea, then Clara, Blanca and Alba, covering the period from around the turn of the century to 1975.[1] Although Chile is not named as such, the story is obviously set there. A series of parallels with Chile's turbulent history and with the dramatic story of Allende's own family[2] reveals to the reader that this is a legitimate frame of reference.[3] Politics initially form a backdrop, but as the story progresses they move into the foreground. The dominant male is the tyrannical patriarch, landowner and senator Esteban Trueba, husband of Clara, and father and grandfather of Blanca and Alba respectively. In piecing together the story Alba, the principal narrator, emphasizes the constructed nature of history; she uses the notebooks of Clara, which 'bear witness to life', along with her own memories and first-person interpolations from Esteban himself in his later years. Alba's clearly stated intention is to

From *Bulletin of Hispanic Studies* LXXV (no. 3) (July 1998): 357-365. ©1998 by Liverpool University Press. Reprinted by permission.

ensure that their history is saved from obscurity, presumably so that their story is told to subsequent generations, who will not have to reconstruct the female consciousness gained painfully by the del Valle women.

In *La casa de los espíritus* Allende depicts a number of female characters who have, in varying degrees, an ability to connect with what we may in the West call the preternatural world.[4] This raises questions, which are the subject of this article, about the subtext of the novel, especially the possible implication that women are more intuitive, sensitive and prone to experiences beyond mere rationality than men. As far back as the Middle Ages the supernatural was thought to be caused by hysteria.[5] Hysteria, an etymologically intriguing word if ever there was one, is derived from the Greek word for uterus, *hystera*, showing clearly the emphasis on a connection between women and irrationality. Of course, the term hysteria is not explicitly foregrounded in *La casa de los espíritus* but, as is apparent in the recent controversial research of Elaine Showalter,[6] hysteria is just one way in which women's psychic conflicts can manifest themselves; magic is Allende's symbolic way of representing this in a positive and non-destructive manner. The range of preternatural incidents is narrower than in many other magical realist texts, such as Gabriel García Márquez's *Cien años de soledad*, to which it is often compared. The principal means by which magic manifests itself in the novel is through Clara's clairvoyance, in all its permutations. She can read dreams, predict the future, recognize people's intentions and move objects by means of telekinesis. Her prescience shows itself at an early age. For example, at the age of six Clara correctly predicts the riding accident of Luis, her brother. The preternatural gradually fades as the story progresses, and some critics, such as P. Gabrielle Foreman, have argued that Allende abandons it as 'magical realism gives way in the end to political realism'.[7] This view suggests that political realism (whatever that is) is preferable to magical realism and that the latter is, by implication, not political. This is surely a misreading given that magical realism is amongst the most highly politicized of recent writing. Politics do not have to be worn solely as content on the sleeve; they can be present with greater subtlety in the symbols and structures of texts. Allende reveals an implicit understanding through the use of magic that the personal is the political.

Patricia Hart has coined the term 'magical feminism' to describe Allende's mode of fiction and defines it as 'magical realism employed in a femino-centric work, or one that is especially insightful into the status or condition of women in the context described in the work'.[8] She and others claim that Allende uses magic in her fiction to demonstrate a truth about the female condition for feminist purposes. Hart examines Clara's clairvoyance and convincingly concludes that her capabilities do not produce any hugely beneficial results for anyone, but neither are they harmful. Often, she is unable to protect her family from political or natural disaster, either because they ignore her predictions, or because her clairvoyance fails at crucial times. For example, when Clara is still a child, we are told:

> Predijo la hernia de su padre, todos los temblores de tierra y otras alteraciones de la naturaleza, la única vez que cayó nieve en la capital matando de frío a los pobres en las poblaciones y a los rosales en los jardines de los ricos, y la identidad del asesino de las colegialas, mucho antes que la policía descubriera el segundo cadáver, pero nadie le creyó ... (74)

Although she correctly predicts a death in the family, which turns out to be that of the unfortunate Rosa, she is unable to say whose death it will be or how it will be brought about. Had she known that her father's political opponents would anonymously send a poisoned decanter of brandy the tragedy could have been averted. Hart recounts a number of similar instances and notes that Clara's ability has 'slight practical application'.[9] Not only is the 'relative uselessness' implied;[10] it is directly stated, as when the mysterious clairvoyant, Luisa Mora, comes to tell Alba:

> La muerte te anda pisando los talones. Tu abuela Clara te proteje desde el Más Allá, pero me mandó a decirte que los espíritus protectores son ineficaces en los cataclismos mayores. (322)

This raises the question of what use magic can possibly be if it cannot benefit or protect in any way those who have these special powers. Hart exposes Clara's clairvoyance to various metaphorical readings, suggesting that it could represent sensitivity, intuition or passivity. She favours the reading of clairvoyance as a metaphor for passivity as this is consistent with the 'submergence' of magic towards the end of the novel. It is certainly true that the women become progressively less passive and more politically active through the generations. Alba, for example, defies her grandfather and risks her life by smuggling refugees into embassies, so allowing them to escape persecution after the 1973 *coup* which overthrew the unnamed President Salvador Allende.

Magic is frequently debunked through the juxtaposition of the preternatural with the mundane. For instance, Clara invites friends to the house 'para invocar a los espíritus e intercambiar cábalas y recetas de cocina'

(115). During the Second World War Clara has only a vague idea of events in Europe, but she supports the Allies by knitting socks for the soldiers—a rather mundane form of assistance from a talented clairvoyant! This indicates that there is a certain degree of ironic and comical distancing in the tone of the narrative, although the magic is there in that it has a reality in the world of the text; it is not imaginary. Hart says: 'Isabel Allende may be, consciously or unconsciously, questioning the very morality of continuing to use magical realism as a dominant literary mode in Latin America.'[11] She suggests that Allende may be undermining the magical realist style, the very style within which she has situated herself, and puts forward the view that magical realism may at times be the 'opiate of the oppressed'.[12] Although Hart's analysis has much to recommend it, a rather different, albeit related, interpretation can be placed upon the role of magic in this novel. She is surely mistaken when she writes:

> Like miniatures, the magical touches produce a sense of pleasure when examined close up but they do not alter the overall picture of a novel any more than a miniature can have much impact on the overall decoration of a room.[13]

Similarly, P. Gabrielle Foreman says, 'Allende seems to employ a feminized magical realism as a technique to pull the reader into a political-historical novel ...',[14] implying that the magic is no more than a syrup which sweetens the bitter pill of worthy but unpalatable political history. However, the magical dimension is never a form of embellishment, but is an integral part of the novel. Neither is it a trivial enticement to the reader, since it serves a structural function. The magic does not evaporate because Allende has abandoned magical realism as a literary technique, but because magic represents the 'wild zone' to which some women have access when they are marginalized and powerless in society. Their psychic abilities do not enable the women to make great political changes, rather they are sustained in times of difficulty by the world of spirits; it provides them with a power base. Magic diminishes in the story when it no longer serves a useful social function for the women.

In her essay, 'Feminist criticism in the wilderness',[15] Elaine Showalter engages with the model developed by Shirley and Edwin Ardener, which shows in the form of a Venn diagram the overlapping spheres of men and women, or dominant and muted groups, respectively. This cultural model can assist in the interpretation of *La casa de los espíritus* since it posits the existence of a crescent of female experience unknown to men—the 'wild zone'—which is represented by magic in the novel. Magic can be viewed as either a mechanism for escaping madness, agoraphobia and paralysis, or it could be symptomatic of these conditions, an alternative to suffering and illness caused by the conflicts present in these women's lives. In this case it does provide an escape route, albeit a limited one. Some women have less effective methods of release. For example, Rosa, the beautiful, invents a 'zoológico de pesadilla' (13), which she endlessly embroiders on a tablecloth. She depicts

> bestias [...] mitad pájaro y mitad mamífero, cubiertas con plumas iridiscentes y provistas de cuernos y pezuñas, tan gordas y con alas tan breves, que desafiaban las leyes de la biología y de la aerodinámica. (12)

Blanca also has a similar outlet creating clay figures. In this way they are both able to release their energies in inventing fantastical menageries. They show a desire to represent creatures which transgress the boundaries of the natural world. Unlike Alba, they have neither the knowledge nor the education to allow them to channel their energies in any other way.

As the novel progresses the female characters who have the magical powers fade and Alba writes of the magical world which 'no longer exists'. Foreman observes:

> By the novel's close, Alba has little living access to her magical matrilineage. Only the memory of the magical survives, but this memory helps Alba to survive the penetration of the patrilineal political sphere.[16]

In Foreman's opinion 'the magic in Allende's world is swept away by the political cataclysm she describes'. The magic has been depressed, however, not so much by the political cataclysm, as by the feminist consciousness, emancipation and political commitment of the new generation represented by Alba and her fellow prisoner, Ana Díaz.

This 'wild zone' is rejected to some extent by Blanca and almost completely by Alba, as it signifies a withdrawal from the patriarchal world of business and politics. Withdrawal denotes submissiveness and inaction. It provides sanctuary, comfort, female solidarity, subversiveness, secrecy, but in the final analysis is ineffective at promoting change in the wider society. The limited nature of women's resistance can be seen when Clara is violently struck across the face by her husband, Esteban. She vows, in a classic symbolic female act of defiance, never to speak to him again. Hélène Cixous writes: 'Silence: silence is the mark of hysteria.'[17] Silence can be very powerfully semanticized. Showalter considers that women can risk 'self-destruction through psychic overload' or 'ego death' from a state of super 'receptive sensibility'. She notes that George Eliot observed this as 'the roar on the other side of silence'.[18] Esteban becomes exasperated and realizes he has lost Clara, but she does not leave him, so her muteness, whether willed or not, is hardly the ultimate in feminine rebellion. Although she now refuses to acknowledge the dominant patriarchal discourse, she is in danger of silencing herself out of existence. Despite her magnetic personality and charm she is politically resigned and, as Hart observes, seems to have strongly deterministic beliefs. Repeatedly, the reader sees that where Clara is re-active, Alba is pro-active; where Clara has an external locus of control, Alba has an internal locus of control; Clara offers passive resistance, Alba offers active resistance, and Blanca, the middle generation, hovers between the two. Allende recognizes this, at some level, and so for this reason the magic gradually fades from her novel.

If we focus on two characters and compare Clara, who has access to magic and Férula, who has not, the beneficial effect which magic exerts becomes evident. Férula, Esteban's sister, dedicates much of her life to nursing her bedridden mother. She is described as follows:

> Era todavía una bella mujer, de formas opulentas y rostro ovalado de madona romana, pero a través de su piel pálida con reflejos de durazno y sus ojos llenos de sombras, ya se adivinaba la fealdad de la resignación. Férula había aceptado el papel de enfermera de su madre. Dormía en la habitación contigua a la de doña Ester, dispuesta en todo momento a acudir corriendo a su lado a darle sus pócimas, ponerle la bacinilla, acomodarle las almohadas. Tenía un alma atormentada [...] Era de gestos bruscos y torpes, con el mismo mal carácter de su hermano, pero obligada por la vida, y por su condición de mujer, a dominarlo y a morder el freno. (44–45)

Those last few words, 'clamp down on the bit', speak volumes about her repression. She resents Esteban, whose 'libertad [...] a ella le dolía como un reproche, como una injusticia' (46). Whilst they are living under the same roof an intimate friendship develops between the two women. Clara is aware of Férula's strong affections, but oblivious to the subliminal sexual nature of her attachment. Esteban has a blazing row with Férula, when he says that she is coming between him and his wife with her 'artes de lesbiana' (121). The violence of his language serves to indicate his complete lack of understanding of his sister. If anyone could be accused of driving Clara crazy it would be Esteban himself. Clara is the only friend Férula has ever had and when they banish her from the house they never see her alive again. Years later, when she dies, they find her lying on her bed:

> Engalanada como reina austríaca, vestía un traje de terciopelo apolillado, enaguas de tafetán amarillo y sobre su cabeza, firmemente encasquetada, brillaba una increíble peluca rizada de cantante de ópera. (137)

Her bedroom looks like 'las bambalinas de una mísera compañía de teatro en gira' (136). Férula's exotic costumes provide a kind of outlet for her repressed desires. She does not have magic as a retreat, as Clara does. Nor has she a supportive network of family and friends. Her flamboyant clothes are an ineffective use of subversive energy, except significantly, as a form of self-preservation. Appearing to them as a ghost, the assembled family hear 'el campanilleo metálico de las llaves en la cintura de Férula' (134), symbolizing her physical, emotional and spiritual incarceration.

Despite an appearance of passivity Clara is able to get her own way a great deal. When she is a child she is given to throwing tantrums in order to manipulate her parents. When her father tries to get rid of her newly adopted dog, Barrabás, she says: 'Es mío, papá. Si me lo quita, le juro que dejo de respirar y me muero' (24). Barbara Loach notes that even when young Clara 'demonstrates that she will not be confined to the parameters of acceptable language for females'.[19] Loach cites the incident of Clara's impertinent interjection in church in the middle of a fire-and-brimstone sermon: '¡Pst! ¡Padre Restrepo! Si el cuento del infierno fuera pura mentira, nos chingamos todos ...' (14). Clara is traumatized when at nine years of age she witnesses the autopsy carried out on her older sister. She thinks she has brought about Rosa's demise, having predicted a death in the family. This suggests that she is deluded into thinking she has greater power than is actually the case. It may be an imagined power, but to Clara it is real. She enters her first period of silence and is mute for nine years. There is other evidence of Clara's over-active imagination. On peeping through the kitchen window to witness the autopsy, what she sees, according to Hart, is 'a fantastic tableau constructed from a blend of reality and her childish imagination'.[20] She sees the family doctor 'transformado en un vampiro gordo y oscuro' (40). Similarly, on listening to the wonderful tales of her well-travelled Uncle Marcos, she can 'sentir en su propia carne la quemante mordedura de las víboras, ver al reptil deslizarse sobre la alfombra' (22). Clara's vivid imagination seems to give her the ability to experience a transgression on a different 'diegetic level'.[21] However, on reaching adulthood, she settles for a fairly traditional, domesticated life. On marrying Esteban she is resigned to a loveless marriage.

According to Pam Morris, '[w]oman as other is the location of all that is desired and feared, all that is mysterious, magical, unrestricted and all that must be controlled and mastered'.[22] Esteban's thoughts reveal this ideology exactly, but despite his egotistical and despotic nature, he understands the limitations of his power in their relationship:

> Se daba cuenta que Clara no le pertenecía y que si ella continuaba habitando un mundo de aparecidos, de mesas de tres patas que se mueven solas y barajas que escrutan el futuro, lo más probable era que no llegara a pertenecerle nunca […] Deseaba mucho más que su cuerpo, quería apoderarse de esa materia imprecisa y luminosa que había en su interior … (90)

Through her magic Clara resists being 'controlled and mastered' and, therefore, avoids being merely a possession of her husband. Esteban can never be part of the world of the spirits. Later on in their married life he observes:

> Sentía a su mujer cada vez más alejada, más rara e inaccesible, no podía alcanzarla ni con regalos […] Quería que Clara no pensara más que en él, que no tuviera más vida que la que pudiera compartir con él, que le contara todo, que no poseyera nada que no proviniera de sus manos, que dependiera completamente.
>
> Pero la realidad era diferente, Clara parecía andar volando en aeroplano, como su tío Marcos, desprendida del suelo firme, buscando a Dios en disciplinas tibetanas, consultando a los espíritus con mesas de tres patas que daban golpecitos, dos para sí, tres para no, descifrando mensajes de otros mundos que podían indicarle hasta el estado de las lluvias. (117)

He can try to intimidate her with fits of temper and violence, but in a sense she is able to control him. Even after her death Esteban feels her comforting presence in the house and 'sin embargo procuraba no aventurarse en la región encantada que era el reino de su mujer' (347). He tolerates magic in the domestic sphere, but feels that 'la magia, como la religión y la cocina, era un asunto propiamente femenino' (124). Since magic is considered to be a 'feminine affair', it is, of course, relegated to a low status; like many aspects of women's lives, it is trivialized. Magic is associated to some extent with innocence. Nana tells Nívea: 'hay muchos niños que vuelan como las moscas, que adivinan los sueños y hablan con las ánimas, pero a todos se les pasa cuando pierden la inocencia' (15). However, there are two male characters who have some qualities which border on the magical. Pedro Segundo is able to lead a plague of ants off the farm; Uncle Marcos applies himself to 'estudios cabalísticos', although 'con más esfuerzo y menos acierto' than Clara (73). The fact that these men have limited access to magic lends weight to an anti-essentialist argument, suggesting that magic is not a product purely of female biology but is a product of a muted or marginalized group. Clara has the support network provided by magic; she has a psychological release from the oppression of her macho husband and the wider patriarchal society, and a level of peace and inner contentment of which Férula cannot even dream. Since she has no source of esteem in the male dominated society of her time Clara has little option but to locate an alternative avenue of experience, and in so doing sets in motion a process of eroding the monologism of her society; she dislocates and disrupts the symbolic and social order. Clara is articulating and demarcating her own reality, rather than accepting the male-centred version. Despite her religious zealousness, Férula's faith brings her no joy. She has no access to the magical; she lacks fulfilment, becomes embittered and finds herself ensnared in a patriarchal trap.

The 'wild zone' is a double-edged concept. As Hart observes, Allende 'plants small seeds of ambivalence about the value of Clara's gift'.[23] Allende is ambivalent because the 'wild zone' is a refuge, a support and a site of resistance, but where possible it is better to cope without it. It produces a feeling of identity through resistance and empowerment, but it is not power in the sense that the men know and may be more akin to the power of mystique or enigma. Clara is not given the status of prophet or seer. Often when people seek out her help, it is for small matters. It does not really have the status of even sibylline power, as there is no trace of evil in the spirits with which she communes. It is a form of counter-power, but ultimately it hovers between a female utopia and a prison-house. This feminist reading shows that magic, in the way in which it is treated in this novel, represents a woman's epistemology, stemming from a woman's structure of feeling. Women realize at some level that, in excluding themselves from a masculine sphere, they have colluded in their subjection, in that they have internalized and channelled their energies into perpetuating the mythology relating to womanhood.

Literally, magic can be viewed as part of an actual female reality, but to delimit it in such a way could lead to crude essentialism. Metaphorically, magic can be seen as a cultural construct, as the 'wild zone', a form of psychological protection serving a similar function to the bonds or informal networks which women forge between themselves to preserve their sanity in times of repression. To see the novel on different levels, whatever the metaphorical interpretation, produces a layered, polyvocal reading. Magical realism, as appropriated by Allende, does not so much find a voice for women, since they eventually find a means of articulating themselves through the 'malestream' means appropriated by Alba.[24] Towards the close of the novel Alba is suffering, imprisoned in a tiny claustrophobic cell known as the doghouse; she is considering giving up her struggle to live, when her grandmother appears to her telling her that the point is not to die, but to live and write her testimony. Alba makes the decision to survive since, as Showalter says, it is in certain periods 'self-annihilation that is the hallmark of female aestheticism'.[25] Alba does not succumb, like certain women of earlier eras, to the idea that suicide is a 'grotesquely fantasized female weapon, a way of cheating men out of dominance'.[26] Alba's discovery that she is pregnant provides an ambivalent moment at the end of the novel: she is life-affirming; she carries and promotes life. Yet the knowledge that her child is that of a rapist must surely cast a long shadow over events, even though Allende implies that Alba, because of her raised political and feminist consciousness, has the ability to overcome her terrors and put the past behind her. To die would be to comply with the stereotype of the weak woman.

The magical, as it is used by Allende in this novel, does provide an insight into the experimental and cryptic ways in which women dramatize the conflicts inherent in their lives. Yet she shows how women can be more than the Other; they can be the Other-Worldly, drawing strength from what may be termed the experience of suppression and the 'internalization of otherness' experienced by all women.[27] Magical realism, as a literary strategy used by Allende, dramatizes the painful contradictions inherent in post-colonial, patriarchal society. Magic, as part of lived experience, is shown to become an inadequate and at best an ambivalent force in the lives of women. To say that they gain in confidence is insufficient: they acquire nothing less than a new subject position and a sense of self, but know that there will always be that trace of the Other in their collective consciousness: magic will continue to exist in their matrilineal memory. Undoubtedly, Clara is the most attractive and fascinating character, suggesting perhaps that even in contemporary feminist circles women writers and readers cannot wholly rise above the ideology within which they live and breathe. Clara has an aura,[28] in the widest sense of the term, and once women become like men they lose this, and we both celebrate and mourn for what Freud's contemporary, Weir Mitchell, referred to as our 'mysteria'.[29]

## NOTES

1.  Isabel Allende, *La casa de los espíritus* (Barcelona: Plaza & Janés, 1982). Subsequent page references appear parenthetically in the text.

2.  Isabel Allende was related to President Salvador Allende. Her autobiographical 'letter' to her daughter, *Paula* (London: Harper Collins, 1995), reveals her family history.

3.  This lack of specificity produces a more universal story; the subtext is that this could happen anywhere.

4.  'Preternatural' indicates that which is 'out of the ordinary course of nature; beyond, surpassing, or differing from what is natural ...' (*OED*). It is preferable to 'supernatural', which, although it has a similar meaning, has through its usage become heavily loaded with connotations of vampires and evil which are inappropriate to magical realist writing. Many Latin American writers insist in certain ways upon the literal reality of the preternatural or the fabulous; this is an issue beyond the scope of this article.

5.  See Peter Melville Logan, *Nerves and Narratives: A Cultural History of Hysteria in Nineteenth Century Prose* (California: Univ. of California Press, 1997), 8.

6.  Elaine Showalter, *Hystories: Hysterical Epidemics and Modern Culture* (London: Picador, 1997).

7.  P. Gabrielle Foreman, 'Past-On Stories: History and the Magically Real, Morrison and Allende on Call', in *Magical Realism: Theory, History, Community*, ed. Lois Parkinson Zamora and Wendy B. Faris (London & Durham: Duke U.P., 1995), 286.

8.  Patricia Hart, *Narrative Magic in the Fiction of Isabel Allende* (London: Associated Univ. Presses, 1989), 29–30.

9.  *Ibid.*, 42.

10. *Ibid.*, 44.

11. *Ibid.*, 96.

12. *Ibid.*, 32.

13. *Ibid.*, 156.

14. Foreman, 'Past-On Stories', 295.

15. In Elaine Showalter, ed., *The New Feminist Criticism: Essays on women, literature and theory* (London: Virago, 1986). The essay first appeared in *Critical Inquiry*, VIII (Autumn 1981), 179–205.

16. Foreman, 'Past-On Stories', 295.

17. Quoted by Peter Melville Logan in *Nerves and Narratives*, 9.

18. See Elaine Showalter, *A Literature of Their Own: British Women Novelists from Brontë to Lessing* (London: Virago, 1982), 251.

19. Barbara Loach, *Power and Women's Writing in Chile* (Madrid: Editorial Pliegos, 1994), 16

20. Hart, *Narrative Magic*, 41.

21. For a discussion of narrative or 'diegetic levels' see Wenche Ommundsen, *Metafictions? Reflexivity in Contemporary Texts* (Carlton, Victoria: Melbourne U.P., 1993), 8.

22. Pam Morris, *Literature and Feminism* (Oxford: Blackwell, 1995), 19.

23. Hart, *Narrative Magic*, 40.

24. Loach uses this term in *Power and Women's Writing in Chile*, 34.

25. Showalter, *A Literature of Their Own*, 250.

26. *Ibid.*

27. This phrase is used by Loach in her summary and discussion of Josephine Donovan's work in *Power and Women's Writing in Chile*, 37.

28. This brings to mind Walter Benjamin's observations on the loss of aura in the arts in his essay, 'The work of art in the age of mechanical reproduction', in *Illuminations*, ed. Hannah Arendt (London: Fontana, 1973), 219–53.

29. See Mary Jacobus, 'An Unnecessary Maze of Sign-Reading', in *Reading Woman: Essays in Feminist Criticism* (London: Methuen, 1986).

# Chronology

| | |
|---|---|
| 1942 | Isabel Allende is born in Lima, Peru, on August 2. She was the daughter of Chilean diplomat Tomás Allende and Francisca Llona Barros Allende. |
| 1945 | Allende's parents get a divorce. Allende grows up in Santiago in her maternal grandparents' house. |
| 1953-58 | Allende's mother marries Ramón Huidobro. He is a foreign diplomat and the family moves to Bolivia, Europe, and Lebanon. Allende attends an all girls school in Beirut. |
| 1958 | Allende meets her future husband Miguel Frías. |
| 1959-65 | Allende works for the FAO (Food and Agriculture Organization). |
| 1962 | Allende marries Miguel Frías. |
| 1963 | Allende's daughter Paula is born. |
| 1964-65 | Allende travels through Europe. She lived in Brussels and Switzerland. |
| 1966 | Isabel, Miguel and Paula return to Chile and Allende's son Nicolás is born. |
| 1967-74 | Allende begins writing for *Paula* magazine. She write feminist articles and is in charge of the humor column "The Impertinents." |
| 1970 | Allende's stepfather is appointed Ambassador to Argentina. |
| 1972 | Her play *El Embajador* is performed in Santiago. |

| | |
|---|---|
| 1970-75 | Allende works part time for a television station. |
| 1973-74 | She writes for the children's magazine *Mampato*. Allende publishes two children's stories, *The grandmother Panchita* and *Lauchas y lauchones*. In addition she publishes a compilation of her humor column, *Civilice a su Troglodita.* |
| 1975 | Isabel and Family move to Venezuela. She works for *El Nacional*, the newspaper of Caracas. |
| 1978 | Isabel and Miguel separate temporarily. She moves to Spain for two months before returning to Miguel. |
| 1979-82 | She works as the administrator for the Marroco College in Caracas. |
| 1981 | Allende learns that her 99 year old grandfather is dying. She begins writing him a letter that will eventually turn into the initial draft of *La casa de los espíritus* (*The House of the Spirits*). |
| 1982 | *The House of the Spirits* is published. |
| 1984 | *La Gorda de Porcelana* (The Fat Porcelain Lady) is published. |
| | *De amor y de sombra* (*Of Love and Shadows*) is published in Spain. |
| | French version of *The House of the Spirits* is awarded the Grand Roman d'Evasion Prize. |
| 1985 | English version of *The House of the Spirits* translated by Magda Bogin. It is an immediate success. Allende works as a guest professor at Montclair State University. |
| 1986-87 | Allende spends time as guest lecturer at University of Virginia. She also spends time visiting he daughter, Paula. |
| 1987 | Allende divorces Miguel Friás. *Eva Luna* is published in Spain. *Of Love and Shadows* appears in English. Allende meets the twice-divorced San Francisco lawyer, William Gordon. She falls in love and moves to San Rafael. |
| 1988 | Allende marries William Gordon on July 17. *Eva Luna* appears in English. Allende is Gildersleeve Lecturer at Barnard College. |
| 1989 | *The Stories of Eva Luna* is published in Spain. Allende's essay "Writing as an Act of Hope" is published in *Paths of Resistance*. Allende is a guest writer in the creative writing department at University of California Berkeley. |

| | |
|---|---|
| 1991 | *The Stories of Eva Luna* appears in English. Paula enters Madrid hospital, a few days later she slips into a coma, from which she never emerges. *El plan infinito* is launched at the Santiago Book Fair. |
| 1992 | Paula dies in San Rafael exactly one year after she fell into a coma. |
| 1993 | Harper Collins publishes *The Infinite Plan* in English. *The House of the Spirits* is adapted to public stage in England. On October 22 the screen production premieres in Munich. The film stars Meryl Streep, Glenn Close, Jeremy Irons, Winona Ryder, Antonio Banderas, and Venessa Redgrave. It is an instant success. |
| 1994 | *The House of the Spirits* receives the Bavarian Film Prize on January 14. She receives the Gabriela Mistral prize, Chile's highest cultural honor. *Eva Luna* is adapted for the stage. It premieres in Denver under the title *Stories* on March 25. An Argentinean-Spanish coproduction of *Of Love and Shadows* is released. *Paula* is published in December. |
| 1995 | *Paula* appears in German and Dutch as a novel and climbs to the top position on both countries best seller lists. Paula is translated into English by Margaret Sayers Peden and published by Harper Collins. It climbs to number eight on the New York best-seller list. Allende establishes the Paula Scholarship for students at University of San Jose. |
| 1996 | Allende receives the author of the year award in Los Angeles. January 16 is established as Isabel Allende day. She receives the Harold Washington Literary Award. *Of Love and Shadows* starring Antonio Banderas is released in film version. |
| 1997 | *Aphrodite* is an illustrated nonfiction book covering the topics of food and sex. Many of the recipes in the book are Chilean aphrodisiacs. |
| 1998 | *Aphrodite* is published in English. Allende establishes a research grant on Porphyria, the rare disease that killed Paula. Allende wins the Dorothy and Lillian Gish Award. |
| 1999 | *Daughter of Fortune* is published in Spain and almost immediately translated into English. Allende's son Nicolas marries Lori Barry. |

| | |
|---|---|
| 2000 | *Portrait in Sepia* is published in Spain. Allende appears on the Oprah Winfrey show. |
| 2001 | *The City of Beasts,* a young adult novel taking place in the rainforest, is published in Spain and translated into English by Margaret Sayers Peden. |

# Bibliography

Agosin, Marjorie. "Entrevista a Isabel Allende/Interview with Isabel Allende." Trans. By Cola Frazen. *Imagine: International Chicano Poetry Journal* 1. (Winter 1984): pp. 42–46.

"Allende, Isabel." *Current Biography* 49 (2) (Feb 1988): pp. 3.

Allende, Isabel. "Interview with Isabel Allende." *Democracy Now! Pacifica Network News.* September 10, 1999.

Baldock, Bob. "Isabel Allende (Interview)." *Mother Jones* 19 (5) (Sept-Oct 1994) 21.

Behar, Ruth. "In the House of Spirits." *The Women's Review of Books* 13 (2) (Nov 1995): pp. 8.

Bennet, Caroline. "The Other and the Other-Wordly: The Function of Magic in Isabel Allende's *La casa de los espíritus. Bulletin of Hispanic Studies.* LXXV (no. 3) (July 1998): pp. 357–365.

Carvalho, Susan de. "Escrituras y Escritoras: The Artist-protagonist of Isabel Allende." *Disurso Literario* 10 (no. 1)(1992): 59–67.

Cohn, Deborah. "To See or Not To See: Invisibility, Clairvoyance, and Re-visions of History in *Invisible Man* and *La casa de los Espíritus.*" *Comparative Literature Studies* 33 (4) (Fall 1996): pp. 372.

Correas de Zapata, Celia. *Isabel Allende: Vida y Espíritus.* (Mexico: Plaza & Janés, 1998).

Crystall, Elyse. "An Interview with Isabel Allende." *Contemporary Literature* 33 (4) (Winter 1992): pp. 584.

Diamond Nigh, Lynne. "Eva Luna: Writing as History." *Studies in Twentieth Century Literature* 19 (no. 1) (Winter 1995): pp. 29-42.

Earle, PG. "Literature As Survival, Allende *The House of the Spirits.*" *Contemporary Literature* 28 (4) (1987) 543-554.

Espadas, Elizabeth. "Isabel Allende's *La Casa de los Espíritus:* Between the Chronicle, the Testimonial, and the Love Story." *MACLAS: Latin American Essays* 3 (1989): pp. 133-140.

Foreman, P. Gabrielle. "Past-on Stories: History and the Magically Real, Morrison and Allende On Call." *Feminist Studies* 18 (2) (Summer 1992): pp. 369.

Foster, Douglas. "Isabel Allende Unveiled (interview)." *Mother Jones* 13 (10) (Dec 1988): pp. 42.

Frenk, Susan. "The Wandering Text: Situating the Narratives of Isabel Allende." *Latin American Women's Writing: Feminist Readings in Theory and Crisis.* ed. Anny Brooksbank Jones and Catherine Davies. (Oxford: Clarendon Press, 1996).

Garcia Johnson, Ronie-Richele. "The Struggle for Space: Feminism and Freedom in *The House of the Spirits.*" *Revista Hispanica Moderna* 67 (1) (1994 June): pp. 184-93.

Gautier, Marie-Lise Gazarian. "Isabel Allende." *Interviews with Latin American Writers.* Elmwood Park, Ill: Dalkey Archive Press, 1989.

Hart, Patricia. *Narrative Magic in the Fiction of Isabel Allende.* (Rutherford, N.J.:Fairleigh Dickinson University Press, 1989.)

———. "'Magic Books' and the Magic of Books." *Narrative Magic in the Fiction of Isabel Allende.* (Rutherford, N.J.: Fairleigh Dickinson University Press, 1989.): pp. 70-85.

———. "Magic Feminism in Isabel Allende's *The Stories of Eva Luna.*" *Multicultural Literatures through Feminist/Poststructuralist Lenses.* (Knoxville: The University of Tennessee Press, 1993): pp. 103-136.

Helsper, Norma. "Binding the Wounds of the Body Politic: Nation as Family in *La casa de los espíritus.*" *Critical Approaches to Isabel Allende's Novels.* ed. Sonia Riquelme Rojas and Edna Aguirre Rehbein. (New York: Peter Lang, 1991): pp.49-58.

Hughes, Kathryn. "California Scheming." *New Statesman and Society*. (2 July 1993): pp. 38-39.

Jenkins, Ruth Y. "Authorizing Female Voice and Experience: Ghosts and Spirits in Kingston's *The Woman Warrior* and Allende's *The House of the Spirits*." *MELUS* 19 (3) (Fall 1994): pp. 61.

Kovach, Claudia Marie. "Mask and Mirror: Isabel Allende's Mechanism for Justice in *The House of the Spirits*." *Postcolonial Literature and the Biblical Call for Justice*. Gallagher, Susan VanZanten (ed.): 1994.

Levine, Linda Gould. "Isabel Allende." *Spanish American Women Writers: A Bio-Bibliographical Source Book*. ed. Diane E. Marting. (New York: Greenwood Press, 1990): pp. 20-30.

Logan, Joy. "Aphrodite in an Apron; or, the Erotics of Recipes and Self-Representation in Isabel Allende's *Afrodita*." *Romance Language Annual* 10 (no. 2) (1998): pp. 685-689.

Martinez Z., Nelly. "The Politics of the Woman Artist in Isabel Allende's *The House of the Spirits*." *Writing the Woman Artist: Essays on Poetics, Politics, and Portraiture*. Jones, Suzanne W. (1991).

Meyer, Doris. "'Parenting the Text': Female Creativity and Dialogic Relationships in Isabel Allende's La Casa de los Espíritus." *Hispania*, 73 (May 1990): pp. 360-365.

Moody, Michael. "Isabel Allende and the Testimonial Novel." *Confluencia: Revista Hispaniacutenica de Cultura y Literatura* 2 (Fall 1986): pp. 39-43.

Perricone, Catherine R. "Iconic/Metaphoric Dress and Other Nonverbal Signifiers in *De Amor y de Sombra*. Critical Approaches to Isabel Allende's Novels*. ed. Sonia Riquelme Rojas and Edna Aguirre Rehbein. (New York: Peter Lang, 1991): pp. 83-96.

———. "Genre and Metarealism in Allende's *Paula*." *Hispania* 81 (no. 1) (March 1998): pp. 42-49.

Pinet, Carolyn. "Choosing Barbarás: Dog as Text & Text as Dog In Isabel Allende's *La Casa de los Espíritus*." *Hispanofila: Literatura-Ensayos* 123 (May 1998): pp. 55-65.

Rehbein, Edna Aguirre. "Isabel Allende's *Eva Luna* and the Act/Art of Narrating." *Critical Approaches to Isabel Allende's Novels*. ed. Sonia Riquelme Rojas and Edna Aguirre Rehbein. (New York: Peter Lang, 1991): pp. 179-190.

Riquelme Rojas, Sonia and Edna Aguirre Rehbein. *Critical Approaches to Isabel Allende's Novels*. (New York : Peter Lang, 1991).

Rodden, John. "The Responsibility to Tell You: An Interview with Isabel Allende." *The Kenyon Review* 13 (1) (Winter 1991): pp. 113.

———. *Conversations with Isabel Allende*. (Austin: University of Texas Press, 1999).

Ruta, Suzanne. "Lovers and Storytellers." *The Women's Review of Books* 8 (no. 9) (Spring 1991): pp. 60.

Shea, Maureen E. "Love, Eroticism, and Pornography in the Works of Isabel Allende." *Women's Studies* 18 (2-3). (September 1990): pp. 223.

Shields, E. Thomson Jr. "Ink, Blood, and Kisses: La Casa de los Espíritus and the Myth of Disunity." *Hispanofila: Literatura-Ensayos* 99. (May 1990): pp. 79-86.

Simon, Linda. "The Odyssey of an Evangelist's Son." *The Wall Street* (May 24, 1993): pp. A8.

Smith, Amanda. "Isabel Allende (interview)." *Publishers Weekly* 227 (May 17 1985): pp. 119.

Sullivan, Joan Therese. *Visions and Spirits: The Supernatural in Three Contemporary Novels*. (San Francisco: San Francisco State University Press, 1991).

Swanson, Philip. "Tyrants and Trash: Sex, Class and Culture in *La casa de los espíritus*." *Bulletin of Hispanic Studies* LXXI (no. 2)(April 1994): pp. 217-237.

Tayko, Gail. "Teaching Isabel Allende's *La casa de los espíritus*." *College Literature* 19 (3) (Oct-Feb 1992): pp. 228.

Urquhart, Jane. "Tales from Isabel Allende's Passionate, Magical World." *Quill and Quire* 56 (no. 11) (November 1990): pp. 25.

Zamora, Lois Parkinson. "The Magical Tables of Isabel Allende and Remedios Varo." *Comparative Literature* 19-20 (No. 3-1) (October 1992-February 1993): pp. 228-232.

Zamora, Lois Parkinson. "The Magical Tables of Isabel Allende and Remedios Varo." *Comparative Literature* 44 (no. 2) (Spring 1992): pp. 113-143.

# Contributors

HAROLD BLOOM is Sterling Professor of the Humanities at Yale University and Henry W. and Albert A. Berg Professor of English at the New York University Graduate School. He is the author of over 20 books, including *Shelley's Mythmaking* (1959), *The Visionary Company* (1961), *Blake's Apocalypse* (1963), *Yeats* (1970), *A Map of Misreading* (1975), *Kabbalah and Criticism* (1975), *Agon: Toward a Theory of Revisionism* (1982), *The American Religion* (1992), *The Western Canon* (1994), and *Omens of Millennium: The Gnosis of Angels, Dreams, and Resurrection* (1996). *The Anxiety of Influence* (1973) sets forth Professor Bloom's provocative theory of the literary relationships between the great writers and their predecessors. His most recent books include *Shakespeare: The Invention of the Human*, a 1998 National Book Award finalist, and *How to Read and Why*, which was published in 2000. In 1999, Professor Bloom received the prestigious American Academy of Arts and Letters Gold Medal for Criticism.

PATRICIA HART is a professor of Spanish at Purdue University. Her areas of expertise are Peninsular Spanish Twentieth Century Literature, Catalan Literature and Translation, Film in Spain and Latin America. Her publications include *The Spanish Sleuth and Narrative Magic in the Fiction of Isabel Allende*. She has published numerous times in journals such as *Cine-Lit II, Cincinnati Romance Review, MLA. Discusro: Revista de Estudios Iberoamericanos*, and *The Catalan Review*.

191

E. THOMSON SHIELDS JR. is an associate professor of English at East Carolina University. His areas of interest are Director, Roanoke Colonies Research Office American Literature to 1820 (English, Spanish, Southern, North Carolinian), Native American Literature, General American Literature, Bibliography and Research Methodologies

DORIS MEYER is the Roman S. and Tatiana Weller professor of Hispanic Studies at Connecticut College. Meyer is the author of numerous articles and books, including *Victoria Ocampo: Against the Wind and the Tide* (UT Press).

CATHERINE R. PERRICONE is a professor of Spanish at Lafayette College in Easton Pennsylvania. She is a prolific writer and has numerous publications in journal such as *Romance Notes, SECOLAS Annals: Journal of the Southeastern Council on Latin American Studies, Antipodas, South Eastern Latin Americanist, Hispania, The Americas Review, The Language-Quarterly, and The USF-Language-Quarterly.*

EDNA AGUIRRE REHBEIN is a critic and a scholar who edited *Critical Approaches to Isabel Allende's Novels* and has been published in *World Literature Today.*

NORMA HELSPER is an associate professor of Spanish International Communications and Culture at SUNY College at Cortland. She is a scholar of great talent who has numerous publications.

SUSAN DE CARVALHO received her PhD from University of Virginia and is now an associate professor of Spanish-American literature at the University of Kentucky. Her primary interest is in the 20th century novel. She has published articles on Pablo Neruda, Isabel Allende and Gabriel Garciá Márquez. She is currently working on a book called *The Road to Macondo: Garcia Marquez' Early Journalism.*

RONIE-RICHELLE GARCÍA-JOHNSON is an assistant professor of environmental policy at Duke University. She has her doctorate in Political Science with an emphasis in World Politics and Comparative Politics.

CLAUDIA MARIE KOVACH is a professor of English at Neumann College. Her work has been published in the journal *Studies in Language and Literature and the book Postcolonial Literature and the Biblical Call for Justice.*

PHILIP SWANSON is chairman of the Spanish Department at the University of Aberdeen in Scotland. He has published many articles in journals including, *Forum for Modern Language Studies, New Novel Review: Nueva Novela Nouveau Roman Review, Bulletin of Hispanic Studies, Studies in Twentieth Century Literature*.

LYNNE DIAMOND-NIGH earned a Ph.D. in Romance Languages from the University of Oregon, and is the founding editor of the *New Novel Review*. Her current work is on the relationship between literature and the visual arts in contemporary Europe. She also intends on writing a book and developing course offerings on the history of the book.

CAROLYN PINET is an adjunct instructor of Spanish in the Department of Modern Languages & Literatures at Montana State University-Bozeman. She is an accomplished writer whose work can be found in *Hispanic Journal, Hispanofila, Rocky Mountain Review of Language and Literature, and Romance Notes*.

CAROLINE BENNETT is a scholar and critic whose work has been published in the *Journal of Educational Administration* and *The Bulletin of Hispanic Studies*.

# *Acknowledgments*

"'Magic Books' and the Magic of Books," by Patricia Hart. From *Narrative Magic in the Fiction of Isabel Allende*. © 1989 by Fairleigh Dickinson University Press. Reprinted by permission.

"Ink, Blood, and Kisses: La casa de los espíritus and the Myth of Disunity," by E. Thomson Shields Jr. From *Hispanofila:Literatura-Endsayos* (May 1990): 79-86. © 1990 by University of North Carolina. Reprinted by permission.

"Parenting the Text": Female Creativity and Dialogic Relationships in Isabel Allende's La Casa de los Espíritus," by Doris Meyer. From *Hispania* 73 (no. 2) (May 1990): 360-365. © 1990 by the American Association of Teachers of Spanish and Portuguese, Inc. Reprinted by permission.

"Iconic/Metaphoric Dress and Other Nonverbal Signifiers in De Amor y de Sombra," by Catherine R. Perricone. From *Critical Approaches to Isabel Allende's Novels*. © 1991 by Peter Lang Publishers. Reprinted by permission.

"The Act/Art of Narrating in Eva Luna," by Edna Aguirre Rehbein. From *Critical Approaches to Isabel Allende's Novels*. © 1991 by Peter Lang Publishers. Reprinted by permission.

"Binding the Wounds of the Body Politic: Nation as Family in La Casa de los Espíritus," by Norma Helsper. From *Critical Approaches to Isabel Allende's Novels*. © 1991 by Peter Lang Publishers. Reprinted by permission.

"Escrituras y Escritoras: The Artist-Protagonist of Isabel Allende," by Susan de Carvalho. From *Discurso Literario* 10 (no. 1) (1992): 59-67. © 1992 by Susan de Carvalho. Reprinted by permission.

"The Struggle for Space: Feminism and Freedom," by Ronie Richelle Garcia-Johnson. From *Revista Hispanica Moderna* 67 (no. 1) (June 1994): 184-193. © 1994 by Ronie Garcia-Johnson. Reprinted by permission.

"Mask and Mirror: Isabel Allende's Mechanism for Justice in the House of the Spirits," by Claudia Marie Kovach. From *Postcolonial Literature and the Biblical Call for Justice* (1994):74-90. © 1994 by University Press of Mississippi. Reprinted by permission.

"Tyrants and Trash: Sex, Class and Culture in La Casa de los Espirítus," by Philip Swanson. From *Bulletin of Hispanic Studies* LXXI (no. 2) (April 1994): 217-237. © 1994 by Liverpool University Press. Reprinted by permission.

"Eva Luna: Writing as History," by Lynne Diamond-Nigh. From *Studies in Twentieth Century Literature* 19 (no. 1) (Winter 1995): 29-42. ©1995 by *Studies in Twentieth Century Literature*. Reprinted by permission.

"Genre and Metarealism in Allende's Paula," by Catherine R. Perricone. From *Hispania* 81 (no. 1) (March 1998): 42-49. ©1998 by the American Association of Teachers of Spanish and Portuguese, Inc. Reprinted by permission.

"Choosing Barrabas: Dog as Text & Text as Dog in Isabel Allende's *La casa de los espirítus*," by Carolyn Pinet. From *Hispanofila* 123 (May 1998): 55-65. © 1998 by University of North Carolina. Reprinted by permission.

"The Other and the Other Worldly: The Function of Magic in Isabel Allende's *La Casa de los Espirítus*," by Caroline Bennett. From *Bulletin of Hispanic Studies* LXXV (No. 3) (July 1998): 357-365. ©1998 by Liverpool University Press. Reprinted by permission.

# Index